SMYLLIE'S IRELAND

Protestants, Independence, and the Man Who Ran the Irish Times

Caleb Wood Richardson

INDIANA UNIVERSITY PRESS

This book is a publication of

Indiana University Press
Office of Scholarly Publishing
Herman B Wells Library 350
1320 East 10th Street
Bloomington, Indiana 47405 USA

iupress.indiana.edu

Manufactured in the United States of America

Cataloging information is available from the Library of Congress.

ISBN 978-0-253-04123-4 (hdbk.)
ISBN 978-0-253-04124-1 (pbk.)
ISBN 978-0-253-04127-2 (web PDF)

1 2 3 4 5   24 23 22 21 20 19

SMYLLIE'S IRELAND

IRISH CULTURE, MEMORY, AND PLACE

Oona Frawley, Ray Cashman, and Guy Beiner, *editors*

CONTENTS

ACKNOWLEDGMENTS

STUDENTS SOMETIMES ASK ME HOW ANYONE EVER WRITES a book. Here's how, in eight easy steps:

First, choose the right graduate program. Paul Seaver, Paul Robinson, James Sheehan, Richard White, and Jack Rakove were models of scholarly rigor and personal generosity. Peter Stansky provided help, advice, counsel, constructive criticism, and occasionally quiche for the better part of a decade, and the historian I am today is almost entirely his doing. Chad Martin, Amy Robinson, Rodney Koeneke, John Broich, Chris Wilson, Jesse Kauffman, Rachel Nunez, Emily Greble, James Ward, Kevin Carey, James Carolan, Anna Chang, Kris Salata, Joe Sacco, and Dan Maidenberg all helped me maintain some sense of perspective. The Lady Vaizey's hospitality is much appreciated. Thanks are also due to grants from the Stanford History Department and the Stanford School of Humanities and Sciences as well as to the Fred W. Oakford Graduate Fellowship.

Second, get to know librarians and archivists—the eternally unsung heroes of the scholarly world. The special collections and archival staff at the National Archives and the National Library, Dublin; University College Cork; University College Dublin; the National Archives, Kew; the University of Victoria; the University of Southern Illinois at Carbondale; the Hoover Institution; Stanford University Libraries; and the University of New Mexico Libraries all responded to my impertinent requests with good humor and great advice. Acknowledgements are also due to the following for permissions granted: the *Irish Times*, *New Hibernia Review*, *Éire-Ireland*, and the Harvard Law Library.

Third, find great people to work with. The faculty and staff of the History Department at the University of New Mexico had me unceremoniously foisted upon them but have never once reminded me of this. One of the greatest pleasures of my professional career is being able to listen to the complaints of colleagues at other institutions whose departments are dysfunctional, disagreeable, or worse. I get to smile and say, quite honestly, that I really have no idea what they're talking about. And I was lucky enough to have not only a great department but also a great set of colleagues outside my department. Trying to build an Irish Studies program from scratch is easy if you have a coconspirator as impressive as Sarah Townsend. Interdisciplinary collaboration is a breeze when you get to work with people such as Maria Szasz and Mary Power. Lori Gallagher has provided a model of generosity and dedication to the field that will never cease to inspire me.

Fourth, get yourself a scholarly network. I found mine in and around the American Conference of Irish Studies and the American Conference for Irish Studies–Western Regional. Brian Ó Conchubhair, Nick Wolf, Anna Teekell, Jim Walsh, Audrey Eyler, Charlotte Headrick, Kathy Heininge, Donna Potts, Traolach O'Riordain, Dave Emmons, Myles Dungan, Matt Spangler, Glen Gendzel, Tony Bucher, David Brundage, Nick Harrington, Matt Horton, Brian McCabe, and Camille Harrigan have changed my mind about conferences, and Ian d'Alton, Ida Milne, David Lloyd, Jim Rogers, Vera Kreilkamp, and Jim Donnelly have all been extraordinarily supportive of my work at moments when I was not at all sure that it deserved it. Matthew Stibbe was generous in sharing his extensive knowledge of Ruhleben Camp and Colonel William Gibson his unparalleled expertise in the history of Irish golf.

Fifth, find a world-class press. When I first began telling people that I had signed a contract with Indiana University Press, they would sigh and say, "Ah, Indiana," as if they were remembering prewar Paris in springtime. It turns out that Indiana's reputation for being a pleasure to work with is understating it considerably. Kate Schramm's patience is apparently endless, and the professionalism and enthusiasm of Jennika Baines—the kind of scholar-editor that most people don't believe exists anymore—is truly a wonder to behold. Thanks also to the anonymous peer reviewers of this work in manuscript: your thoughtful comments and suggestions were enormously helpful.

Sixth, associate yourself with good families, and ideally plan ahead so that you're born into one. Denis and Bev Pirio and Stephanie and Steve Parrish have been relentlessly encouraging. My parents, Bill and Carol Richardson, have showered me with affection, support, and healthy snacks for as long as I can remember, and even before. Micah, Catherine, and Desmond have tolerated my absent-mindedness with far more good humor than I have any right to expect.

Seventh, if you're going to have children, be sure to have great ones. Townes and Harrison did everything in their power, at every stage of the process, to distract me from my research and writing, and I can't thank them enough for it.

Eighth, if at all possible, marry Sarah Pirio. Most of what I do, when it comes down to it, is just showing off to try to get her attention, and this book is no exception.

SMYLLIE'S IRELAND

INTRODUCTION

What do you do when your country leaves you behind?
In the early twentieth century, this was the question faced by hundreds of thousands of southern Irish Protestants, who found themselves transformed into aliens in their own land. The period of the Irish Revolution—the series of events between 1912 and 1923 that included a fight over Home Rule, the Easter Rising and War of Independence, the partition of the island into separate states, and the Civil War—is the most obvious landmark in this story. By the early 1920s, the religious divide between the two polities on the island was as clear as it would be between India and Pakistan decades later, with southern Protestants on the wrong side of the line. There is a good reason that many of the classic histories of southern Protestant influence end on or about December 6, 1921, the day the Anglo-Irish Treaty was signed.[1] It seems characteristic of this remarkably undramatic group that they let Michael Collins get to the phrase first, but southern Irish Protestants, too, could have said that they were "signing their death warrant" with the treaty.

In fact the alienation of southern Protestants had begun much earlier and would last much longer than that period. From Catholic Emancipation to Celtic Tiger, members of this group found themselves on the wrong side of Irish history. Few of its members alive in 1912 could remember a time when they had been anything but a "descendancy," and few born that year would live to witness "how the Catholics became Protestant" at the turn of the twenty-first century.[2] Since the group's peak in the late eighteenth century, when the southern Protestant minority had attained a position of power and influence in Ireland comparable to that once held by Germans in the Baltic or Swedes in Finland, they had been losing ground. The Act of Union eliminated their parliament, Daniel O'Connell's successful campaign for Catholic Emancipation diluted their votes, and a rising middle class chipped away at their economic power. By the late nineteenth century, their largest threats came from those they might have assumed to be their friends. The three most serious blows to southern Irish Protestant power in the late nineteenth and early twentieth centuries were dealt by Charles Stewart Parnell, a Wicklow landlord who led a nearly successful campaign for Irish Home Rule; Gerald Balfour, the chief secretary for Ireland whose attempts to "kill Home Rule with kindness" nearly killed off Unionist dominance in local government; and George Wyndham, a Conservative member of parliament who sponsored a series of Land Acts that encouraged the breakup of large estates.

As a result, even before the tumultuous period of 1912 to 1923, the position of southern Irish Protestants had begun to weaken. But as a dividing line, the period still matters. Until that point, southern Protestants could still point to Jonathan Swift, Henry Grattan, Parnell, and Theobald Wolfe Tone to make the case that Protestants as well as Catholics deserved a place in Ireland's history. From a cultural perspective, in the 1890s and early 1900s the leading lights of the Celtic Revival seemed to prove that a Protestant could be as Gaelic as anyone else. They may have been a minority, but it was a minority that played an outsize role. But during the revolutionary period even that claim to status disappeared. Part of this was due to guilt by association: in a revolt against British power, southern Irish Protestants, many of whom professed some degree of attachment to Britain, were natural scapegoats. Part of it was that southern Irish Protestants found themselves made irrelevant by their co-religionists in the North: most of the Protestants who mattered in Irish politics in the 1910s and '20s were Ulster Unionists. Part of it, too, was the group's own tendency toward quietism and political compromise—hardly qualities that get one noticed during a revolution. Finally, even southern Protestants sympathetic to the changes were unable or unwilling to recognize the extent to which the political ground shifted beneath their feet during this period; few were able to make the transition from Home Rulers to nationalists.

But it was not just that southern Irish Protestants suddenly found themselves out of step—they also seemed out of luck. Decline was not inevitable, but it must have started to feel that way to many in the group as missed opportunities piled up. Home Rule, which could have reconciled southern Protestants' local and imperial loyalties, failed, in part because of the efforts of Edward Carson, one of their own who transformed himself into a symbol of Ulster Unionism. The idealism of the outbreak of the First World War, which promised a fight for the rights of small nations that could have potentially united Irish Protestants and Irish Catholics, disappeared in the trenches. Despite the prominent roles played by some southern Protestants in the Easter Rising, the event wrong-footed the group as a whole; by the time they began to comprehend radical nationalism's significance they had become, willingly or unwillingly, its enemy. The abortive Irish Convention of 1917—which, in terms of policy, represented the last best chance for southern Protestants to contribute their own answer to the Irish Question—was another missed opportunity.[3] During the War of Independence, some hoped that southern Protestants could play the role of interpreter, explaining Ireland to Britain and vice versa. Instead, southern Protestants became targets, with dozens shot and hundreds harassed by the IRA. The murder of thirteen men and boys around Dunmanway, County Cork, during a period of truce in April 1922 has come to epitomize the worst of what some have called an attempt at "ethnic cleansing."[4] Even the outbreak of the Civil War—a conflict of nationalist against nationalist, from which southern Protestants could have reasonably hoped to stand aside—offered little respite. Now Protestants were blamed for supporting the Free State: some managed to make it through the revolution only to have their Big Houses burned in 1923—not because they resisted the new order, but because they had agreed to adapt to it by becoming senators.[5] The Irish Revolution proved that southern Irish Protestants had become an infinitely adaptable enemy. Edmund Burke's warning in the 1790s had finally come true: the term *Protestant* had ceased to identify a set of religious beliefs or practices and had become "nothing more or better than the name of a persecuting faction . . . [defined] not by what it is, but by what it is not."[6] What southern Protestants were not, it seemed, was authentically Irish.

After 1922 the group faced a stark choice: exodus or alienation. Many southern Protestants left the country, "returning home" to the more congenial environment of mainland Britain. The Protestant population in the South fell by more than 30 percent in the period between the 1911 and 1926 censuses. A decline of that proportion among any group is significant; in a country in which Protestants represented only about 10 percent of the population, it was devastating.[7] In County Kildare, the Protestant population fell by approximately 70 percent during this period.[8] Tipperary town lost 88 percent of its Protestants. In smaller towns and in rural areas, this decline amounted to near erasure from the landscape. In 1926, there were only eleven Protestants remaining in Fethard-on-Sea, County Wexford.[9] Partly as a result of their diminished numbers, over the next few decades the remnants of the political power of southern Irish Protestants vanished. As Protestants in the North were consolidating their influence, southern

Protestants were losing theirs. *Protestant* in the north came to evoke the imposing façade of Stormont while the term in the south meant only a burned-out Big House. Before independence, Protestants could interpret sectarian feeling as a form of respect: at least they were still powerful enough to be hated. But after independence, the greater threat was a kind of malign neglect.

Three events are often used to illustrate the diminished position of southern Irish Protestants in the mid-twentieth century. First, in 1931, Catholic bishops and a public boycott quashed the appointment of a Protestant to the post of county librarian in Mayo—a blatant example of religious discrimination that, some Protestants noted, seemed to trouble them far more than their Catholic neighbors. Second, in 1951, again in response to pressure from the Catholic hierarchy, the government abandoned Minister of Health Noel Browne's proposals to reduce infant mortality in Ireland via a form of social insurance. Although Protestants were not directly targeted in the defeat of the Mother and Child Scheme, their lack of influence in the debate—and its proof of the power of the Catholic Church over not only the government but also the medical profession, in which Protestants felt they had a proprietary stake—meant that they felt its failure particularly strongly. Third, in 1957 the collapse of a mixed marriage in Fethard became an event of national significance when the Protestant wife of a Catholic farmer fled to the security of Belfast to avoid having to raise her children Catholic—which was required under the terms of the *Ne Temere* decree. This prompted her former neighbors to boycott local Protestant business-people, who they suspected of having helped her escape. In some ways, the Fethard affair offered some consolation to Protestants. Some government ministers condemned the boycott, and it was, after all, a boycott, which hearkened back to a time when the group was influential enough to attract such formal protests. But like the Mayo Librarian and Mother and Child affairs, it only underscored how little southern Protestants mattered in independent Ireland. Even their tragedies were somehow unimpressive.[10]

The one bright spot in the modern history of southern Protestant-ism—the group's continued prominence in business and professional life—began to fade as well as old networks gave way to new ones. Those on the bottom end of the socioeconomic spectrum fared even worse. Sociologists and folklorists have recorded heartbreaking accounts of isolation among working-class Protestants. Even those who escaped actual physical violence suffered psychological damage that in many cases reached down through the generations. These stories remind us that the most tragic element of any historic power shift is that those who suffer most are those who never had much power to begin with.[11] It also reveals that the most damaging aspect of discrimination against Protestants in Ireland was its silence: for most of the twentieth century, they were effectively written out of Irish history.

In recent years, southern Protestants have attracted renewed interest among historians and sociologists. The experiences they have uncovered are more complex and more interesting than the "decline and fall" motif would have one believe, but the titles of their works demonstrate the continuing power of the received narrative: *Buried Lives, Untold Stories, Outside the Glow.*[12] The story of southern Irish Protestants since independence, then, would seem to be a story of failure.

But it is not the whole story.

Recent research has shown that while Protestants in some areas, and during some periods, left the country at high rates, their decline—especially when the period between the 1911 and 1926 censuses is put in its broader context—was not as overwhelming as it may seem. This was, in part, because that decline had more to do with demographic and economic change than with sectarianism. A significant portion of the 30 percent that left the country were British civil and military officials, victims only of a transfer of power from one administration to another.[13] Irish independence did not solve the problem of Irish poverty for Catholics or for Protestants, and members of both groups continued to emigrate as they had done for centuries. The difference was that Protestants seemed less willing or able to reproduce themselves, either biologically or by attracting new members.[14]

Instances of persecution—violent, in doorways in Dunmanway, or social, on farms (or businesses) in Fethard[15]—were undoubtedly devastating to the individuals and families involved, but when put in the broader context of the experience of minorities in the modern world, Irish Protestants fared reasonably well. Even if all the worst fears of the proponents of the "ethnic cleansing" analysis were proven true, the revolutionary violence in Ireland would still not impress most historians of central or eastern Europe. The most generous estimation of Protestants killed in Ireland would produce a number that would equate to weeks, if not days, of the death toll involved in the roughly contemporaneous Soviet campaign against their own internal "aliens," the Cossacks.[16] Anne Dolan reminds us that in Ireland, "our massacres and atrocities were measured in small numbers . . . and we probably should not lose sight of that."[17] Similarly, it is important to contextualize examples of "soft sectarianism" such as the case of the Mayo librarian, the defeat of the Mother and Child Scheme, and the Fethard boycott within Irish society more broadly. Anti-Protestant bias is only one and not necessarily the most important element in these controversies. Differing views about the position of women in Ireland, about the power of local government, and about the relationship between the institutions of church and state need to be taken into account as well, not to mention individual ambition and personal resentment.[18]

Finally, the "decline" of Protestant political and economic power, while the hardest aspect of all to assess statistically, is almost certainly overstated by apologists for the group and by its critics. There is more to politics than what happens in Leinster House, and if there is such thing as an Irish "establishment," not being Catholic enough has never been quite the barrier to entry that it might appear from the outside.[19]

Recent writers have warned against overstating the economic success of Protestants and have criticized Kurt Bowen's characterization of the group as a "privileged minority," pointing out, justifiably, that this does not take into account the experiences of lower-class or lower-middle-class Protestants, of which there were many.[20] Conor Cruise O'Brien made a somewhat similar point when he observed that Irish Catholics tended, wrongly, to see all Protestants as "colonels and dentists."[21] Even so, by the late 1950s, when Protestants made up 5 percent of the Irish population, they still occupied 20 percent of the administrative, executive, and managerial positions in Ireland—and 24 percent of directors, managers, and company secretaries were Protestants. Protestants were overrepresented in the middle and upper middle class. And, at all levels, they were slightly more likely to report that they were "in gainful employment" than were Catholics.[22]

As a result, the concept of a "privileged minority" remains useful by reminding us that success—or, for that matter, just managing, thank you very much—can be as historically invisible as failure.[23] It is true that the poor or marginalized are often denied the right to tell their stories. It is also true that the rich or reasonably satisfied often do not bother to tell theirs. The problem with what Ian d'Alton has memorably termed the "grand tragedy" interpretation of southern Irish Protestant history is that it oversimplifies.[24] Whether that tragedy is performed before a backdrop of a burning Big House, a crumbling tenement, or a wall of demographic data, all people whose stories do not fit that narrative of decline are left out. Those Protestants who "made it" in independent Ireland—in all of the various ways that people can "make it" in any country, in any period—drop out of the story. And the researcher motivated by the entirely understandable desire to rescue a minority from the "condescension of posterity" actually ends up misrepresenting that group in a new way.[25]

This book is an attempt to tell a different story about southern Irish Protestants. Instead of highlighting the group's failures, it explores their successes. Rather than focusing on alienation, it emphasizes integration. And it rejects a narrative of disappearance and decline in favor of something more positive. Once, on the train from Dublin to Cork, I sat across from an octogenarian who—in my graduate-student certainty, earned through weeks of reading Elizabeth Bowen and Molly Keane in the National Library—I just *knew* had to be Protestant, and "Anglo-Irish" at that. She was wearing an ancient dog-hair-ridden tweed field coat; a weeks-old copy of *Spectator* stuck up from her handbag; her posture and skin had that indefinable quality that can be attained only by spending decades around horses. We struck up a conversation. I spent far more time than I had any right to telling her about my research, and she spent the rest of the trip avoiding giving me any information about her at all—until the end. We had pulled into the station and were packing our things. She wished me luck on my work and then said, almost as an aside, "No 'twilight,' please. Every book I've read about us has too much 'twilight.'"[26] If this book is anything, then, it is a "twilight"-free history of southern Irish Protestants: the least such a vital people deserve.

R. M. Smyllie, best known as the editor of the *Irish Times* in the 1930s, 1940s, and early 1950s, was one of these southern Protestants who does not fit the "decline and fall" model: he is one of those who "made it" in independent Ireland. A study of his life and the lives of those in his extensive social network reveals some of the qualities or strategies that successful southern Irish Protestants drew on to make their way in twentieth-century Ireland.

The first of these was a commitment to one's locality. Born in Scotland but raised in Sligo, Smyllie grew up in an area in which southern Protestants played an influential role. His father—an accomplished musician, journalist, newspaper editor, and county councillor—was in many ways the kind of thoroughly engaged turn-of-the-century Protestant bourgeois that nationalists and some historians like to forget ever existed. No one seemed to have informed Smyllie senior that his people were dying relics of a colonial order. In the pages of his newspapers and in countless local meetings, he made a small-*u* unionist, small-*c* conservative, large-*S* Sligoman's case for his people's place in Irish life. In chapter 1, I explore the Smyllie family's life in Sligo just before the revolution, attempting to open a window onto an underexplored area of the southern Irish Protestant experience. Not all lived in Dublin, or in big houses, or on small farms, and they were actively involved in the affairs of their cities and towns. That involvement was not always easy—Smyllie senior clashed as often as he worked with the good burghers of Sligo—but it revealed a deep commitment to his local area.

The second key to success for southern Irish Protestants was reckoning with one's British heritage. Smyllie junior took the typical path of someone of his class and confession, attending Sligo Grammar School and Trinity. He seemed destined to follow his father into provincial journalism. But this plan was interrupted in 1914 when, while working as a tutor for an American family visiting Germany, he was captured and interned. Smyllie spent the first part of Ireland's revolutionary decade in Ruhleben, the civilian internment camp just outside Berlin that, for a while, became one of the most famous prisons in the world. Ruhleben held civilian prisoners of war officially designated as "British," a category that included virtually anyone with British ties that happened to be in German territory at the outbreak of the war. But over the course of the war, this diverse group of inmates actually did create a kind of utopian version of a British community, with its own economy, its own university, its own newspapers, and its own system of private clubs and sports teams and drama groups and musical ensembles. In some ways Ruhleben resembled an Anglophile's ideal version of a small Cotswold town more than a prison camp except that it was in no way provincial: its inhabitants defined their often-contested nationality in terms that were both international and transnational. For them, Britishness had less to do with nation or empire than a commitment to a set of values, beliefs, and practices. In chapter 2, I examine the way that, for Ruhleben internees such as Smyllie and for southern Irish Protestants more generally, a sense of cultural connection to Britain was in no way incompatible with a strong political commitment to Ireland.

The third characteristic of successful Irish Protestants was maintaining a strong sense of one's broader place in Europe. After the war, Smyllie gained a position on the *Irish Times*, which at the time was widely considered to be the journalistic voice of the Protestant upper-middle class. When Smyllie joined the staff, the paper was in search of a new role for itself. Some of its core readers had dropped off the subscriber list by leaving the country, those who stayed were rapidly aging, and the paper's traditional stance now seemed not only anachronistic but quixotic. The paper's editor, John Healy, although often caricatured as a hidebound pedant of the old school, was aware that his paper had to change, and Robert Maire Smyllie seemed the man for the job: an articulate, forward-looking, internationally minded representative of southern Irish Protestantism's new generation. In chapter 3, I examine some of Smyllie's most prominent assignments on the paper in the 1920s and 1930s: reporting from the Paris Peace Conference and writing accounts of his travels in Czechoslovakia. In his reporting on the Peace Conference, Smyllie speaks both to and for southern Irish Protestants who were trying to make sense of Ireland's new position in the postwar world. Although most of his dispatches from Paris do not directly concern Ireland, the implication is clear: Ireland must look beyond its borders in order to see itself clearly. Smyllie's travelogues about Czechoslovakia—which were eventually published in book form, and which earned him the recognition of the Czechoslovakian government—made an even stronger case for an internationalist perspective. That tendency to look outward for solutions to Ireland's problems was something that Smyllie shared with the wider southern Irish Protestant group. As the twentieth century wore on, it would become one of their defining characteristics.

A fourth way that Protestants made their way in independent Ireland was by becoming "patrons." Ireland forgives much of those who find their métier, and southern Protestants who found theirs were accepted into the new state: when it came down to it, no one really cared what your religion was if you could build a business, train horses, keep financial books, pull a tooth, write a poem, or paint a picture or a house better than anyone else. Some southern Irish Protestants found their way into Irish life at that intersection of literature, art, music, jobbery, backstabbing, and self-promotion that characterized Dublin's "poet's pubs" in the middle of the twentieth century. Smyllie, for a time, was the undisputed—although never unresented—king of this environment, with the power to feed a starving modernist or buoy the hopes of an aspiring civil servant-cum-watercolorist with a single commission. And he played the role to the utmost. Smyllie, holding court at the Palace Bar, was the kind of Dublin bohemian who made visitors from Soho or Nollendorfplatz wonder if their own affectations were quite eccentric enough. But in chapter 4, I attempt to illuminate the extent to which this apparently lawless netherworld was in fact a highly organized and rigidly stratified hierarchy and one that allowed Smyllie to carve out a space for himself in Dublin society.

In chapter 5, I explore the fifth way in which southern Irish Protestants "made it" in independent Ireland: by becoming "liberals." In some ways, this was a kind of liberalism by default: if de Valera's Ireland was defined as "conservative"—as it was by his contemporary critics, and as it continues to be by some historians of the period—then its critics were "liberal."[27] Similarly, if Catholicism represented received opinion, then Protestants were, by definition, those who challenged that opinion. As a result, Protestants were often at the forefront of debates over what, in retrospect, look like "liberal" or "progressive" policies. The Mother and Child Scheme, for instance, took on some of the character of a Protestant crusade, despite Protestants playing a relatively small part in a complex and wide-ranging debate.[28] Because of this association with liberalism, Protestants became a target for nationalist critics who questioned the motivation behind, rather than the substance of, southern Protestant opposition to Catholic policies: this was the voice of the burned-out landlord complaining about his former tenants. In 1942 Smyllie and his paper found themselves at the heart of a debate over literary censorship. Three very different sorts of books were banned for violating Catholic practice, and the *Irish Times* leapt to their defense. In the ensuing discussion—which consumed hours of the Irish Senate's meeting time and countless column inches in both the *Irish Times* and the pages of its journalistic competitors—Smyllie and his circle made a strong case for a broader, more "liberal" definition of what it meant to be Irish.

In chapter 6, I examine a question of loyalty. Were southern Irish Protestants more attached to Britain or Ireland? That loyalty was tested during the Second World War, which put southern Irish Protestants in a predicament that was, in some ways, just as uncomfortable as it had been in the First World War. Remaining in neutral Ireland made it very difficult for southern Irish Protestants to rationalize their commitment to even the loosest version of a British Commonwealth: they had abandoned it during its darkest hour. On the other hand, if fighting for Britain offered a kind of consolation, by doing so southern Irish Protestants ran the risk of proving their critics right. They were more British than Irish after all, and now they wore the uniforms that proved it. Smyllie's position was clear: he fully supported the British war effort, up to and including refusing to hire men of military age during the war. And he involved the paper in a war of its own against Ireland's press censors, who were tasked with making sure that Ireland's media would be free of any suspicion that the country favored one side or the other in the conflict. Smyllie's campaign against the censors is perhaps the most heavily analyzed period of his career. He is sometimes presented as a relentless critic of neutrality, taking every opportunity to expose what he believed was an unjust and immoral attempt to mislead the Irish people about what was really going on, motivated by—depending on one's attitude toward Smyllie—a conservative attachment to Britain or a liberal belief in freedom of the press. But a closer examination of his interaction with the censors reveals a different story. Smyllie disagreed with Irish neutrality personally, and he thought the censorship was absurd. But he also believed that it was his duty as an Irish citizen to work within the system, even when—especially when—this meant pointing out the government's errors at every opportunity. And over time, he came to appreciate the arguments made by the "other side," including the case for neutrality. In taking this stance, he reflected a fairly common attitude among southern Protestants. Ireland was still their home, even if they fought for another country.

In chapter 7 I examine an obvious but important question: how different were southern Irish Protestants after all? One obvious marker would seem to be attitudes toward the Irish language. Although the *Irish Times* had long been critical of compulsory Irish language education—an editorial position that Smyllie inherited from Healy and carried on enthusiastically when he took over—Smyllie, like many southern Protestants, had a much more complicated attitude toward the language. He had, after all, studied and briefly taught the language while in Ruhleben. But his most constructive contribution to the Irish language debate was hiring the *Irish Times*'s first Irish-language columnist, Brian O'Nolan. O'Nolan was Catholic, a fluent speaker and writer of Irish, and a nationalist—of a sort; he was, in some ways, the last person one would expect to find a home at the *Irish Times*. Writing under the pseudonym of Myles na gCopaleen, however, O'Nolan turned the language inside out and was often more critical of its staunchest defenders than Smyllie would have ever dared to be. The back-and-forth between Smyllie and "Myles"—which was often a literal back-and-forth, as O'Nolan's column usually appeared on the *Irish Times*'s editorial page—revealed that on a host of topics, these two men from very different backgrounds shared a critical view of Ireland. They were not as different as they seemed.

Finally, in chapter 8, I examine how Smyllie's story fits into perhaps the most pernicious misconception about southern Protestants—what I have termed the "Anglo-Irish Fallacy." The group has long suffered from its association with a motley cohort of aristocratic and semiaristocratic grandees known, with varying degrees of error, as the "Anglo-Irish," the "Ascendancy," the "Anglo-Irish Aristocracy," or "Big House Protestants." Literary critics unfamiliar with Ireland are prone to employing one or the other of these terms to refer to all Irish Protestant writers and artists not named O'Casey; even otherwise responsible historians have been known to misuse the phrase.[29] Many of the misperceptions about southern Protestants generally can be traced to the error of mistaking this part for the whole—those Eugenio Biagini has called "'small-house' Protestants" were, after all, the majority within the minority.[30] It is easy to understand the appeal for the historian: the exodus from castle to semidetached is a lot more picturesque than the shift from Rathmines to a slightly less expensive street in Rathmines. And it is only the most principled nationalist who can resist the temptation to characterize one's enemy as treasonous, heretical, *and* posh. But like most of the stereotypes about southern Protestants, this oversimplifies. The result is that southern Irish Protestants without a title in their background were and are especially sensitive about being mistaken for those who do. Perhaps the only experience shared by virtually every southern Irish Protestant is having a non-Protestant assume that one is richer than one is. However, while it is incorrect to think all Protestants lords, it is also true that members of the group were remarkably successful in maintaining their position in Irish society. The shrewd social networkers of the mid-twentieth century would never have allowed themselves to fail as spectacularly as the "Anglo-Irish" did. In this chapter, I trace how Smyllie—who was not Anglo-Irish but who deeply enjoyed making people think he was—was at the center of a revitalized Irish "Establishment" during the period. Southern Irish Protestants, it turns out, were remarkably successful at making sure that they remained successful.

Despite its largely chronological organization, *Smyllie's Ireland* is not a full-dress biography of R. M. Smyllie, in part because his personal papers have not been collected, much less catalogued. Considering Smyllie's former employees' accounts of his organizational strategies, it is unlikely that such an archive could possibly be compiled. His tendency to write anonymously or under pseudonyms makes it difficult to clearly distinguish his work from that of his employees. He wrote so much, and so much of that under the influence of a looming deadline, whiskey, or both, that a comprehensive survey would probably resemble Borges's "Library of Babel," where "for every rational line or forthright statement there are leagues of senseless cacophony, verbal nonsense, and incoherency."[31] And besides, any such archive would capture only Smyllie's written work, proving a hopelessly incomplete portrait of a figure whose influence should be measured in conversations as well as column inches.

Second, and more importantly, it is not a full-dress biography because it is doubtful that Smyllie's life warrants such an effort. He was a writer and an editor but only occasionally brilliant at either job. The paper he edited is certainly worthy of consideration, but it has already gotten it, in impressive recent work by scholars of Irish cultural history and journalism.[32] Arguably, the *Irish Times* changed Irish journalism: but Smyllie played a transitional, rather than a pivotal, role in that transformation.[33] He deserves a great deal of credit for supporting Irish arts and letters at a time when Irish arts and letters needed all the help they could get, but he never had the money or the influence to become a great benefactor along the lines of Augusta Gregory, Hugh Lane or Sarah Purser. It is entirely appropriate that Smyllie's contribution to Irish culture is commemorated not by a journalism school, or a bursary, or a literary prize, but by the back room of the Palace Bar. Finally, although Smyllie was a staunch opponent of censorship and an influential political and social critic, his line of argument was never rigorous or sustained enough to warrant a place alongside distinguished contemporaries such as Hubert Butler.[34]

In fact, Smyllie's flaws as a biographical subject make him particularly well suited to a project that aims to explore the broader experience of southern Protestants after independence. Rather than biography, this book should be read as microhistory, or perhaps even as a series of microhistories. The reader might notice that Smyllie disappears, for pages at a time, from the narrative that follows; this is deliberate, and it is an indication that *Smyllie's Ireland* is a book about a much wider group of people than its eponymous subject.

All of which raises the question: why put Smyllie—who may be representative of this group but is not, by any means, typical—at the center of the story? Why not tell the general story of the "fall and rise" of Protestants during the period?

The answer is that there is no "general story." Each southern Protestant responded differently during this period, for all sorts of reasons. There were regional variations: the stories of Protestants in Cork do not necessarily match those of Protestants in Donegal. Rural and urban Protestants experienced independent Ireland in different ways. Gender mattered—Samuel

Beckett and Elizabeth Bowen both qualify as "southern Irish Protestants," which is good enough reason for treating the category cautiously. This was a diverse group in terms of class, incorporating everyone from dockworkers to earls. There were also religious differences. "Southern Protestantism" encompassed a wide range of people in a wide range of denominations, many of whom held firm to their sects with an enthusiasm that rivaled or even surpassed that of the Catholic majority. Finally, and perhaps most importantly, there were individual differences of personality. Southern Protestants had no political party, no central organizing committee, no government in exile to speak for them. So each faced modern Ireland himself or herself, with all the inconsistency and incoherence that implies. Generosity, determination, optimism, and confidence are all part of the southern Protestant story; so are selfishness, snobbery, fatalism, and hopelessness. Smyllie's story encompasses all of these.

But Smyllie also had one crucial quality that made him representative of the larger group: like many (perhaps most) southern Irish Protestants, he refused to be defined by decline. His story, like the stories of so many of the members of his minority, is a patriotic one. He loved his country, even if it did not always seem to love or even particularly like him.

Notes

1. See, for instance, Patrick Buckland, *Irish Unionism: The Anglo-Irish and the New Ireland* (Dublin: Gill and Macmillan, 1978); J. C. Beckett, *The Anglo-Irish Tradition* (London: Faber and Faber, 2009); and Terence de Vere White, *The Anglo-Irish* (London: Victor Gollancz Ltd., 1972).

2. The origins of both phrases are controversial. For "descendancy," see Hubert Butler, "The Bell: An Anglo-Irish View," *Irish University Review* 6, no. 1 (Spring 1976): 66–72; and David Fitzpatrick, *Descendancy: Irish Protestant Histories since 1795* (Cambridge: Cambridge University Press, 2014). For Catholics becoming Irish, see R. F. Foster, *Luck and the Irish: A Brief History of Change, 1970–2000* (London: Allen Lane, 2007) and David McWilliams, *The Pope's Children: Ireland's New Elite* (Dublin: Gill and Macmillan, 2005.)

3. R. B. McDowell, *The Irish Convention 1917–18* (London: Routledge and Keegan Paul, 1970).

4. See Peter Hart, "The Protestant Experience of Revolution in Southern Ireland," in *Unionism in Modern Ireland: New Perspectives on Politics and Culture*, ed. Richard English and Graham Walker (London: Macmillan Press Ltd, 1996), 81–98.

5. Terence Dooley, *The Decline of the Big House in Ireland: A Study of Irish Landed Families 1860–1960* (Dublin: Wolfhound Press, 2001), 190.

6. Edmund Burke, "Letter to Richard Burke, Esq., on Protestant Ascendency in Ireland, 1793," in *The Writings and Speeches of Edmund Burke*, vol. 6 (Boston: Little Brown, 1901), 393.

7. John Coakley, "Religion, Ethnic Identity and the Protestant Minority in the Republic," in *Ireland and the Politics of Change*, ed. William Crotty and David E. Schmitt (Harlow, Essex: Addison Wesley Longman Limited, 1998), 90.

8. "Table 8B: Percentage Increase or Decrease from 1911 to 1926 of Persons of Each Religion in Each County and County Borough in Saorstat Eireann," Irish census 1926.

9. "Table 7: Number of Persons of Each Religion in Each Town of 1,500 or More Inhabitants (and Smaller Towns Possessing Local Government) in Saorstat Eireann on 18th April, 1926, Showing Percentage Changes from 1911 to 1926," Irish census 1926.

10. Stephen Mennell, introduction to *Untold Stories: Protestants in the Republic of Ireland 1922-2002* (Dublin: Liffey Press, 2002,) 8–11.

11. Probably the most valuable and important of these collections will be the Irish Protestant Folk Memory Project at the National Folklore Collection at University College Dublin, which has begun collecting fairly recently. See Peter McGuire, "The Secret Lives of Ireland's Protestants," *Irish Times*, February 9, 2017.

12. See Heather W. Crawford, *Outside the Glow: Protestants and Irishness in Independent Ireland* (Dublin: University College Dublin Press, 2010); Robin Bury, *Buried Lives: The Protestants of Southern Ireland* (Dublin: History Press, 2017); Colin Murphy and Lynne Adair, *Untold Stories: Protestants in the Republic of Ireland, 1992–2002* (Dublin: Liffey Press, 2002); Michael McConville, *Ascendancy to Oblivion: The Story of the Anglo-Irish* (London: Quartet Books, 1986); and R. B. McDowell, *Crisis and Decline: The Fate of the Southern Unionists* (Dublin: Lilliput Press, 1997).

13. Andy Bielenberg, "Exodus: The Emigration of Southern Irish Protestants during the Irish War of Independence and the Civil War, *Past and Present*, no. 218 (February 2013): 202.

14. Fitzpatrick, *Descendancy*, 180. The current consensus can be found in Andy Bielenberg, "Southern Irish Protestant Experiences of the Irish Revolution," in *Atlas of the Irish Revolution*, ed. John Crowley, Donal Ó Drisceoil, and Mike Murphy (New York: New York University Press, 2017), 770–80.

15. Catherine O'Connor, "Southern Protestantism: The Inter-relationship of Religious, Social and Gender Identity in the Diocese of Ferns 1945–65" (PhD thesis, University of Limerick, 2007).

16. Peter Holquist, "'Conduct Merciless Mass Terror': Decossackization on the Don, 1919," *Cahiers de Monde Russe* 38, nos. 1–2 (1997): 127–62. Important comparative studies involving Ireland include Tim Wilson, "Ghost Provinces, Mislaid Minorities: the Experience of Southern Ireland and Prussian Poland Compared, 1918–1923," *Irish Studies in International Affairs* 13, no. 1 (2002): 61–86; John Coakley, "Independence Movements and National Minorities: Some Parallels in the European Experience," *European Journal of Political Research* 8 (1980): 215–47, 61–86; and T. K. Wilson, *Frontiers of Violence: Conflict and Identity in Ulster and Upper Silesia, 1918–1922* (Oxford: Oxford University Press, 2010).

17. Anne Dolan, "Divisions and Divisions and Divisions: Who to Commemorate?" in *Towards Commemoration: Ireland in War and Remembrance 1912–1923*, ed. John Horne and Edward Madigan (Dublin: Royal Irish Academy, 2013), 151.

18. Tim Fanning, *The Fethard-on-Sea Boycott* (Dublin: Collins Press, 2010).

19. Daithí Ó Corráin, *Rendering to God and Caesar: The Irish Churches and the Two States in Ireland, 1949–73* (Manchester: Manchester University Press, 2006) 88–93.

20. Kurt Bowen, *Protestants in a Catholic State: Ireland's Privileged Minority* (Kingston and Montreal: McGill-Queens University Press, 1983). See also Crawford, *Outside the Glow*, esp. 137–68.

21. "Ireland's Quiet Protestants," *Economist*, May 21, 1998.

22. "Table 1A: Persons of Each Religion at Each Census" and "Table 11: Males and Females in Occupational Groups Classified by Religion," Irish Census 1961.

23. Niall Meehan's exploration of Protestant business networks via an analysis of advertisements in the *Irish Times* is one ingenious approach to this problem. See Niall Meehan, "Shorthand for Protestants: Sectarian Advertising in the *Irish Times*," *History Ireland* 17, no. 5 (September/October 2009), 46–49.

24. Ian d'Alton, "'A Vestigial Population'?: Perspectives on Southern Irish Protestants in the Twentieth Century," *Éire-Ireland* 44, nos. 3–4 (fall/winter 2009): 41.

25. E. P. Thompson, *The Making of the English Working Class* (New York: Vintage Books, 1966), 12.

26. She was referring to a common trope in writing about this group during this period: historians and literary scholars will often refer to the "twilight" in the sense of the "last hours" of southern Irish Protestants, occurring in the early twentieth century.

27. Ronan Fanning, *Éamon de Valera: A Will to Power* (London: Faber & Faber, 2015).

28. Eamonn McKee, "Church-State Relations and the Development of Irish Health Policy: The Mother and Child Scheme, 1944–1953," *Irish Historical Studies* 25, no. 98 (November 1986): 159–94.

29. See, for instance, Caleb Richardson, "Transforming Anglo-Ireland: R.M. Smyllie and the *Irish Times*," *New Hibernia Review* 11, no. 4 (geimhreadh/winter 2007): 17–36.

30. Eugenio Biagini, "The Protestant Minority in Southern Ireland," *Historical Journal* 55, no. 4 (2012): 1172.

31. Jorge Luis Borges, "The Library of Babel," in *Jorge Luis Borges: Collected Fictions*, trans. Andrew Hurley (New York: Penguin Books, 1998), 114.

32. See Terence Brown, *The* Irish Times: *Fifty Years of Influence* (London: Bloomsbury, 2015); Mark O'Brien, *The* Irish Times: *A History* (Dublin: Four Courts Press, 2008); Ian d'Alton, "A Protestant Paper for a Protestant People: The *Irish Times* and the Southern Irish Minority," *Irish Communication Review* 12, no. 1 (January 2010): 65–73; Dermot James, *From the Margin to the Centre: A History of the* Irish Times (Dublin: Woodfield Press, 2008); and John Martin, *The* Irish Times *Past and Present: A Record of the Journal Since 1859* (Belfast: Belfast Historical and Educational Society, 2008).

33. Mark O'Brien highlights the important role that Smyllie played in the Mother-and-Child Debate, as well as placing the editor's contributions in their larger context. See Mark O'Brien, *The Fourth Estate: Journalism in Twentieth-Century Ireland* (Manchester: Manchester University Press, 2017,) especially pages 104–7.

34. Smyllie's social criticism could never withstand, for instance, the incisive treatment that Butler's receives in Robert Tobin, *The Minority Voice: Hubert Butler and Southern Irish Protestantism, 1900–1991* (Oxford: Oxford University Press, 2012).

1

LOCALS

R. M. SMYLLIE WAS NOT THE FIRST IN his family to court controversy. In the spring of 1900, when his father was editor of the *Sligo Independent*, Smyllie senior had publicized a report by a Local Government Board inspector. The inspector had criticized the Sligo Board of Guardians for its treatment of workhouse inmates, and Smyllie senior—always happy to highlight any mismanagement by the nationalist-dominated board, particularly when it involved the poor—had given the report full coverage in his newspaper. In response, the Board of Guardians banned Smyllie from their meetings.

Smyllie showed up at the next meeting anyway. When asked to leave, he refused. The Guardians alerted the porter, who decided to call for reinforcements. Smyllie prepared for a fight while also alerting a justice of the peace (JP) in attendance "that it was [the JP's] duty to prevent any assault being committed in his presence." The JP's first impulse was to circumvent the problem by simply leaving the room, allowing the assault to continue in his absence. But then Edward Foley, a fellow member of the board, a prominent brewer, and later a mayor of Sligo, pointed out that it was "contrary to the spirit of any Irish gentleman to ask three men to attack one man." A better option, he suggested, would be trial by combat: one member of the board should defend the group's honor via a one-on-one fight with Smyllie.[1]

No one took Foley up on this offer, so the police were called. Foley pointed out, with some justification, that this was a pointless gesture, "as the police, he said, would only preserve the peace, and Mr. Smyllie was quite peaceable."[2] Smyllie stood his ground, and the affair ended with a deadlock. The meeting broke up. Smyllie was the last to leave.

This event could be read as a fin de siècle precursor of the declining power and influence of southern Protestants later in the century, foreshadowing even more severe forms of exclusion and alienation yet to come. At the time, however, the *Irish Times* probably hit closer to the mark when it characterized the incident as an amusing lark, another case of a provincial eccentric showing up the powers that be. According to the paper, "the incident . . . caused much amusement in Sligo."[3] This was not a case of a southern Protestant making a last stand for a doomed race. Smyllie senior was playing a role much more integral to Irish society, both before and after independence: the local character.

Localism was a crucial part of southern Irish Protestant identity, as it was and as it continues to be to Irish identity generally.[4] Except during unusually tense periods of political or sectarian upheaval, local roots trump most other allegiances; the gang of blow-ins from one county over is far more "foreign" than the family with the German last name who has lived in the townland for generations. Hubert Butler, one of southern Irish Protestantism's most cosmopolitan defenders, is proof of this: for all his international connections he was, first and foremost, a Kilkennyman. A passionate genealogist, archaeologist, preservationist and "country scholar," Butler had a global reach that served to complement, rather than supersede, his love of the Nore River valley.[5] "I have always believed that local history is more important than national history," wrote this evangelist for the restoration of southern Protestants to Ireland's national story. "Where life is fully and consciously lived in our own neighbourhood, we are cushioned a little from the impact of great far-off events which should be of only marginal concern to us," observed this most passionate advocate for eastern Europe's relevance to the West.[6]

Attachment to one's neighborhood, in fact, was one of the defining characteristics of southern Irish Protestants, both before and after independence. Some of this followed the conventionally "Anglo-Irish" model of Protestant as patron. Protestants served their local communities through scholarship, uncovering the history, archaeology, or natural history of their areas. The early volumes of the *Journal of the County Kildare Archaeological Society* contain numerous contributions from and tributes to a number of "Anglo-Irish" figures, perhaps most prominently Sir Walter Fitzgerald, whom the society still recognizes with an annual prize. Although the Irish Georgian Society is now a national organization with an international profile, its modern founder, Desmond Guinness, was famously inspired by one particular part of Dublin. Leaving the Shelbourne Hotel, he saw workmen removing roof slates from houses in Kildare Place and realized that he had found his mission.[7] "Anglo-Irish" figures less prone to intellectual forms of leisure served as masters of local hunts, which involved them deeply in the economic and social lives of a kind of "country" that does not necessarily appear on official maps.[8]

For those with less lofty backgrounds, southern Protestant localism took the form of involvement in a whole set of voluntary organizations. On one level, being active in one's local church implies transcendence—of local, national, even metaphysical boundaries. But, at least within that portion of their activity that took place in this world, most southern Irish Protestants experienced their faith in an intensely local way. Martin Maguire has described Church of Ireland parishes as "self-governing republics," each maintaining its own finances, its own media operation, and a whole set of parish organizations, both charitable and social.[9] Examining the associations listed in one inner-city parish's magazine in 1930, Maguire counted sixteen different social groups. In a parish in better-off Clontarf, he found an astonishing thirty-nine, ranging from the Children's Scripture Company to the Minstrels' Troupe to the Ping Pong Club.[10] This fondness for associations was by no means limited to members of the Church of Ireland, either: reports of the annual meeting of the Adelaide Road Presbyterian Church congregation in 1941 reveal the existence of active branches of the Women's Missionary Association, the Ladies' Committee, the Girls' Auxiliary, the Old Age Fund, the Orphan Society, the Praise Committee, and the Knitting Party, among others.[11]

Even international Protestant voluntary organizations differed greatly according to locality. Norma MacMaster, who grew up in Cavan in the 1940s and 1950s, remembers that her fellow Presbyterians took their faith and its role in the Irish story very seriously. "We were proud of our faithfulness to our tradition in spite of 'famine and sword,' proud that we had withstood the onslaughts of the once-established Anglican Church and the Roman Church, proud of our values," she remembered. "[We'd] have cheered King Billy on."[12] One would assume a group with these commitments would be natural and passionate Orangemen. But in fact, according to MacMaster, in Cavan the Orange Order took on a very different character than it did across the border. To borrow R. V. Comerford's phrase, Cavan Orangeism appears to have been more pastime than patriotism.[13] History was one thing, writes MacMaster, but "when it came to Orangeism, well that was an entirely different matter! To be Orange was an optional extra, a frivolous frill that threw a blade of colour into otherwise dull lives in July and August."[14] Whereas a few miles across the border the movement took on a whole mass of sectarian and political associations, translated into the locality of Cavan it was just another leisure activity. Presumably, after marching season, the sashes went back into the press, and the Presbyterians of Cavan returned to their Ping Pong Club.

For southern Protestants, local affairs allowed them to be involved in ways that were often denied them at the national level. In the received narrative of southern Protestant decline, one of the often-cited landmarks is the Local Government (Ireland) Act of 1898. This replaced the existing system of local government, made up of grand juries and baronial sessions, both of which were overwhelmingly dominated by Protestant and Unionist landlords, with directly elected councils. While scholars who emphasize the significance of the act are looking in the right place—local government does matter—they often fall victim to two of the great pitfalls of writing about southern Protestants. They overestimate the relevance of the "Anglo-Irish" to the group as a whole, and they underestimate the diversity of avenues to political—and nonpolitical—activity in local life. It is true that the Local Government Act significantly reduced the political influence of the Protestant minority. It is also true that there are numerous ways of making one's voice heard, and being actively engaged in one's locality is one of the most effective of these. The experience of the head of the Smyllie family in the 1890s through the 1910s is an example of how focusing on local and regional issues allowed southern Protestants to overcome whatever deficit attached to their faith and supposed allegiances.

Smyllie moved to Sligo from Glasgow in the late 1880s, working as a journalist on the conservative *Sligo Independent* newspaper. If Sligo seems an odd career choice for a young turn-of-the-century journalist on the move, it is important to remember that the town was a thriving port, and one with a long history of Protestant settlement. Smyllie's path had been well trod by Scottish Protestants, and by the middle of the eighteenth century half of the inhabitants of Sligo town were Protestant. If by the 1880s that population had declined, and if it did not quite retain the "magnetic appeal to the Protestants" that it had once had, it was still an important commercial city with a relatively large number of Protestants and with close ties to Ulster.[15] It was also—no small draw for a conservative journalist looking to make his name—notorious for corruption, governed by a combination of bodies medieval, modern, and everything in between. By the 1880s, it had become a byword: an analyst of British elections used Sligo as an example of "general corruption" so endemic that it had almost become the status quo.[16] The presence of rich Protestant and "Anglo-Irish" families such as the Pollexfens, Coopers, Gore-Booths, and Wynnes must also have been an attraction, promising patronage both financial and social. And the area boasted a range of social, charitable, and sporting organizations that often crossed sectarian boundaries. It is not accidental that, in his *History of Sligo*, the "Anglo-Irish" scion William Gregory Wood-Martin lumps "religion" into a somewhat vestigial chapter along with sport, recreation, education, and language: one's faith was only one of many aspects of identity in Sligo.[17]

Smyllie appears to have met his wife, Katherine Follis, in Sligo. She was a native of Kerry who was the principal of the Calry School. They were married in 1892. The marriage was, in a sense, a mixed one—Robert was Presbyterian, and Katherine was Church of Ireland—although Katherine appears to have adopted her husband's faith at some point between the 1901 and 1911 censuses.[18] Although by the time they married the Smyllies already had distinguished careers in journalism and education, it appears that what brought them together—and what first got them noticed in Sligo—was music. In 1890, Robert appeared as bass soloist in Alfred Robert Gaul's once enormously popular *The Holy City*. It was in the first concert of the ninth season of the Sligo Musical Society, and Smyllie did not disappoint, contributing an encore of "Deep in the Mine" that was "much relished."[19] "Miss Follis," as she then was, was also musical, being described as "a highly accomplished vocalist" in their wedding announcement.[20] By 1893 Smyllie was advertising his services as a teacher of the "Tonic-Solfa System"—a once-popular method of teaching sight singing, deeply rooted in the Presbyterian tradition. "During the past week a pupil of his, Miss A. Armstrong succeeded in obtaining the first grade certificate of the Tonic-Solfa College, London," announced the *Sligo Champion* in January 1893. "It is sufficient to say on the subject that Miss Armstrong was but in three months in training under Mr. Smyllie."[21]

In some respects, Smyllie's musical activities followed the southern Protestant mode. Much of his talent he put to spiritual use: he was organist and choirmaster as well as precentor (lead singer) of the Sligo Presbyterian Church.[22] In 1897, the Sligo Presbyterian Musical Association presented him with a silver baton in honor of the "improvement which he had effected in their musical service."[23] Many of his concerts were held under the auspices of local Protestant grandees: the patrons of the Sligo Musical Society included prominent landowners such as Gore-Booths, the Coopers, and the

Wynnes. But either his talent was too great or Sligo Protestant circles were too small for him to be contained within sectarian boundaries. By 1909, Smyllie had become, according to the *Fermanagh Herald*, "a household word in Sligo . . . within recent years there has been no artist who has created such a favourable impression upon a music-loving and discriminating public."[24] As Patrick Deignan has shown, Sligo musical circles were fairly diverse; if anything, the minority played a majority role in what were quite religiously mixed organizations.[25] Still, it says something about Smyllie's musical abilities that the *Herald*, a nationalist paper, praised him in such terms, especially since he had just founded a conservative competitor in the *Sligo Times*. But then again, they were praising the kind of southern Protestant who would gladly appear in a concert sponsored by the exclusively Catholic Ancient Order of Hibernians. And the kind that would play a crucial role in establishing Sligo's own Feis Ceoil.[26] Three decades later, his son would also complement his journalistic career with a strong involvement in the arts—although Robert Maire Smyllie would focus on literature rather than music.

Smyllie elder's interactions with local bodies in Sligo were not always so comfortable. In 1895, while still on the staff of the *Sligo Independent*, he became involved in a controversy over street preaching. During the 1890s, a small number of Protestant evangelical organizations, most of which were based in England, began proselytizing in Irish cities and towns, provoking a strong response from church and civil authorities and an occasionally violent reaction from the public. In Sligo during the summer of 1895, in response to this evangelism, a riot broke out where preachers were stoned and a local deaf-mute Protestant boy was beaten. When the suspected perpetrators were brought to a hearing, a nationalist-dominated bench dismissed all of the charges.[27]

For Smyllie, the affair—which combined anti-Protestant bigotry, populist violence, and an assault on freedom of speech—was irresistible. He publicized every affront to the preachers in the *Sligo Independent*, to the point that the nationalist *Sligo Champion* felt compelled to defend the Protestants of Sligo against association with Smyllie:

> Now, we ask who were the very first to object to those "Protestant Missionaries" coming to Sligo to preach "the glad tidings?" The respectable Protestants of the town! At a representative meeting of Churchmen held in the vestry room of St. John's Church, on the Friday before the first attempt was made at street-preaching, the following resolution was unanimously adopted:—"Resolved: That we, the churchmen of the parish of St. John and Calry, hereby declare

that we disapprove of the projected visit of Open-air Missionaries to Sligo; that we believe the requirements of religious worship are amply secured by the existing organisations, and that we believe our opinion to be representative."

Smyllie and his fellow writers could console themselves with "being martyrs to the cause of liberty," but that would not stop the *Champion* from speaking up for true Protestantism.[28] No "Scotch reared bigot or irresponsible nobody from the Salt Market of Glasgow" would dictate terms to the people of Sligo.[29] By December of that year, Smyllie's association with street preaching had grown to the point that he himself was attacked.[30] He drew a revolver against his assailant and eventually ended up appearing in court, although the case was withdrawn "in the hope that by such an agreement peace would be secured in the town."[31]

But it did not end there. At the end of the year, a large group of Catholics met in Sligo to discuss the issue of street preaching. By this point Smyllie's name was common currency. The mayor, P. A. McHugh, reminded the assembled crowd that while the preachers had left the scene of the crime, their defender remained. "They fled full soon on the month of June, and they left poor Smyllie fighting," he announced in a piece of doggerel that was met with "loud laughter and groans." Next the crowd heard a letter from John Clancy, recently ensconced as Bishop of Elphin. He attacked "the studied sentences of Smyllie's clerical assistants," regretting that Smyllie and his minions had allowed "loud-voiced evangelisers, redolent of garlic and whiskey," to transform "our peaceful towns, where for ages Catholics and Protestants were on the most intimate terms of friendship" into "a 'pandemonium,' where blasphemies against our faith are vociferated in the public streets, and insults to our Catholic feelings are dinned into our ears." "There is a higher law than the law of England," concluded the bishop, "and more important interests than liberty of speech." The rest of the meeting went on along similar lines: the editorial line of the *Sligo Independent* was jeered, every mention of Smyllie's name was booed, and the meeting broke up having adopted "the attitude of endeavouring to maintain peace, but refusing to submit to insult (loud cheers)."[32]

To its credit, the *Sligo Champion* did not fail to report one important, if somewhat unexpected, feature of this meeting: throughout the entire proceedings, Smyllie sat in the front row of the platform, taking it all in. One gets the sense that he would not have missed it for the world. This willingness—even eagerness—to engage with one's critics would be shared by his son and by some of southern Protestantism's most important representatives.

But nothing better captures Smyllie's commitment to local affairs than the paper that he founded and edited between 1909 and 1914. During the existence of Smyllie's *Sligo Times*, Sligo had two conservative newspapers, the *Times* and the *Independent*, as well as a nationalist weekly, the *Sligo Champion*. Two conservative papers in one town was unusual, although not unheard of: there were conservative or unionist papers throughout provincial Ireland well into the 1910s, including in Carlow, Galway, Meath, Kilkenny, Limerick, Longford, Waterford, and Wicklow. Some of these were quite influential. Although its name is now most often associated with the rugby club, the *Cork Constitution* was one of the leading unionist voices of its time.[33] But many of these papers were, for lack of a better word, provincial. They reported on county councils, provided accounts of borough courts and petty sessions, and publicized committee and charity meetings. If one were to skip their editorial pages, it would be difficult to tell a nationalist from a unionist paper in turn-of-the-century Ireland. Both would probably feature a tedious report of the recent meeting of the local school committee; both would probably include a few "special" reprints from national papers concerning events in Parliament; both, if the papers were successful, would be full of advertisements for local haberdashers and kitchen necessities ("'Purity' Flour: The Brand for Everybody: Same Quality for the Peasant as for the King.")[34]

Nevertheless, that editorial page mattered to the public, who decided which paper to subscribe to according to its political position, and to the paper's editors and owners, who hoped to promote their particular viewpoint while also maintaining the paper as a going concern. Smyllie was taking a risk founding a second conservative paper in this small city, but he was doing so because he believed in his cause: he had decided that his former employer, the *Sligo Independent,* was not conservative enough. "We can only say that the Conservative policy (?) [*sic*] of the 'Sligo Independent' only excites laughter and ridicule amongst those conservatives whose Conservatism is worth being taken into account," he wrote in one of the early issues of the paper.[35] For Smyllie, the *Independent* was too confrontational, too disconnected from the life of the city, too much a caricature of southern Protestantism's worst features, to truly represent conservatism's values in Sligo. In some ways, Smyllie senior did for conservatism in Sligo what his son would do for the "Anglo-Irish" in Ireland, and his efforts to integrate his beliefs into a changing country would be echoed by many other southern Protestants in many other areas of Irish life.

What, then, made an Irish provincial newspaper truly "conservative," according to Smyllie? A policy of moderation, for one: "A great and wise Conservative once said that everything good in the political sense is to be found between extremes." It also meant encouraging civil debate: the *Sligo Times*'s "conservatism will not partake of . . . the abusive characteristics which are the distinguishing features of some of our contemporaries." Finally and most importantly, it meant being embedded in its local community:

> From all classes of the community the editor of this paper has received the warmest encouragement, the kindliest expressions of esteem, and the more practical, but no more welcome, promises of support. We come amongst the people of Sligo garbed in no false robe or colour. Our politics are well known to all, and it is gratifying to us to know that gentlemen whom we have opposed politically in the past have been the first to offer us their good wishes because, as one stern and unbending nationalist—Mr. John Gilmartin—remarked, they prefer an open opponent to a secret foe.[36]

It was not enough to promote conservative principles. The point was to do so in a way that would engage rather than alienate the local community.

Each issue of the *Sligo Times* included a "Picture Gallery" feature, highlighting prominent locals. This was not just good business, although it was that—the continuing survival of the *Sligo Times* required the backing of local merchants. But it was also an opportunity for Smyllie to develop and promote his particular version of conservatism and to restore southern Protestants to the Irish story though a local approach. The first to receive this honor was Major Charles Kean O'Hara, who might seem the personification of southern Irish Protestantism at its most exclusive. He was a member of the O'Haras of Annaghmore, a Gaelic family whose history serves as a kind of shorthand for the Irish Protestant experience: they converted from Catholicism in the early 1600s, thus escaping the confiscations of the next two centuries. They then went on to serve as high sheriffs, deputy lieutenants, and MPs; befriended Edmund Burke; helped suppress the 1798 rebellion; opposed the Union; provided relief during the Famine; and married into an Anglo-Irish family, the Coopers, in the 1860s. C. K. O'Hara was lord-lieutenant of the county, was active in unionist politics, and even led his own pack of hounds, the O'Hara Harriers.[37] But for Smyllie, O'Hara was a model Irishman, full stop: "In politics he is an unwavering conservative, true to the principles and the traditions of his race, but his sympathies are wide, his opinions broad, and even those who most strongly differ from him recognise in him the personification of all that is noblest, most highminded and best in the Irish character."[38]

Later "Picture Gallery" features made similar cases, both for Protestants such as George Pollexfen and Catholics such as John O'Dowd; what bound them, according to Smyllie, was service to their local community.[39] Doing what was right for Sligo transcended sectarian and national political differences.

None of this is to say that the *Sligo Times* believed that one's attachment to locality should take the place of broader loyalties. Reports of the naval arms race between Britain and Germany brought out Smyllie's most lyrical side: "Germany is the Power that may be, but it will never become the power that Is [*sic*] until the men of British blood forget the noble traditions of their race, and allow the old flag that has braved the battle and the breeze to sink into inglourious ignominy. That day, we believe, will never dawn."[40] Much of the same imagery featured in another editorial a few months later, this one on the topic of empire: "The Imperial idea means something fundamentally different from an alliance for specific purposes. It is deeper, more intimate, more expressive of the essential unity of the British race . . . the disruption of the Empire would be a blow at that higher civilization of which the dawn is now breaking in rosy splendour upon us."[41]

Smyllie was an unabashed unionist, heavily publicizing the activities of local unionist organizations and speaking at a rally himself in August 1912.[42] And his old-fashioned devotion to king and country did not forget the first part, either. Although as a matter of policy he promoted a vision of Ireland that included a wide range of different political views, when the king died in 1910 he could not imagine but that all of "the Irish people believed absolutely in the good faith of King Edward."[43] This attachment to old conventions would be shared by his son, who fought tooth and nail against removing the "Court and Personal" section from the *Irish Times*.

But although Smyllie could certainly outdo the most sentimental patriots when he wished, it was much more common for him to bring national politics down to the local level. Sometimes this meant urging his readers to stop worrying so much about nation and instead focus on country. "If instead of tubthumping and prating about the merits of Home Rule," he suggested, "the men and women of Ireland were to settle down quietly to work together irrespective of creed or politics, for the betterment of the country, what a different Ireland we would have!"[44] A few days before the general election of December 1910, he appealed to Sligo's nationalists in the best way he knew how:

> Have our nationalist friends considered that they now enjoy to the fullest extent local Home Rule? They have the absolute control of all local taxation; they have filled all places of honour and emolument by [sic] those who agree with them religiously and politically. In this whole country not a single representative position has been allotted to a Unionist, nor would one have the slightest chance of being elected to any position of profit, against a Nationalist, although Unionists contribute so strongly to the general taxation. We regret that this should be the case, but we have made no protest as we are quite conscious that in former times we were not altogether free from blame in this respect.[45]

The passage captures some of the fundamental conflicts within southern Protestantism in the early twentieth century. Its view of history is simultaneously apologetic and accusatory; its take on politics is both entirely reasonable and yet utterly blind to the nationalist perspective. There is a reason that "local Home Rule" never inspired its own political movement. On the other hand, to those such as Smyllie, whose world virtually ended at the county if not city limits, it makes perfect sense.

But another aspect of this passage became significant only in retrospect. Despite his assertion that his kind would not have "the slightest chance of being elected to any position of profit," just under a year after publishing the editorial Smyllie was elected to the Sligo County Council. He was, his paper crowed, "the only Conservative who has come forward for election in Sligo since the first polls under the Local Government Act of 1898, and for the first time in over ten years a Conservative will take his seat on the Corporation."[46] It was a shocking result for those who did not know Smyllie or Sligo. The *Irish Independent* reported with amazement that Smyllie defeated two nationalist challengers in the "overwhelmingly Nationalist" North Ward.[47] The nationalist *Strabane Chronicle* took the opportunity to interpret this as a sign of tolerance, reporting that while "one of the arguments used against Home rule was that no Unionist was a member of the Sligo Corporation," Smyllie's election "disproves the allegation that Catholics and Nationalists are bigoted in municipal matters."[48] But even this generous interpretation could not overcome the small victory Smyllie had achieved for the power of localism.

In at least one respect, Smyllie did not disappoint those who had elected him: he was a consistent and relentless critic of corruption and misuse of public funds. In 1912, he was appointed to represent the Corporation in an examination of a nearby waterworks. Water was leaking out of a reservoir, which raised the possibility that, during hot weather, the reservoir might dry up completely. Smyllie drew up a report on the matter, and when he presented it, another councilor questioned whether this was really a problem at all. An excerpt from the meeting provides a flavor of the discussion that ensued:

> Councillor Hanley—Isn't the water up to its nominal height now?
> Mayor—It is.
> Councillor Hanley—What more do we want?
> Councillor Smyllie—Mr. Hanley knows nothing about it. He is ignorant of the facts.
> Councillor Hanley—I certainly object to you jumping at me in that way.
> Councillor Smyllie—You don't understand the facts.
> Councillor Hanley—Your report is not worth considering.
> Councilor Smyllie—I protest against such a statement. It is an honest report. Evidently you are not worth considering.[49]

Smyllie also supported and heavily publicized the meetings of the "Co. Sligo Ratepayer's Defence Association," the forerunner of the "Ratepayer's Association" movement, one of the most important routes to Protestant involvement in local politics in the decade before independence.[50] In his recent thesis, which examines Protestant life in Sligo from 1914 to 1939, Patrick Deignan captures the importance of the Sligo Ratepayer's Association (SRA) in the life of the city during and after the First World War. The SRA was founded partially in response to a series of negative reports about Sligo's finances. The group was at its strongest beginning in 1917, when a group of businessmen—both Protestant and Catholic—banded together to try to reform the finances of the Sligo Corporation. As Deignan shows, it had a significant influence on Sligo politics, even inspiring the introduction of a new system of voting. Rather than the first-past-the-post system, the Sligo Corporation established a combination of Proportional Representation (PR) and Single Transferable Vote (STV), both of which give minorities a greater chance for representation. In January 1919, Sligo became the first municipality in the United Kingdom to use Proportional Representation in an election, and the result was a reason for Protestant optimism: five of the eight newly elected SRA councilors were Protestants.[51]

But the 1917 version of the SRA was not the first attempt by Protestants to retain a voice in Sligo politics. Ratepayers' associations had popped up throughout the country beginning in the early 1910s, with candidates winning elections in Protestant strongholds such as Pembroke and Dalkey and making a strong showing in Cork.[52] Their message was simple: they were paying too much in tax, and their tax money was being misspent by local authorities. Because many of those local authorities happened to be nationalists, the SRA movement was associated with Protestants and Unionists, to the point that some nationalists believed it to be a kind of fifth column: John O'Dowd, a Sligo MP, declared them "a gang of narrow Orange bigots."[53] But in fact, in Sligo and elsewhere, this was an issue that cut across the usual lines of Irish politics, uniting middle-class Catholics with Protestants who had something to lose to what they believed to be a corrupt system. David Fitzpatrick, in his analysis of a similar group in Clare, has written that an attempt to ban the organization in that county "brought more Protestants into common cause with Catholics than, perhaps, any episode since the Union."[54] Taxes were a local issue that transcended religious divisions, and Smyllie devoted much of his time in office to exposing the way "they"—by which he meant officialdom—were spending "our"—by which he meant Sligo citizens'—money. After independence, many southern Protestants would raise similar concerns, although from a less conservative standpoint; Smyllie the younger, for instance, would criticize the government for not spending enough on social welfare.

But if the nationalists of Sligo feared that Smyllie was the vanguard of a unionist counterrevolution, their fears were quickly allayed. On the two great issues of the day—votes for women and the labor movement—he held fast to the moderate position that he had laid out in his early editorials. He was supportive of women's suffrage, but not quite yet. He and his newspaper had backed women's suffrage from the beginning—"we have sympathy with the women who are seeking the vote by proper methods"[55]—but he also wrote that "we fear the present times are too unsettled . . . to grant [suffragists] their desires."[56] Similarly, when Sligo became one of Ireland's centers of trade union activity, culminating in the election of several members of the Irish Transport and General Workers' Union (ITGWU) to the council and the participation of Sligo's workers in several national strikes, Smyllie occupied the middle ground. Michael Wheatley has argued that because of the prominence of Protestants among Sligo's business leaders, trade union activity was closely linked with nationalism: in Sligo, standing up against the bosses meant standing up against Protestants.[57] Smyllie recognized that it could have this implication and spent much of his time making the case that this was a local issue: the real division was between the people of Sligo and outsiders. "We sympathise with the working classes in their struggles to improve their condition," he wrote in 1911, "but we have no hesitation in advising them to beware of paid English agitators, who do not care a straw how many Irish families may be starved with hunger and cold so long as they gain their own desires."[58] As always, his argument was for moderation: "violence of language and rioting can never be expected to settle a problem so difficult as the one we are considering." This could never be the work of Sligomen, after all. "Of course the great majority of the working men of Sligo would not be guilty of wanton insult and destruction of property," he wrote in 1913, "but in their name deeds have been done which are certain to injure their cause."[59]

When it came to his work on the council, he was even less radical. One of his first actions after being elected was to support a resolution on censorship put forward by the Ancient Order of Hibernians. "The provincial towns of Ireland are flooded weekly with newspapers which give details of divorce cases with all their sensual developments, the reading of which constitutes a grave danger to young people," Smyllie wrote in an editorial. "We welcome the movement to stamp out pernicious literature."[60] And many of his own contributions were much more modest than attacking "officialism" among his fellow councilors or backing the SRA: he put forward a motion to put the unemployed to work repairing Sligo streets, opposed a movement to ban cycling on city footpaths, and supported a plan to build houses for laborers.[61] Rather than pushing any sort of grand ideological agenda, he spent most of his time trying to ease the daily frustrations of the citizens of Sligo. In 1911, he made national news by drawing attention to the Byzantine complexities involved in sending a telegram from Sligo to Drumcliffe, a town just north of the city. A telegram sent from Sligo went first to Dublin, then to Enniskillen, then to Bundoran, and then to Grange, from which it was carried by bicycle to Drumcliffe. By the time it reached its final destination, it had traveled just under three hundred miles in order to reach a town five miles north. This was the kind of outrage that could unite all the people of Sligo.[62]

Even when it came to the issues that in many respects got Smyllie into politics in the first place, his touch was light. During a particularly virulent period of criticism of Sligo's finances in the spring of 1912, Smyllie used the *Times* to highlight every one of the Corporation's misdeeds. But here again he was standing up for the people of Sligo, not for nationalists or unionists or Catholics or Protestants. Even when he boasted, he did so in local terms. By August 1912, he was particularly proud to announce that "the *Sligo Times* has a larger circulation than any other Conservative paper published in the North-West."[63] Again, the "North-West" was what mattered, not Ireland or Britain. Even early on, when touting the paper to potential advertisers, he had chosen to quote the nationalist *Roscommon Herald* endorsement of the *Sligo Times*: "[it] is of course a Unionist organ . . . its politics are of a genial type, and already it has found some of its strongest adherents amongst the Nationalists in the country." "Everybody likes Mr. Smyllie," wrote the *Herald*, in a eulogy that Smyllie must have particularly appreciated, "and nobody bothers too much about his politics."[64]

The father's influence on the son's work was clear. In some ways, the *Irish Times* of the 1930s and 1940s would come to resemble a national version of the *Sligo Times* of the 1910s. Both papers focused on Irish affairs but acknowledged British connections; both papers encouraged the Protestant minority not only to accept but to embrace an active role in contemporary Irish life. Above all, both would bear the mark of an editor deeply embedded in the city in which he worked: Smyllie junior would become as much a fixture of Dublin life as his father had been in Sligo.

One of the great flaws of the "alienation and decline" model of southern Protestantism is how it flattens the way life is actually lived. Focusing on the local can correct for this. Even in the turbulent lead-up to the revolutionary decade of the nineteen-teens and twenties, Catholics and Protestants, unionists and nationalists, and that always considerable group of people who fall in between all of the historian's neat categories had to find a way to live together. And at times they probably even enjoyed it a little.

Perhaps the best expression of this in Smyllie senior's life appears in a small paragraph in the *Sligo Champion* from 1907. James "Pat" Rowan was leaving town. Rowan was the sort of local grandee who could be found in nearly every small city in Ireland—a businessman and man-about-town whose "name was one to conjure with at all the sporting and athletic meetings in the county of Sligo for many years past,"[65] exactly the kind of figure who plays an enormous role in his area but leaves little historical record behind. To mark the occasion, the mayor, Michael Keane, hosted a reception in Rowan's honor. Among the list of attendees, few would end up on the subscriber lists of Smyllie's paper when he would found it a few years later; fewer still, probably, would attract his criticism in the pages of the *Sligo Times* or across the table in a county council meeting. But they were all there together that night.

The group delivered a formal farewell to Pat, presented the guest of honor with a parting gift, toasted a variety of bodies ranging from "The Ladies" to "The Commercial Prosperity of Sligo" to "The Professions" to "The Press," and then were treated to "recitations, songs, etc." by the more artistic contingent, a group that included Smyllie. The reporter present at the meeting highlighted two songs in particular: Thomas Davis's "A Nation Once Again" and Robert Burns's "Auld Lang Syne."[66]

It would be interesting to know which of these last two songs Smyllie joined in on. Both, it is true, were written by Protestants. But neither author's views would have been particularly welcome on the pages of the *Independent* or the *Times* or in the Smyllies' dining room in Union Place. Nevertheless, it is likely that Smyllie sang both. He sang for Pat, and he sang for that small part of Ireland called Sligo that he loved. And he probably meant every word that night.

Notes

1. *Irish Times*, March 6, 1900.

2. Ibid.

3. Ibid.

4. See Tom Inglis, "Local Belonging, Identities and Sense of Place in Contemporary Ireland," IBIS Discussion Paper #4, Institute for British-Irish Studies, University College Dublin, accessed March 1, 2017, http://www.ucd.ie/ibis/publications/discussionpapers/localbe longingidentitiesandsenseofplaceincontemporaryireland/p%26d_disscussion_paper_4.pdf.

5. Robert Tobin, *The Minority Voice: Hubert Butler and Southern Irish Protestantism, 1990–1991* (Oxford: Oxford University Press, 2012), 206.

6. "Beside the Nore" in Hubert Butler, *Independent Spirit: Essays* (New York: Farrar, Strauss and Giroux, 1996), 41.

7. See Desmond Guinness, introduction to *The Irish Georgian Society Records of Eighteenth-Century Domestic Architecture and Decoration in Dublin* (Dublin: Irish Georgian Society, 1969), v–ix, and Erika Hanna, *Modern Dublin: Urban Change and the Irish Past, 1957–73* (Oxford: Oxford University Press, 2013).

8. See W. E. Cairnes, "Fox-Hunting in Ireland," *National Review* 40 (1903): 430–42, and the Earl of Mayo and W. B. Boulton, *A History of the Kildare Hunt* (London: St. Catherine Press, 1913). For an interesting treatment of the irony of the county—a foreign imposition—as a unit of local identity in Ireland, see David Dickson, "County Histories, National Narratives and Missing Pieces: A Report from Ireland," accessed February 1, 2017, https://webcache .googleusercontent.com/search?q=cache:ULQVEpl5_XsJ:https://www.victoriacountyhistory .ac.uk/sites/default/files/page-attachments/dickson_-_local_histories.doc+&cd=1&hl=en&ct =clnk&gl=us.

9. Martin Maguire, "The Church of Ireland in Dublin Since Disestablishment," in *The Laity and the Church of Ireland, 1000-2000*, ed. Raymond Gillespie and W. G. Neely (Dublin: Four Courts Press, 2002), 279.

10. Ibid., 292.

11. *Irish Times*, March 10, 1941.

12. Norma MacMaster, *Over My Shoulder: A Memoir.* (Dublin: The Columba Press, 2008), 45, 80.

13. R. V. Comerford, "Patriotism as Pastime: The Appeal of Fenianism in the mid-1860s," *Irish Historical Studies* 22, no. 87 (March 1981): 239–50.

14. MacMaster, *Over My Shoulder*, 80.

15. Toby Barnard, *A New Anatomy of Ireland* (New Haven: Yale University Press, 2002), 2.

16. Miles Walker Mattinson, *The Law Relating to Corrupt Practices at Elections* (London: Waterlow and Sons Limited, 1883), 103.

17. William Gregory Wood-Martin, *History of Sligo, County and Town, from the Revolution of 1688 to the Present Time.* (Dublin: Hodges Figgis and Co., 1892), 387.

18. Irish census, 1901, 1911.

19. *Sligo Champion*, November 22, 1890, 3.

20. *Sligo Champion*, July 23, 1892, 2.

21. *Sligo Champion*, April 1, 1893, 3.

22. *Sligo Champion*, July 23, 1892, 2.

23. *Dublin Daily Express*, February 25, 1897, 5.

24. *Fermanagh Herald*, October 30, 1909, 8.

25. Patrick Deignan, "The Protestant Community in Sligo, 1914–1949," (PhD thesis, NUI Maynooth, 2008), 372.

26. *Sligo Times*, June 16, 1911.

27. Matthew Kelly, "The Politics of Protestant Street Preaching in 1890s Ireland," *Historical Journal* 48, 1 (2005): 105.

28. *Sligo Champion*, August 24, 1895, 4.

29. *Sligo Champion*, February 15, 1896, 4.

30. *Lisburn Herald, and Antrim and Down Advertiser*, December 14, 1895, 3.

31. *Sligo Champion*, January 4, 1896, 2

32. *Sligo Champion*, December 28, 1895, 12.

33. Mark O'Brien, *The Fourth Estate: Journalism in Twentieth-Century Ireland* (Manchester: Manchester University Press, 2017), and Marie-Louise Legg, *Newspapers and Nationalism: The Irish Provincial Press, 1850–1892* (Dublin: Four Courts Press, 1999).

34. *Sligo Times*, March 6, 1909, 6.

35. *Sligo Times*, August 21, 1909, 6.

36. *Sligo Times*, February 20, 1909, 4. John Gilmartin was chairman of the Sligo Board of Guardians.

37. See O'Hara Papers, National Library of Ireland, Accession No. 5626.

38. *Sligo Times*, February 20, 1909.

39. *Sligo Times*, February 27, 1909, March 6, 1909.

40. *Sligo Times*, April 10, 1909, 5.

41. *Sligo Times*, January 8, 1910, 7.

42. *Sligo Times*, August 6, 1912, 7.

43. *Sligo Times*, May 21, 1910, 7.

44. *Sligo Times*, March 9, 1912, 7.

45. *Sligo Times*, December 4, 1910, 7.

46. *Sligo Times*, October 21, 1911, 7.

47. *Irish Independent*, October 21, 1911, 8.

48. *Strabane Chronicle*, October 28, 1911, 7.

49. *Freemans Journal*, November 1, 1912, 10.

50. *Sligo Times*, February 4, 1911, 4

51. Deignan, "Protestant Community," 140–50.

52. *Irish Times*, January 21, 1911, 4; January 17, 1911, 5.

53. Deignan, "Protestant Community," 147.

54. David Fitzpatrick, *Politics and Irish Life 1913–1921: Provincial Experience of War and Revolution* (Dublin: Gill and Macmillan, 1977), 71.

55. *Sligo Times*, May 17, 1913, 5.

56. *Sligo Times*, July 6, 1912, 8.

57. Michael Wheatley, *Nationalism and the Irish Party* (Oxford: Oxford University Press, 2006), 139.

58. *Sligo Times*, September 28, 1911, 7.

59. *Sligo Times*, September 6, 1913, 5.

60. *Sligo Times*, November 25, 1911, 7.

61. *Sligo Times*, April 13, 1912, 4; November 22, 1913, 5.

62. *Irish Times*, December 23, 1911, 12.

63. *Sligo Times*, August 6, 1912, 7.

64. *Sligo Times*, March 6, 1909, 4.

65. "From *Sligo Champion*," *Tuam Herald*, March 23, 1907, 4.

66. Ibid.

2

WEST BRITS

IT REPRESENTED A DREAM FULFILLED. FEW HAD THOUGHT that such an achievement was even possible under the circumstances—in a country at war, under constant surveillance by the authorities. It had not been easy. German support had been, at best, halfhearted, and the scheme's leaders had disagreed on everything from scheduling to the roles that each member should play. Nevertheless, the actions of that week represented a statement of resistance and a promise that the voice of the people would never be silenced. The events of Easter 1916 would be remembered.

By all accounts, the Tercentenary Shakespeare Festival, held at the Gefandgenenlager (Prison Camp) Ruhleben from April 23 to April 30, 1916, was a success, even by the generally high standards of Ruhleben productions. Despite a tiny budget, the most rudimentary costume and set design, and the limitations imposed by an all-male cast, the organizers could congratulate themselves on an impressive achievement. The event, which included not only productions of *Twelfth Night* and *Othello* but also music and lectures, had thoroughly lived up to the unabashedly earnest statement of purpose contained in the official program: "This Festival is offered to the subjects of the British Empire interned at Ruhleben, as a tercentenary commemoration that cannot be without a special significance to all who reverence the ideals that spring from English soil and live in the English tongue."[1] The festival committee had every reason to believe that they had fulfilled their rather lofty goal. One of its members in particular—a young Trinity graduate from Sligo named R. M. Smyllie, who had not only served on the committee but had appeared as Rodrigo—was especially proud.[2]

If localism was essential to southern Protestant identity, this in no way conflicted with the group's connection with Britain. In fact, the two were inextricably linked. Smyllie senior's call for "Local Home Rule" had been rooted in his unshakeable belief that Sligo was just as important to Britain as Dublin, Liverpool, Melbourne, Hong Kong, or Bombay.[3] The local mattered because it was part of the larger whole: when he defended the rights of street preachers in Sligo, he did so because he believed the people of Sligo should fully appreciate their rights and responsibilities as British citizens.

Although scholars have extensively analyzed "Britishness" among Protestants in Northern Ireland, they have not paid the same amount of attention to that aspect of southern Protestant identity.[4] Some of this is probably due to good manners on the part of non-Protestants anxious not to be seen as indulging in D. P. Moran-style ethnonationalism and on the part of Protestants wanting to distinguish themselves from their more vociferous counterparts in Northern Ireland. It is also difficult to measure this quality in southern Protestants in any concrete way because—aside from the fact that "Britishness" is an amorphous concept at best—southern Protestants had few ways of "proving" their allegiance to Britain in the twentieth century, apart from enlisting in the armed forces in time of war. Also, in some ways, their status as Protestants superseded their other associations. Even if the majority felt that "to be Irish was to be Catholic and to be British was to be Protestant," when Protestants made news—during the Mayo librarian controversy, during the Mother and Child Scheme debate, or during the Fethard boycott—they did so not because they were "British" but because they were not Catholic.[5]

The complexity of early twentieth-century citizenship law also plays a role. As Jack White has explained, even after the 1937 Constitution and its gestures toward a complete break from Britain, "Irishmen still travelled back and forth across the Irish Sea without any form of passport control. They were still eligible for jobs in Britain, even in the civil service or the armed forces. They could still, in certain cases, hold British passports. If they lived in Britain, they were even entitled to vote and to stand for parliament."[6] According to British law, the Irish did not actually cease to be British subjects until 1949, and even then Irish citizens who were alive on or before January 1, 1949 could apply to keep that British citizenship. In some ways, the reason that the "Britishness" of early twentieth-century southern Irish Protestants is understudied is entirely straightforward: many of them never considered for a moment that they might be anything else. Until 1949, and in some cases long afterward, they were no less British than anyone else in the British Isles.

Another reason that the "Britishness" of southern Irish Protestants is underexplored can be traced to the looming presence of the "Anglo-Irish" fallacy. This meant not only that Protestants were often mistakenly associated with a certain class but also that they were assumed, like the "Anglo-Irish," to be torn between two identities, neither of which was "British." R. F. Foster's description of Elizabeth Bowen feeling "most at home in mid-Irish Sea" is sometimes expanded to encompass the group as a whole, evoking an image of a people caught between two states.[7] For many southern Irish Protestants, however, a connection with Britain, rather than with England specifically, was a more potent source of identification. Many of the loyalties that shaped the lives of the group were British, not English: a working-class Dublin Orangeman might have felt torn between his faith and the United Kingdom before independence and perhaps between his faith and his membership in a British-based labor union afterward.[8] A middle-class Cork businessman might have felt forced to choose between his fellow urban professionals, closely integrated with a British world of business and trade, and his coreligionists in Ireland.[9] Even Bowen's own identity was much more complicated than just "English vs. Irish": she had to make her way through a whole host of different "British" allegiances, up to and including her relationship with the Canadian diplomat Charles Ritchie.[10]

For some southern Irish Protestants, the idea that one could be fully Irish while at the same time part of a political, economic, and cultural system that had strong connections with Britain was so obvious as to be unremarked upon. Much of Elizabeth Bowen's exploration of her diverse loyalties is, in fact, an attempt to carve out a place for her people in both Irish and British history simultaneously.[11] In a radio interview, Bowen chose a slightly different metaphor than Foster's: "the Anglo-Irish . . . you have a foot in each country, a foot on each side, which sounds an extremely uncomfortable physical metaphor when you think how wide the Irish Sea is."[12] We sometimes forget that both Foster's and Bowen's metaphors evoke not only being between two states but being in an indeterminate location between them—not to mention being in a space that, for Bowen's entire lifetime, was either explicitly or implicitly claimed as British, not English. The geographer Halford Mackinder's idea of the Irish Sea as the "British Mediterranean" continued to inform British policy, even after his confident tone had gone out of fashion.[13] Many southern Irish Protestants were invigorated rather than demoralized by feeling Irish in a larger British world, believing themselves to be making a unique contribution to Irish and to British life at the same time.

While his father was standing up for freedom of speech and attacking government corruption, Smyllie junior had been quietly making his way up the traditional provincial southern Irish Protestant ladder of success: winning prizes at Sligo Grammar School,[14] serving as president of the Sligo County Chess Club,[15] attaining a Junior and School Exhibition to Trinity College Dublin.[16] His politics, such as they were, were contrarian. A few months after the Parliament Act of 1911, at the Sligo Grammar School Debating Society, he spoke in support of the proposition that the House of Lords should be abolished.[17] When he went up to Trinity, he spent much of his free time at a newspaper agent's shop, discussing politics with Thomas MacDonagh, Joseph Plunkett, and Thomas Clarke. But in that setting, he remembers, "I was a violent Carsonite . . . and often used to argue the Unionist toss with Tom Clarke when the two of us were alone in the shop."[18]

Perhaps this rather detached and philosophical approach to politics factored into Smyllie's decision to take a job as a tutor for the son of an American businessman traveling in Germany in the summer of 1914. Smyllie was not particularly impressed with his charge: he had never and would never see the point of Americans, particularly those who called their parents by their first names.[19] But at least he would see part of the continent and get paid to do so. If the dark clouds of war were gathering, he hardly noticed.

As a result, he thought little of it when, on July 31, 1914, his employer asked him to post a telegram for him from Bad Nauheim. But at the post office, the German authorities accused Smyllie of attempting to send a message in code. As Smyllie did not have a passport and could not remember the name of the hotel in which the family was staying—"for all I knew it may have been the Ritz or the Murphy Arms"—he was arrested as an English spy. "At this stage," Smyllie remembered in 1939, "I made a futile effort to protest against the appellation of 'Englishman,' and tried to explain that an Irishman was something different. But these were the days before the Constitution of Eire had been invented, and the Nauheim detective had never even heard of our beloved island."[20] Although in this case his employer interceded on his behalf, he could defend his employee for only so long, and Smyllie spent the next three months being repeatedly called before the authorities and then released. It was not until November that he, along with thousands of other British citizens, was permanently interned in Ruhleben.

The camp, located just outside Berlin, was located on the site of a prewar racecourse, a coincidence that struck at least one observer: "it may or may not have been intentional—the refined cruelty of a practical joke—that all the British, so fond on their native heath of horse racing, should be interned on a race track which, from that moment, never saw a horse."[21] Most Berliners today know Ruhleben as the western terminus of the U2 line, and even a century ago the camp was close to the train tracks. As a result, although the camp's name means "quiet life," internees were constantly aware of how close they were to the metropolis.[22] The grounds covered about ten acres of land, and the buildings consisted of eleven barracks, three grandstands, a boiler house, and a restaurant; as the war went on, additional barracks and a YMCA building were added.[23] At various times, the camp held between 2,300 and 4,300 men.

The men were housed in stables, and in the first winter of the war they were packed into the small, dirty, poorly insulated quarters indiscriminately. J. C. Masterman, later a distinguished Oxford academic and a member of MI5 during the Second World War, remembers that while "if the four-year period is treated as a whole, we were well treated by the Germans . . . this statement does not apply to the first four or five months."[24] The first "camp captain," Joseph Powell, describes how most early internees were hauled in and subject to long railway journeys, after which they were crowded into tiny stables with little sanitation and no real medical care.[25] In addition, during the first cold winter, the stables were inadequately heated and lit: "horses do not read or write," remembers one internee, "and the Ruhleben stables had little lighting."[26]

It was a diverse group in terms of occupation. According to Masterman, their number included sailors (involved in the merchant service rather than the navy); businessmen; academics and other professionals; a number of trainers and jockeys; athletes; workmen "more skilled than not," according to Masterman; and a number of "others."[27] Another internee describes them as "almost a cross-section of British society, from the manor house to the slum; scarcely a trade or profession was unrepresented."[28] Matthew Stibbe's more statistically precise estimate reveals that a plurality (roughly 35 percent) of the camp's inhabitants were sailors and fishermen, followed by 24 percent businessmen and clerks, 18 percent professionals (including academics, students, and musicians), and about 17 percent workmen of various skill levels.²⁹

Every internee in and visitor to Ruhleben remarked on the diversity of the camp's inhabitants. Daniel J. McCarthy, a professor at the University of Pennsylvania who worked as a camp inspector for the American embassy, was struck by the wide range of backgrounds: "The British tourist from some German cure or summer resort, the music student or teacher from Munich or Berlin; the successful business man, banker, broker, merchant, professional men, all slept in the same horse stalls, marched in barrack line to the same kitchen for food in company with some two hundred and fifty negroes from the China coast, the Strait Settlements or South Africa, with sailors and fishermen from Grunsby, stokers from some tramp merchant-man and, *mirabile dictu*, several hundred British Germans, most of whom could not speak a word of English."³⁰

Israel Cohen, an internee, had an equally colorful take: "There were spruce clerks and long-haired musicians, music-hall artists and pictorial artists, burly Grimsby fishermen in top-boots and dusky Maltese sailors with earrings, mercantile marine captains with gold-braided coats, and university students with college blazers; there were professional foot-ballers and golfers, jockeys and trainers, chauffeurs and waiters, touts and adventurers."³¹

In the early days of the camp, the group was also diverse in terms of its political loyalties. The internment camp at Ruhleben was designed to contain noncombatant British males between the ages of seventeen and fifty-five. In this case, "British" was broadly defined: it meant British citizens living in Germany, people born in Britain to German parents, and inhabitants of the British Empire. There were many in the camp that were British by birth or parentage but German in every other way, up to and including their allegiances. John Patrick Bradshaw, one of the Irish internees, remembers that "the vast majority of the interned were certainly genuine British subjects, but a very large number had but a vague notion of their nationality."³² The internees quickly divided into two groups. On one side were the "P.G.s," those that the British loyalists had determined were "Pro-German." On the other were "Englishmen pure and simple," the "Stock Engländers," as the P.G.s called them. Both of these categories were more complex than they seem. The P.G.s were, after all, not so "pro-German" that they had volunteered to fight. On the other side, as Israel Cohen pointed out, "Stock Engländer" "included representatives not only of the four divisions of the

United Kingdom and of most of their counties, but also of nearly every part of the British Empire—Canada and South Africa, Australia and New Zealand, India, Jamaica, and the Straits Settlements": all of whom had very different interpretations of what being "British" meant.[33]

But in fact, what both inhabitants and observers of Ruhleben found most remarkable was not the diversity of its inhabitants. It was how quickly and how completely those inhabitants forged a new, "British," society in the camp. Masterman remembers how "the change from a motley collection of prisoners herded into a camp to an active and integrated society was both rapid and memorable, and it was brought about by the prisoners themselves. In effect the prisoners took over the camp from their captors and ran it in their own way."[34] Joseph Powell, the first "camp captain" elected by the internees, dedicated his memoir of life in camp to describing how the internees forged a common identity. His elision of the terms "English" and "British" is significant: "This book is written to set forth, in detail, the facts on which it was based, and to show how a number of Englishmen, raked in from the German cities, dumped in a swamp, and housed in stables, set to work to found a British colony and build a British city within a few miles of the enemy's capital, and to place on record the hard work done by many men in many different departments of endeavor."[35]

Many internees and observers used imperial and colonial terms to describe the Ruhlebenites' activities. "During the winter of 1914-1915 Ruhleben was settled by the British," writes J. Davidson Ketchum.[36] Perhaps the most memorable expression of this came from a German-reared internee. "We who have had a German education seem to have lost our bearings; we wander about the camp like stray dogs, not knowing what to do," a German doctor of chemistry told Powell. "You who have had an English education set to work at once as if you were emigrants colonizing a new country."[37]

Within months, Ruhleben had come to resemble a small, unusually vibrant, provincial town. It had its own economy. Part of this was due to desperation: in the early days of the camp, prisoners were forced to find a way to supplement insufficient rations provided for them by the German authorities, and they did so through the black market. Part of it was due to economic surplus: as time went on, and aid packages from relatives and charitable aid groups started making their way into the camp, prisoners sold or traded excess goods. By the end of 1916, there were so many parcels arriving that the Central Prisoners of War Committee of the British Red

Cross, along with the Order of St. John of Jerusalem, were brought in to supervise their distribution.[38]

But the camp's economic development was also a response to something deeper within the Ruhlebenites' self-conception: they simply refused to accept their status as prisoners and, as a result, created the conditions for a service economy. "I found it impossible to get British prisoners to perform the ordinary work of cleaning up the camp, and so forth, always expected of prisoners," wrote James W. Gerard, who, as American ambassador, served as a liaison between the UK government and the inhabitants of Ruhleben. "So, with the funds furnished me from the British Government, the camp captain was compelled to pay a number of the poorer prisoners to perform this work."[39] As money began to circulate throughout the camp, the more enterprising internees began to create places for that money to be spent. By early 1915, visitors to Ruhleben's shopping district could purchase a range of dry goods; have their clothes tailored, their shoes cobbled, and their watches repaired; buy books and have their own publications printed; refill their supply of tobacco; patronize a "light refreshment counter for the sale of lemonade and malt beer in summer, and tea and coffee in winter"; and even visit private latrines.[40] As a result, fairly early into their period of captivity, Ruhlebenites were better off than most—better off than German or British soldiers at the front, and better off than civilian prisoners in other camps. As time went on, they even became better off than their captors. As economic conditions in the rest of Germany worsened, it got to the point that "a much better tea could be had with the prison officers than with the camp commander."[41] Joseph Powell remembers how, when he first came to Ruhleben in 1914, he had overheard a German woman expressing her happiness that English internees were being denied food. During his last months in the camp, he recalled, German women were begging for food from some of those same prisoners.[42]

Ruhleben also had its own government. Initially, the internees were under direct supervision: the Germans assigned one German officer and three soldiers to each barrack. But these were replaced with a gradually expanding internee-staffed bureaucracy that one contemporary observer compared to "the Rise of the Commons in England."[43] First, each barrack elected its own "interpreter," which soon morphed into the position of "barrack captain." Next, those captains formed themselves into a committee, and by early 1915 Wallace Ellison, who had been working in a shoe factory in Frankfurt when the war broke out, came up with an entirely new political system, in which prisoners would govern themselves.[44] From that point on, according to Joseph Powell, "Ruhleben was really a bit of England—a small British colony as it were, planted in the heart of the enemy's country."[45] By 1917, it had its own camp constitution as well as a formal system of elections of officers and a schedule of audits for camp finances.[46] By 1918, they even held their own mock parliamentary elections.[47]

Ruhleben had its own social order. At the top, it was dominated by a clubland whose unwritten rules were just as severe as those of Pall Mall. "Establishment of clubs seems inherent to the Anglo-Saxon nature," observed Ambassador Gerard. "Ten or more persons would combine together and erect a sort of wooden shed against the brick walls of a barrack, hire some poorer person to put on a white jacket and be addressed as 'steward,' put in the shed a few deck chairs and a table and enjoy the sensation of exclusiveness and club life thereby given."[48] Early on, a group known as the "Snobs" sequestered themselves in a building known as the "Summer House" and "prophetically announced, to the amused astonishment of the Camp, that there would be an annual meeting of members on every 6th of November."[49] The Twenty-Five Club and the Phoenix Club served other constituencies of varying status. The "Corner House" catered to musicians and visual artists, the Dramatic Society to actors and directors; there were clubs for marine engineers and clubs restricted to members of particular barracks.

This kind of exclusivity was limited: Israel Cohen estimates that only about one-twentieth of the camp was involved in clubs.[50] But it was an influential minority. When a German private expressed resentment about the "air of easy superiority to circumstances" exhibited by members of the Corner House by throwing some of their deck chairs in a ditch, the club's members complained to the camp's second-in-command, Baron von Taube. The baron, who "saw himself as a gentleman who knew what was due to gentlemen," ordered the soldier to apologize.[51] And this influence extended beyond the camp. When an American journalist "paid a professional visit to the [Summer House] and ventured to air his pro-Germanism . . . a report of the incident which reached England brought about his expulsion from a club to which he belonged in London."[52] Presumably, that report was written on club stationery: several Ruhleben clubs had their own privately printed letterheads.[53]

Ruhleben even had its own university. The Ruhleben Camp School offered courses in everything from Anglo-Saxon literature to machining and, by the end of the war, was actually offering certificate programs accredited by the University of London. A whole host of only slightly less highbrow societies filled in the few educational gaps not covered by the Camp School: the Arts and Sciences Union, the Historical Circle, the Horticultural Society, the Social Problems Discussion Circle, and the English Literature Circle; the most discerning seekers of intellectual improvement could choose between the Literary and Debating Society and the Debating Society.[54]

The only thing taken more seriously than money, government, social life, or education at Ruhleben was leisure. Sport—in all of its various forms—was a critical part of Ruhleben life. There were rugby, soccer, cricket, tennis, track and field, boxing, hockey, fencing and baseball clubs as well as a small society devoted to a sport apparently invented in Ruhleben, "Water Billiards." ("Since England rules the sea I thought a game with water would interest every Englishman," wrote the inventor of the game. "It behoves [sic] us to master the waves.")[55] Internees even built their own five-hole golf course. Gambling was common, although formal casino games had to go underground when Baroness von Taube started losing too much money at the roulette table.[56] And for the inveterate amateurs, there were always bank holiday celebrations: one August the camp held its own fete, complete with a coconut shy and a presentation of a silver cup to the patroness of the event, the baroness.[57] It had a thriving theater scene. Ruhleben had its own censor of plays, J. H. Thorpe, who had prepared for the position by being director of the Otis Lift Company in Berlin before the war.[58] And its musical offerings were truly world-class, with Ernest MacMillan, later conductor of the Toronto Symphony Orchestra, programming a range of concerts and recitals.

Despite their official designation as "British," internees of Ruhleben were much more likely to identify by locality than nationality, especially in the early years of the war. The titles of some of the many clubs and organizations founded in the camp tell this story: the London and Home Counties Society, the Yorkshire Society, Cymdeithas Gymraeg, Scots Circle, South African Society, Canadian Society, Irish Society, Lancastrian Association (which was even more specific, breaking its membership down into "Manchester men, Bolton Trotters, Oldham Rough-Yeds, Bury Muffs, Eccles Cakes, as well as others from Crowbent, Chequerbent [and] Cockeymoor" in a recruiting advertisement).[59] The fact that there was a "British Association" in Ruhleben only proves how little the internees took their ostensibly common identity for granted.[60] Even the sports were organized along national rather than "British" lines: in 1914, the "Ireland" rugby side (featuring right wing R. M. Smyllie) played "Scotland and Colonies" in an "International Match."[61]

At the same time, many of the clubs and activities in Ruhleben reflected a cosmopolitanism that went far beyond the local, national, or imperial. For a group of "British" internees separated from their homeland in a world at war, Ruhlebenites were anything but narrow-minded. Even if one did not join one of the explicitly internationally minded clubs—the Deutscher Zirkel, the Society for German Drama and Literature, the Société Dramatique Francaise, Il Circolo Italiano, Círculo Castellano de Ruhleben, the Russian Circle, the Anglo-Russian Literary Circle, and the Anglo-Belgian Society, to name a few—European culture was everywhere in the camp.[62] Dramatic societies staged Ibsen and Strindberg; symphonies and smaller ensembles performed Beethoven and Brahms; literary groups devoured as much Tolstoy and Dostoevsky as Masefield and Maugham.

The inhabitants of Ruhleben, like southern Irish Protestants after independence, saw no contradiction between their different identities. German authorities sometimes mistook this for an opportunity to divide and conquer. Israel Cohen remembers one Burns Night celebration when Baron von Taube "expressed his thanks for the pleasant and instructive programme and concluded with the cry: 'Hoch die Schotten!' (Long live the Scots!)." The assembled company responded with silent embarrassment; the baron was apparently under the misconception that "the Scots, forsooth, were an anti-British nationality."[63]

What, then, held Ruhleben together? Some scholars caution against placing Britishness at the center of the story. Alexandra Ludewig has ingeniously adapted the German sociologist Ferdinand Tönnies's concepts of *Gemeinschaft* and *Gesellschaft* to explain Ruhleben's identity. According to Ludewig, the camp existed somewhere between *Gemeinschaft*—a community, according to Tönnies, held together by bonds of family or kinship—and *Gesellschaft*—an association organized for a particular, often temporary, purpose. The various clubs, teams, organizations, and societies formed by Ruhlebenites were not entirely utilitarian—shared values played a part—but "in the main derived from need . . . the social capital invested was most unlikely to extend beyond the period when they were forced together and interact[ed] on a daily basis."[64] In a related analysis, Matthew Stibbe suggests that "the British identity of the camp was not something which could be taken for granted amid the relatively large number of prisoners with German names or from German or Russian backgrounds."[65] Ton Hoenselaars warns against assuming "rather too uncritically" the idea that the camp was united by "the existence and development of a sense of corporate British identity," suggesting instead that a cosmopolitan Europeanism predominated.[66]

On the other hand, what is striking about the society that sprung up in Ruhleben is how "British" it turned out to be. While its inhabitants often made decisions based more on pragmatism than patriotism, they did so in ways that were distinctly in line with what they believed to be the best British traditions: the camp's government tended toward decentralized, democratic decision-making. (And, in fact, when it veered off this course, it provoked a sharp response: in September 1915, when the Entertainments Committee was deemed too autocratic and unrepresentative, members of the Ruhleben Dramatic Society, Musical Society, and Irish, French, and German societies went on strike.)[67] Its cosmopolitanism manifested itself in a British context: Stibbe notes that its diverse cultural offerings "resembled a microcosm of the Edwardian metropolis in its heyday."[68] And the appreciation for non-British culture went only so far. William O'Sullivan Molony remembers that while he and other internees responded well to Shakespeare, Sheridan, and John Masefield ("there was a poised and vivid wholesomeness in their writings") as well as Gilbert and Sullivan ("a veritable balm"), "the only dangers that beset us . . . lay in the presentation of the Russian and Scandinavian authors, and in this respect I shall never forget the gloom that settled upon us after seeing Ibsen's Master Builder acted on our stage."[69] Even the different areas of the camp took on British names: the shopping district was called "Bond Street," an area where literary types congregated was named "Fleet Street," an open space was known as "Trafalgar Square."[70] (By contrast, the only camp landmarks given German names were the latrines: "Spandau" was on the east side of camp and "Charlottenburg" on the west.)[71]

In some ways the most extensive examination of the Britishness of the Ruhleben community comes from J. Davidson Ketchum, an internee in the camp who later became a professor of psychology at the University of Toronto. Ketchum's *Ruhleben: A Prison Camp Society* is less a memoir than a kind of retrospective example of participant observation. He treats the camp as a case study in human organization: "this camp provides the fullest picture known to me of the actual growth of a human society, from its origin in a miscellaneous collection of individuals to its culmination in a complex social order."[72]

Ketchum emphasizes how, in the first few months in the camp, internees were conscious of a break with the past: their prewar identities suddenly ceased to matter, as they were transformed into prisoners. But they were reborn when they gained a renewed sense of national loyalty: "The common definition was of course at hand; strangers to one another, separated by great differences of background and education, they were yet one and all *British subjects*. Most of them had simply taken it for granted before August 1914, and some had almost forgotten it during long years on the Continent. By the act of internment, however, the Germans had defined them all as a single group, and had done so on the sole basis of their nationality. The solidarity that resulted was therefore a national solidarity, deeply infused with patriotism."[73]

That solidarity was preserved through a strict code: being "British," for the prisoners of Ruhleben, came to mean adhering to certain norms. Those norms covered behavior and attitude: "the camp was tolerant of much that would be disapproved of elsewhere—profanity, obscenity, gambling, drunkenness—but it never tolerated self-pity or complaining of one's fate."[74] "The whole code was summed up in the significant phrase, 'Be British!' and no other injunction had comparable force as long as the camp lasted."[75] In time, that code of behavior came to supersede other more conventional definitions of "British" as a national identity or set of political allegiances: "Indeed, as differences within the population became more obvious, 'British' came to refer almost exclusively to conduct. It stood for all the social virtues—courage, generosity, honesty, justice, fair play—and this breadth of meaning made it a powerful instrument of control. 'Britishers!' became like 'Comrades!' among communists, a constant reminder that group norms must be upheld."[76] Being "British" came to be mean being involved in the intense associational activity of the camp. You were "British" because of what you did and how you did it rather than because of where you came from. Ketchum memorably sums this up as the "transmutation of pastimes into values."[77]

Many of those southern Irish Protestants who remained in Ireland after independence shared this view. When the Reverend C. B. Armstrong, warden of St. Columba, addressed the Church of Ireland's patrician celebrations of 1932, he began by lamenting the loss of "our birthright and heritage of British tradition and culture which I am not ashamed to regard as the finest in the world," but went on to explain that he was speaking of "traditions of honour, straight-dealing, and tolerance" (not to mention "literature and history") rather than ethnicity or identity.[78]

Perhaps nothing better captures the way that this phenomenon worked among the Irish internees of Ruhleben than their reaction to the revolutionary Roger Casement's short-lived attempt to recruit Irish internees in Ruhleben to the nationalist cause. Both sides attempted to persuade prisoners—military as well as civilian—to switch sides during the war, especially targeting national or ethnic minorities. The British government converted Feltham Borstal, in Middlesex, into a more comfortable camp for prisoners believed to be potentially "sympathetic to the Allies," including Danes and Slavs. The Italians gave Czechs better treatment; Austro-Hungarians tried to "turn" Poles caught fighting for the Russians; the French attempted to win prisoners from Alsace-Lorraine over to the French cause. Germany set up a special camp at Limburg for Irish military prisoners of war, giving them special privileges in the hope of establishing an "Irish Brigade" that could lead a rebellion against Britain. Roger Casement's mission to Ruhleben was an attempt to bring Irish civilians around as well.[79] He first visited the camp in January of 1915, and as he wrote in his diary, he found "163 nominal 'Irish' there—Catholics . . . I think all should be released as an act of goodwill to Ireland by Germany."[80]

According to J. C. Masterman, few in the camp knew who Casement was—which was not unusual, considering Casement's status at the time and the camp's limited contact with the outside world. They knew only that camp authorities were bringing in Irishmen to meet with a distinguished visitor. Casement had little initial success. He interviewed three candidates for the brigade: John Bradshaw of County Antrim, William Coyne from Mayo, and Thomas Hoy from Tyrone. They were allowed a day in Spandau, and when they returned to the camp, they came bearing pamphlets, including one called "Ireland Under British Rule."[81] But a few days later they "very unobtrusively left the camp."[82] Later, they were joined by George Chatterton Hill, who founded a German-Irish Society and wrote a pamphlet on "Irland und seine Bedeutung für Europa" (Ireland and its importance for Europe).[83]

But in general, in Ruhleben and even in Limburg, Casement had little success. He admitted this himself in a letter to his contact in the German Foreign Office, Count Georg von Wedel, in January 1915: "I daresay a sham corps of sorts could be formed by tempting the men with promises of money; but an appeal to their 'patriotism' is an appeal to something non-existent."[84] In fact, according to Casement, the problem even in Limburg was that the loudest voices among the Irish in the camps were pro-British. He contacted von Wedel again in April, to ask him to purge Limburg of a group "that are either not Irish at all, or are so strongly Pro-British that they seriously hinder the effort to form an Irish Brigade . . . they should be carefully collected together and removed altogether from Limburg, and disposed of in other camps of British prisoners along with *bona fide* Englishmen."[85] James Gerard's account of Casement's reception in Ruhleben—he "finally discontinued his visits, after obtaining about thirty recruits, because the remaining Irishmen chased him out of camp"—was overdramatic but not entirely inaccurate.[86] William O'Sullivan Molony, whose father came from an old County Clare Catholic family but who had himself been raised Church of England, was not unsympathetic to Casement's mission but, like "the main body of men of Irish race," returned to his barrack and "sought the companionship of [his] English friends."[87] Casement's visit not only put him off Irish politics, it established "a distrust . . . for all negative and damaging patriotic sentiments that failed to embrace the real human requirements of a nation and of international co-operation at large."[88] Masterman's account is perhaps the most succinct: "The indignation of one [internee], later editor of the *Irish Times*, was typical of the reception of Casement's suggestion that Irishmen should join him against the English."[89]

When Hugh Cimino, a British doctor who had spent a short time in Ruhleben, published his account of his time, he singled out one "Sm. from Sligo" as a particular leader. "He was a born organizer of concerts and tea-parties, a promoter of companies for raising funds for poor sailors," he remembered. "For me he was the most sympathetic figure in that camp. . . . Personally I believe Sm. will end as an M.P."[90]

Although Smyllie does not feature in the list of the "26 Prisoners Most Prominently Mentioned in Camp Magazines" painstakingly compiled by J. Davidson Ketchum, he was an unusually active member of the camp.[91] He was a member of the Corner House club.[92] He played viola in the orchestra.[93] He was a member of the police force, although he claims to have been expelled after he "disgraced [himself] by an idiotically inefficient effort to escape."[94] He was involved in sports, playing both right and left wing in a series of rugby matches and taking part in track and field events, often against Olympic-level athletes.[95] He was actively involved in Ruhleben's thriving dramatic scene. He was a natural choice for Irish plays—he was Daniel Burke in *Shadow of the Glen* and Maurya in *Riders to the Sea*—but he also seems to have been one of the first choices when casting Irish characters in non-Irish plays. He played Lord Francis Etchingham (an Irish Lord) in Maugham's *The Tenth Man*, Sir Gerald O'Hara in the same playwright's *Lady Frederick*, and Dr. Terence McGrath in H. V. Esmond's *When We Were 21*. But he did not limit himself to Irish roles: he played Taras in Tolstoy's *The Cause of It All*, Walter Lenz in Oscar Blumenthal and Gustav Kadelburg's *Die Grosstadtluft*, and Marco Stringhetti in Giulio Rinaldi's *Spiriti Oltra Moderni*.

What is most striking, particularly for those who knew Smyllie only during his period at the *Irish Times*, was how active he was in promoting Irish culture. He was an educator in the Irish Section (translated as *An Cumann Eireannach*) of the Celtic Department of Ruhleben Camp School, lecturing on "The Home Rule Movement," "Trinity College, Dublin," and "As Others See Us" and offering "elementary and beginners' classes" in the Irish language. "LEARN YOUR OWN LANGUAGE!" announced An Cumann Eireannach's prospectus: "The possession of a national language gives concentration, force, colour, and individuality to the national mind and soul. . . . The Irish language is at once a bond and a bulwark, a mine of poesy and a family possession."[96] Later he was even elected *uachtaran* of An Cumann Eireannach (which kept its Irish name but adopted the slightly grander English title of "Irish Literary and Historical Circle.")[97]

But perhaps Smyllie's most direct involvement with Irish culture while in Ruhleben was through drama. It is clear that for all his activities, his heart was with the Ruhleben Irish Players. He not only produced but appeared as the Widow Quin in the Players' production of *Playboy of the Western World*.[98] He also produced Lady Gregory's *The Workhouse Ward* and *Cathleen ni Houlihan* and played numerous roles: Peter Keegan in *John Bull's Other Island*, Mrs. O'Kelly in *Conn the Shaughraun*, J. J. Weldon in George A. Birmingham's *General John Regan*, the Ballad Singer in *The Rising of the Moon*, and Mrs. Tarpen in *Spreading the News*.[99]

Smyllie also quite literally wrote the book on the Ruhleben Irish Players. In honor of its first annual general meeting in April 1916, he produced an illustrated secretary's report, bound and printed by J. S. Preuss, printer by appointment to the royal court. He describes the origins of the group. After seeing a notice about a St. Patrick's Day celebration posted by another member of the camp, he "made the acquaintance of the said gentleman with the result that we jointly called a mass meeting of the Irishmen in the Camp."[100]

The two of them decided to put on an original sketch, cowritten by Smyllie, called *The Night of the Wake*. A script for the play survives in the Ettinghausen Collection at Harvard. It is clear why it has not attracted the attention of even the most open-minded enthusiasts of obscure Irish drama. The plot involves two young Irishmen returning home from Ruhleben. Its humor runs the gamut between broad (one character describes the Ruhleben orchestra as "so fine and classical that you couldn't tell whether they were playing or tuning up") and incomprehensibly referential. But it appears to have delighted the Ruhleben audience, to the point that two more performances were added, and Smyllie was rewarded by the authorities with a day's leave in Berlin.[101] Productions of *Cathleen ni Houlihan*, *Spreading the News*, and the *Rising of the Moon* followed.

Next the Players were approached by the Entertainments Committee. According to Smyllie, they requested "that our next play should be one in which the scene was not a public house or shebeen." The Players obliged: "in order to keep in their good books as far as possible, George Bernard Shaw's 'John Bull's Other Island' was chosen. It is not an 'Irish' play in the Abbey sense of the word, in fact it is more a political philosophical treatise than anything else. Nevertheless it gives a more or less correct idea of the better class Irish peasant, a type which is missing in most of the Abbey repertory plays, and for this reason we decided to have it produced."[102]

Performing Shaw, however, required that the Players break one of its rules, which was a ban on non-Irish performers. Smyllie, again in language that would surprise his postwar readers, explains that he "had been very much in favour of this rule, as [he] considered that the work which we were doing could not be done satisfactorily by outsiders." Nevertheless, they invited English actors to play the roles of Tom Broadbent and Hodson. In somewhat ambiguous language, Smyllie describes how one of these performances "caused a great impression on the audience—they were nearly all Englishmen—and all we regret is, that he is not an Irishman and therefore cannot become a member of our Society."[103] None of this, of course, would in any way have raised doubts about the links between Ireland and England—they were all British together, after all.

Smyllie spent the entire war in Ruhleben. On December 9, 1919, the *Irish Times* featured an article by "An Irish Ruhlebenite" on "The Irish in Ruhleben: Their Jests and Hardships." Ostensibly a review of Joseph Powell's

History of Ruhleben, which the author describes as "a valuable record" albeit a "colourless" one that makes for "dull reading," most of the article focuses on the Irish experience of the camp. The essay is signed "R.M.S.," and later trademarks of Smyllie's style abound: clichés, untranslated foreign terms, and unfavorable comparisons ("Ruhleben provides a good model for our pretentious Utopian architects, whose efforts, so far, have been a dismal failure") all feature prominently. Throughout, "R.M.S." equates Irishness with loyalty to Britain—and disloyalty to Britain as a betrayal of Ireland. He begins by dismissing the actively pro-German Irish prisoners as not worthy of their name: "There were a couple of hundred Irishmen in the camp; and there was also Mr. Chatterton-Hill. This true son of Erin, who pronounced Drogheda 'Drawheeda,' with the accent on the 'hee,' did not stay long with his compatriots. . . . That Mr. Chatterton-Hill ever saw Ireland is doubtful. Certainly his contribution to the *Continental Times* and *Irische Blätter*— the monthly organ of the German-Irish [*sic*] Society—betrayed a colossal ignorance, not only of Irish psychology, but even of historical facts and actual happenings."[104] The author goes on to describe Casement's visit and the departure of Coyne, Hoy, and Bradshaw but assures his audience that "the rest—that is to say all who were worthy of the name [of 'Irishman']— accepted the responsibilities of their British citizenship." Overt expressions of nationalist separatism, according to "R.M.S.," were "suitable to befuddle officious German record keepers or bemuse visiting American observers but were never really taken seriously."[105] That was not the way things were done in Ruhleben.

It would be needlessly tendentious to argue that the best way to prepare for life as a Protestant in southern Ireland after independence was to spend a few years in a German internment camp. But the comparison is not entirely absurd. In both groups, being externally defined as "British" actually strengthened rather than weakened their relationship to that transnational identity. Many Ruhlebenites, like many southern Irish Protestants, never thought of themselves as British until they were seen that way by others. At the same time, for Ruhleben internees as well as for southern Protestants, "British" came to mean something other than political allegiance: it had more to do with an approach to life than a loyalty to a union, monarchy, or empire. As such, it could coexist with all sorts of other attachments. In the case of southern Irish Protestants, it could continue to play an important role in their identity even when they had, passively or actively, chosen to remain in Ireland and become "Irish." In this sense, southern

Irish Protestants did not necessarily become less "British" any more than the devoted Italophiles of Ruhleben's Il Circulo Italiano did. As the sociologists Joseph Ruane and David Butler have pointed out, it is crucial that in examining what might appear to be "culturally distinct historical communities," we must always remember to "explore the ethnographic reality behind the labels and be alert to other meanings."[106] To the inhabitants of Ruhleben and to southern Protestants in Ireland, "Britishness" did not necessarily mean what their captors or their fellow Irishmen understood it to mean. "I am delighted that I can be an Irish Republican and a British what-have-you at one and the same time," Smyllie would write in 1953. "It is quite fun."[107]

Notes

1. Program, 1916 Tercentenary Shakespeare Festival, Folder 10, seq. 340, Maurice Ettinghausen Collection of Ruhleben Civilian Internment Camp papers, 1914–1937, Harvard Law School Library, Harvard University.

2. Ibid., seq. 1058, 1059.

3. Granted, Sligo does not make it onto the erstwhile Labour MP Tristram Hunt's list of *Ten Cities That Made an Empire* (London: Allen Lane, 2013).

4. For a brief overview of a voluminous body of scholarship, see James McAuley and Jonathan Tonge, "Britishness and Irishness in Northern Ireland since the Good Friday Agreement," *Parliamentary Affairs* 63, no. 2 (2010): 266–85. One of the pioneering studies in this area is Claire O'Halloran, *Partition and the Limits of Irish Nationalism: An Ideology under Stress* (Atlantic Highlands, NJ: Humanities International Press, 1987), esp. 31–56.

5. Stephen Mennell, Mitchell Elliott, Paul Stokes, Aoife Rickard and Ellen O'Malley-Dunlop, "Protestants in a Catholic State—A Silent Minority in Ireland," in *Religion and Politics: East-West Contrasts from Contemporary Europe*, ed. Tom Inglis, Zdzisław Mach, and Rafał Manzanek (Dublin: University College Dublin Press, 2000), 73.

6. Jack White, *Minority Report: The Protestant Community in the Irish Republic* (Dublin: Gill and Macmillan, 1975), 109.

7. R. F. Foster, "The Irishness of Elizabeth Bowen," in *Paddy and Mr. Punch* (London: Penguin, 1993), and see Neil Corcoran, *Elizabeth Bowen: The Enforced Return* (Oxford: Oxford University Press, 2008).

8. Martin Maguire, "'Remembering Who We Are': Identity and Class in Protestant Dublin and Belfast, 1868–1905," in *Essays in Irish Labour History: A Festschrift for Elizabeth and John W. Boyle* (Dublin: Irish Academic Press, Dublin, 2008).

9. Ian d'Alton, "Southern Irish Unionism: A Study of Cork Unionists, 1884–1914," *Transactions of the Royal Historical Society* 23 (1973): 71–88.

10. Matt Eatough, "Bowen's Court and the Anglo-Irish World System," *Modern Language Quarterly* 73, no. 1 (2012): 69–94. See also Victoria Glendinning, *Love's Civil War: Elizabeth Bowen and Charles Ritchie, Letters and Diaries 1941–1973* (London: Simon & Schuster UK, 2010).

11. See not only Elizabeth Bowen, *Bowen's Court* (New York: Ecco Press, 1979) but also "The Big House," *The Bell*, October 1940, reprinted in *Elizabeth Bowen's Selected Irish Writings*, ed. Éibhear Walshe (Cork: Cork University Press, 2011), 47–52.

12. "Frankly Speaking: Interview, 1959," in *Listening In: Broadcasts, Speeches and Interviews by Elizabeth Bowen*, ed. Allan Hepburn (Edinburgh: Edinburgh University Press, 2010), 326.

13. Robert J. Mayhew, *Enlightenment Geography: The Political Languages of British Geography, 1650–1850* (New York: St. Martin's Press, 2000), 238–41. The maritime border between the United Kingdom and Ireland was only formally agreed on in 2014.

14. *Irish Times*, December 23, 1911, 12.

15. *Irish Times*, September 20, 1913, 16.

16. *Dublin Daily Express*, October 31, 1911, 8.

17. *Sligo Times*, February 25, 1911, 7.

18. *Irish Times*, July 19, 1943, 3.

19. *Irish Times*, December 17, 1921, 10.

20. *Irish Times*, September 10, 1939, 9. As war did not break out until the following week, Smyllie later wondered if he was in fact the first British subject to take part in the war.

21. Daniel J. McCarthy, *The Prisoner of War in Germany: The Care and Treatment of the Prisoner of War with a History of the Development of the Principle of Neutral Inspection and Control* (New York: Moffat, Yard and Company, 1917), 205.

22. Alexandra Ludewig, "Visualising a Community in Incarceration: Images from Civilian Internees on Rottnest Island and in Ruhleben during the First World War," *War & Society* 35, no. 1 (February 2016): 57.

23. Matthew Stibbe, *British Civilian Internees in Germany: The Ruhleben Camp, 1914–1918*. (Manchester: Manchester University Press, 2008), 53.

24. J. C. Masterman, *On the Chariot Wheel: An Autobiography* (Oxford: Oxford University Press, 1975), 100.

25. Joseph Powell and Francis Gribble, *The History of Ruhleben: A Record of British Organisation in a Prison Camp in Germany* (London: W. Collins Sons & Company Ltd., 1919), 2.

26. J. Davidson Ketchum, *Ruhleben: A Prison Camp Society* (Toronto: University of Toronto Press, 1965), 17.

27. Masterman, *On the Chariot Wheel*, 102.

28. Ketchum, *Ruhleben*, 3.

29. Stibbe, *British Civilian Internees*, 15.

30. McCarthy, *Prisoner of War*, 206.

31. Israel Cohen, *The Ruhleben Prison Camp: A Record of Nineteen Months' Internment* (London: Methuen & Co., Ltd., 1917), 115.

32. John Patrick Bradshaw manuscripts, National Library of Ireland MS 35/288/1, 86.

33. Cohen, *Ruhleben Prison Camp*, 102–4, 113.

34. Masterman, *On the Chariot Wheel*, 102.

35. Powell and Gribble, *History of Ruhleben*, v.

36. Ketchum, *Ruhleben*, 153.

37. Powell and Gribble, *History of Ruhleben*, 41.

38. Stibbe, *British Civilian Internees*, 118.

39. James W. Gerard, *My Four Years in Germany* (New York: George H. Doran Company, 1917), 178.

40. Powell and Gribble, *History of Ruhleben*, 88.

41. Gerard, *My Four Years*, 188.

42. Powell and Gribble, *History of Ruhleben*, 10–11.

43. "Report on the Note from His Excellency the American Ambassador in Berlin on the Conditions Existing at That Date (June 8th) in the Internment Camp at Ruhleben, Germany," Foreign Office Papers 383/69, National Archives, Kew.

44. Powell and Gribble, *History of Ruhleben*, 65. See also Wallace Ellison, *Escaped! Adventures in German Captivity* (London: W. Blackwood and Sons, 1918).

45. Powell and Gribble, *History of Ruhleben*, 68.

46. Ibid., 224.

47. Ettinghausen Collection Box 5, 8, 4316.

48. Gerard, *My Four Years*, 182.

49. Cohen, *Ruhleben Prison Camp*, 112.

50. Ibid., 128.

51. Powell and Gribble, *History of Ruhleben*, 141.

52. Ibid., 140.

53. Ketchum, *Ruhleben*, 229

54. Ettinghausen Collection Box 2, 1, 729.

55. Ettinghausen Collection, Box 3, 10, 2261.

56. Powell and Gribble, *History of Ruhleben*, 155.

57. Cohen, *The Ruhleben Prison Camp*, 130–31.

58. Powell and Gribble, *History of Ruhleben*, 183.

59. Ettinghausen Collection Box 2, 4, 870.

60. Ettinghausen Collection Box 2, 1, 729.

61. Ettinghausen Collection Box 3, 8, 2043.

62. Ettinghausen Collection Box 2, 1, 729.

63. Cohen, *Ruhleben Prison Camp*, 60.

64. Ludewig, "Visualising a Community," 62.

65. Stibbe, *British Civilian Internees*, 79–80.

66. Ton Hoenselaars, "In Exile with Shakespeare: British Civilian Internee Theatre at Ruhleben Camp, 1914–1918," *Shakespeare in Southern Africa* 23 (2011): 3.

67. Masterman Collection, Box 2, 354, Harvard Law School Library, Harvard University.

68. Stibbe, *British Civilian Internees*, 81.

69. William O'Sullivan Molony, *Prisoners and Captives* (London: Macmillan and Co., 1933), 97.

70. Powell and Gribble, *History of Ruhleben*, 69.

71. Ketchum, *Ruhleben*, 149.

72. Ibid., xiii.

73. Ibid., 37–38.

74. Ibid., 67.

75. Ibid., 75.

76. Ibid., 94.

77. Ibid., 214.

78. William Bell and N. D. Emerson, *The Church of Ireland A.D. 432–1932: The Report of the Church of Ireland Conference Held in Dublin, 11th–14th October, 1932, to Which Is Appended an Account of the Commemoration by the Church of Ireland of the 1500th Anniversary of the Landing of St. Patrick in Ireland* (Dublin: Church of Ireland Printing

and Publishing Co., Ltd., 1932), 223–24. See also Ian d'Alton, "Religion as Identity: The Church of Ireland's 1932 Patrician Celebrations," in *Representing Irish Religious Histories: Historiography, Ideology and Practice*, ed. Jacqueline Hill and Mary Ann Lyons (Cham, Switzerland: Palgrave Macmillan, 2017), 197–210.

79. Heather Jones, "A Missing Paradigm? Military Captivity and the Prisoner of War, 1914–1918," *Immigrants and Minorities* 26: 1–2, 37.

80. Angus Mitchell, ed., *One Bold Deed of Open Treason: The Berlin Diary of Roger Casement, 1914–1916* (Sallins, Co. Kildare: Merrion Press, 2016), 133.

81. Frederick William Hanson to Sir Louis Mallet, October 26, 1915, Foreign Office Papers 383/69, National Archives, Kew.

82. Masterman, *On the Chariot Wheel*, 104–5.

83. Reinhard R. Doerries, *Prelude to the Easter Rising: Sir Roger Casement in Imperial Germany*. (London: Frank Cass Publishers, 2000), 96.

84. Casement to Count Georg von Wedel, January 9, 1915, in Doerries, *Prelude*, 76.

85. Casement to von Wedel, April 6, 1915, in Doerries, *Prelude*, 109

86. Gerard, *My Four Years*, 191.

87. Molony, *Prisoners*, 98–99.

88. Ibid., 100.

89. Masterman, *On the Chariot Wheel*, 104–5.

90. Hugh Cimino, *Behind the Prison Bars in Germany: A Detailed Record of Six Months' Experiences in German Prison and Detention Camps*. (London: George Newnes Limited, 1915), 102.

91. Ketchum, *Ruhleben*, 267.

92. Ettinghausen Collection, Box 1, folder 6.

93. *Irish Times*, May 24, 1943, 3.

94. *Irish Times*, April 19, 1944, 3.

95. Ettinghausen Collection, Box 11, folder 1.

96. Ettinghausen Collection, Box 2, Folder 1.

97. Ettinghausen Collection Box 2 Folder 2.

98. Ettinghausen Collection, Box 2, Folder 10.

99. Ettinghausen Collection, Box 2, Folder 10.

100. Ettinghausen Collection, Box 2, Folder 1.

101. Ettinghausen Collection, Box 2, Folder 1.

102. Ettinghausen Collection Box 2, Folder 1.

103. Ettinghausen Collection, Box 2, Folder 1.

104. "'The Irish in Ruhleben: Their Jests and Hardships: The Dublin Rebellion,' by an Irish Ruhlebenite," *Irish Times*, December 9, 1919, 4.

105. "'The Irish in Ruhleben; Their Jests and Hardships; the Dublin Rebellion," by an Irish Ruhlebenite, *Irish Times*, December 9, 1919, 4.

106. Joseph Ruane and David Butler, "Southern Irish Protestants: An Example of De-ethnicization?" *Nations and Nationalism* 13, no. 4 (2007): 633.

107. *Irish Times*, April 25, 1953, 7.

3

CONTINENTALS

ONE OF THE ARCHETYPAL EXPRESSIONS OF SOUTHERN IRISH Protestant identity is W. B. Yeats's speech on divorce in the Irish Senate in 1925. At the same time, no single statement is less representative of the group as a whole, in tone if not in sentiment. For many, this kind of vocal protest constituted "scaring the horses"; the bemused interjections to the speech from the equally southern Irish Protestant chairman of the Senate, James Campbell, Baron Glenavy, during the debate capture some of this reaction. But Yeats's address has come to represent something of the group's views at their most angry.

The debate concerned divorce. Or, rather, the debate concerned a bureaucratic attempt to keep the Irish Senate from actually debating divorce. Officially, it was a discussion of the "Report of the Joint Committee on Standing Orders (Private Business) on the Position in Saorstát Éireann of Bills Relating to Matrimonial Matters." The recommendation of this report was that if an Irish citizen wanted a divorce, it had to be introduced into both houses of the Irish Parliament as a private bill, thus ensuring the de facto outlawing of the practice. In a wide-ranging, carefully prepared speech, Senator Yeats took the opportunity to declare:

> We against whom you have done this thing, are no petty people. We are one of the great stocks of Europe. We are the people of Burke; we are the people of Grattan; we are the people of Swift, the people of Emmet, the people of Parnell. We have created the most of the modern literature of this country. We have created the best of its political intelligence. Yet I do not altogether regret what has happened. I shall be able to find out, if not I, my children will be able to find out whether we have lost our stamina or not. You have defined our position and have given us a popular following. If we have not lost our stamina then your victory will be brief, and your defeat final, and when it comes this nation may be transformed.[1]

This "breathtakingly direct" assertion of "political 'Protestant'" identity has been "enshrined as one of [Yeats's] supreme public moments."[2] It gets pride of place on the "Anglo-Irish People" Wikipedia page.[3] It has even made its way to Australasia, to describe the region's own hyphenated peoples.[4]

But what is less often commented upon is how much of Yeats's focus in this speech is on Europe. R. F. Foster is certainly right to interpret the phrase "great stocks of Europe" as a rhetorical device designed to wrong-foot nationalists who would have expected him to locate Irish Protestants in an English or British tradition. But it is not only that. The rest of his speech is marked by references to Europe that seem less "carefully crafted."[5] He suggests, somewhat ambiguously, that the Catholic clergy in Ireland has "an influence that they do not possess anywhere else in Europe."[6] He points out that divorce "has been adopted by the most civilised nations of the modern world—by Germany, England, America, France and Scandinavian countries."[7] His case for the theological justification for divorce is European: "there is not a scholar of eminence in Europe to-day who considers that the Gospels are, in the strict sense of words, historical documents." Even his more pragmatic argument has a European frame: "Do you think you are going to succeed in what the entire [*sic*] of Europe has failed to do for the last 2,000 years?"[8] Yeats was undoubtedly shaping his argument to emphasize the Irishness of southern Irish Protestants, but his logic was at least as continental as it was national.

This focus on Europe turns a speech that could be seen as morbidly backward-looking—"do you not think we might leave the dead alone?" asked Glenavy at one point—into something more contemporary.[9] Just as many southern Irish Protestants integrated themselves into their local areas or gained a renewed sense of Britishness, so did they rediscover their identity as European in the early twentieth century. This was not in itself new. The relatively small number of Huguenots who fled to Ireland play an outsize role in the southern Protestant imagination, memorialized in streets, churches, cemeteries, and family names throughout Ireland and serving as a much less conflicted source of identification than the more aggressive manifestations of Protestantism that arrived in Ireland before and after them.[10] In addition, many of the new nations established after the First World War, especially in former Habsburg territories, provided examples of countries that managed to contain two or even more religions: Czechoslovakia, Hungary, and Austria were all Catholic majority states with significant

Protestant minorities. The more counterintuitive among the group could look to other mixed nations in which the ratio was reversed, with Protestants the majority and Catholics the minority, but where the same issues of integration and difference remained: Germany, Switzerland, and— especially evocative to Irish Protestants on either side of the border—the home of Prince William, the Netherlands.[11] Alongside these models of religiously diverse societies were less comforting European examples of class distinctions, which some grander southern Irish Protestants would have related to. During the interwar period, White Russians and Prussian Junkers could certainly have made their own versions of Yeats's speech, and the French aristocrat who had to explain to a confused admirer that she was "only the Duchess," not the poet de Noailles, would have related to Yeats's insistence that his group, too, was "no petty people."[12] In some ways, Europe provided more relevant examples for Ireland than Britain or even than the newly independent nations of the British Empire.

As in the case of localism, this renewed focus on European affairs actually brought the minority in line with the majority. Irish nationalists had a long history of European interactions, from the "Wild Geese" to the "Flight of the Earls" to the shipwreck of the *Aud*.[13] Irish Catholics, nationalist or otherwise, had looked to Europe for centuries, for obvious confessional reasons. Those historical and religious connections were even more visible after independence.[14] Finally, Ireland's new role as an independent nation ensured that its diplomatic and political history would be wrapped up with Europe's; it was one of those "small nations" that the First World War had been fought for, even if not all of the supporters of that new era of national destiny saw it that way.[15]

Southern Protestants shared this outward focus during and after the First World War. The war and its aftermath provided direct opportunities for southern Irish Protestants to look beyond the borders of the island, in the form of war charities. The columns of the *Irish Times* were full of these announcements. Five years before she would be burned out of Moydrum House by the IRA, Lady Castlemaine announced in the paper's "Fashionable Intelligence" section that she would again be organizing theatrical entertainments in Athlone in aid of such charities.[16] Lady Arnott hosted art sales in aid of the "Irish Prisoners of War and Belgians in Ireland Fund."[17] The paper publicized the work of groups such as the Irish Branch of the "Friends of Armenia," whose chairman was B. R. Balfour, of Towneley Hall, near Drogheda.[18] Not all of this charity work was on such a grand level. The subscriber lists of the British Red Cross Society and St. John Ambulance Association are full of Protestant family names.[19]

At the end of the war, then, southern Protestants, like the Irish generally, were unusually Europe-focused. As such, it is entirely appropriate that Smyllie's first major assignment for the *Irish Times* was covering the Paris Peace Conference. His account, in a series of long articles beginning in January, demonstrates that Smyllie's style—verbose, fond of untranslated foreign words, pompous and self-deprecating at the same time—emerged fully formed. But it also reveals much about his audience. It was written for Irish Protestants trying to make sense of postwar Europe and Ireland's place in it, and it foreshadowed much about what Europe would come to mean for the group. As Smyllie became more established at the paper, eventually rising to the position of editor, he continued to emphasize the importance of Europe to Ireland. In his reporting on two visits to Czechoslovakia during the 1930s—which were eventually published in book form—he found what he thought was the perfect role model and cautionary tale for the newly independent nation. Smyllie, like many southern Irish Protestants, realized that many of the answers to Ireland's most pressing questions lay further east than either Dublin or London.

This international perspective was not necessarily a priority at the paper Smyllie found himself attached to upon his release from Ruhleben. If anything, the *Irish Times* of the late nineteen-teens was the paper of record of a small, inward-looking, rather provincial imaginary country called "Anglo-Ireland." Like any imaginary country, it had its landmarks. The journalist and historian Brian Inglis lists *Punch*, Gilbert and Sullivan, Trinity Week, the Shelbourne Hotel, the Irish Mail at Euston, Fitzwilliam Lawn Tennis Club, Horse Show Week, the Kildare Street Club, the Island Golf Club, and the *Tatler* as well as the *Irish Times*.[20] The writer Terence de Vere White names "Trinity College; several clubs; Sir Patrick Dun's and Baggot Street Hospitals; a few schools . . . the *Evening Mail*; Guinness's brewery, Jameson's distillery; all save two banks; Jacob's Biscuits; some of the larger stores, and professional offices (local knowledge could identify them by looking at the name)" alongside the paper.[21] Since its foundation in 1859, the *Irish Times* had represented the journalistic voice of a certain class of southern Irish Protestant, particularly in the minds of critics of that class. Stephen Brown expresses this view in his 1937 history of Irish journalism: "The *Irish Times* was from the start and has consistently remained the organ of the Protestant interest in Ireland, its politics being Conservative and Unionist. It steadily opposed all the national movements. It afforded a platform and a rallying cry for all those, Catholics as well as Protestants, whose first allegiance was to England or whose principal preoccupation was the maintenance of the existing order."[22] To a certain extent this association was felt most strongly by the paper's critics: most of the upper- and upper-middle class southern Protestants often described as "Anglo-Irish" would never read an Irish paper as long as a British one was available. But even they accepted the paper as an important landmark. "The *Irish Times*," Brian Inglis remembers, "for all that it might be damned as mealy-mouthed on some subjects, was the only Dublin morning paper that any of our set would have been seen carrying"—and carry it they did, into the Shelbourne and the Fitzwilliam Lawn Tennis Club, across the links of the Island Golf Club and Trinity's quad.[23]

From the beginning, the paper had been run by the kind of solidly respectable gentlemen who, one would think, preferred to forget Europe existed, except when ordering wine or looking for another country's armed forces to ridicule. It was founded in 1859 by a retired British army major, Laurence E. Knox, who sold it in 1873 to Sir John Arnott, the department-store owner, MP for Kinsale, lord mayor of Cork, and founder of Cork's racecourse. The paper's editor for the first quarter of the twentieth century was John Healy, a disappointed clergyman and Redmond supporter. Although a diligent editor, Healy was hardly the man to deal with a rapidly changing country. A staffer later recalled "a man of remarkable inflexibility of mind," famous for insisting that stories should continue *in* rather than *on* whatever page they continued on and for outlining precise mathematical requirements for leading articles ("the main one must always consist of three paragraphs of 22 lines each, the second of a single paragraph of 35 lines.")[24] Healy's staff reflected the paper's upper-middle class origins and carried on its traditions—often because the staff had been there when the traditions began. The paper's general manager, J. J. Simington, worked for the paper from 1878 to 1941. The first reporter Brian Inglis met at the paper in the 1940s had a broader perspective, but he had gained it during the previous century: one of his first assignments was covering the Franco-Prussian War. Lionel Fleming, who also worked for the paper during the war, remembers the *Irish Times* "reflect[ing], gently but sadly, upon such things as an old, 'loyalist', country clergyman might reflect upon them."[25] When Smyllie joined the paper in the early 1920s, the *Irish Times* existed in a sort of late-Victorian fog. If it did not embrace the New

Ireland—much less postwar Europe—it was because it barely recognized its existence.

Despite (or perhaps because of) its title, the newspaper did not enjoy anything like the same position in Irish society that its namesake had in British life. When Healy hired Robert Maire Smyllie as a new reporter in 1918, the young man seemed the perfect agent of change. Smyllie had peerless conservative credentials, but his experience in Ruhleben had broadened his horizons far beyond those of most other applicants for low-paying jobs at low-circulation Irish newspapers. He could be exactly the kind of cosmopolitan figure that could lift the paper out of its doldrums. His first major assignment would be to cover the Paris Peace Conference, the biggest international news story in the world at the time.

This represented a step forward for the paper. Although the *Irish Times* had included a fair amount of international coverage during the war, it had always relied heavily on press association reports and wire services. Its editorials sometimes addressed issues of international importance but with a somewhat detached and superficial tone: when it touched on affairs outside Ireland, it did so only when those affairs might potentially affect Ireland—or the small part of Ireland that the paper represented. At times, the European news coverage in the paper felt as though the paper's staff had been looking for column inches to fill and, in desperation, had done so by paraphrasing the international section of London papers from a few days (or even weeks) earlier.

As such, when Smyllie's first dispatch from Paris arrived, the paper spared no superlatives in assuring its readers that here was something new. "The following message was despatched from Paris by aeroplane post to our London office, and thence telegraphed by our private wire to Dublin," a subheadline announced—an astonishing display of early twentieth-century technological prowess that allowed the report to appear only two days after the meeting opened. Unfortunately Smyllie had little to report on. He had moved more quickly than the meeting itself, and he had to fill several columns describing the meeting room, the gradual entry of the delegates, and his general impression of speeches by Poincaré, Clemenceau, Lloyd George, Wilson, and others. Healy must have wondered if he was going to get his money's worth out of this risky new venture into foreign correspondence.[26]

When formal sessions began the following week, however, Smyllie wasted no time in highlighting the conference's implications for Ireland.

And he began developing four themes that would be characteristic of not only his but many other southern Protestants' thinking about Europe. First, he uses Europe to gently nudge his paper's core readership, demonstrating that postwar Europe provides numerous examples of former elites now cast into the wilderness. The "Anglo-Irish" could no longer rely on their prewar status to see them through. While covering Woodrow Wilson's speech in support of the League of Nations, Smyllie highlighted phrases that must have worried many of his paper's subscribers, such as "the fortunes of mankind lay now no longer in the hands of the select classes, but in the hands of the plain peoples of the earth."[27]

Second, he uses Europe to make a strong case against the idea that the Irish have a monopoly on misery. He could be hard on the "privileged minority" for its privileges, but he was even tougher on the Catholic minority if it believed that it had it worse than anyone else in Europe. "I have discovered that one has to come to Paris in order to find out how well off we are in Ireland," he wrote, "and how, so far as material comforts are concerned, the burden of the war has lain more lightly on our shoulders than, perhaps, on those of any other country in Europe."[28] While it may have been understandable for the Irish in 1919 to feel as though they had been through a period of disruption and upheaval, it was nothing compared to what continental Europeans had suffered through. The idea that the Irish were, by European standards, rather lucky would become a fundamental organizing principle of much of Smyllie's writing about the continent.

Thirdly, he makes the case that the Irish—whether Catholic or Protestant—can learn from the rest of the world. "In Central Europe the intermingling of races is, in parts, so intimate that the Ulster question is simple by comparison. Central Europe is strewn with Irelands."[29] "The Turkish question," he writes on another occasion, "has been a thorn in the side of European diplomatists for even longer than the Irish problem has been the spectre of English politics."[30] He emphasizes that comparison should not be read as equivalence: the Irish situation does not exactly conform to that of other "new" nations aspiring to independence in the postwar world. While "[in Yugoslavia] the fragments of a broken Empire were permitted to reassemble themselves in accordance with their own wishes," he writes, Ireland is in a very different situation. The crucial difference is that the Austro-Hungarian Empire has fallen while the British Empire remains. "As regards the outside world, Ireland would still be part of the United Kingdom, for which there is one stable Government."[31] At the same time, Ireland can learn from the experience of those other nations, even if they are not exact equivalents.

Finally, he uses Europe to remind the Irish—Catholic, Protestant, nationalist, Unionist, or whatever—that they are not nearly as important as they think they are. For Smyllie, a European focus is the best defense against Irish navel-gazing. For one thing, he notes, when foreigners think about the Irish at all, they usually get them wrong, as he discovered when a hotelier mistook him for a Sinn Fein representative and refused to rent a room to such a dangerous radical. "It cost me all my knowledge of French to convince him of my comparatively harmless identity," he reported; "he seemed to think that, because a republic had been proclaimed in the Dublin Mansion House, I must of necessity be a Bolshevist."[32] For another, those foreigners who do understand the Irish don't particularly care about them. "I am afraid that most foreigners refuse to take the Irish question very seriously," he noted, "and the proceedings which have just taken place in Dublin"—here Smyllie is referring to the First Dáil—"seem to have evoked more mirth than sympathy amongst the nations of the Continent."[33] Smyllie clearly relishes the way that a European perspective can reveal uncomfortable truths about foreign perceptions of Ireland. While the rise of Sinn Féin may have been the talk of Ireland in 1919, "one sees almost no reference to the movement in the Paris Press, and, though more space is devoted to the subject in the provincial papers, interest in this side of the Channel is feeble."[34] If anything, those who understand Ireland best are frankly hostile to its aspirations. "As far as America was concerned," Smyllie wrote after meeting with a Cork-born journalist working for an American paper, "Sinn Fein had dug its own grave in Easter Week, and the sympathy of the whole civilized world had been alienated from the 'cause' of Ireland." Then he twists the knife: "I have found a similar attitude among all those whom I have consulted on the subject, and, to be quite frank, I have found the feeling which most nearly approaches sympathy amongst Englishmen themselves."[35]

Smyllie's assignment in Paris was a prestigious and high-profile post for a young man who had only begun his journalistic career, and it represented a risk for a paper that was not necessarily known for its extensive foreign coverage. In some ways, it proved a disappointment. Despite its world-shaping implications, the day-to-day affairs of the conference turned out to be rather mundane—to everyone's surprise, the Paris Peace Conference turned out to be a conference—and Smyllie often had to resort to lengthy digressions about the pleasures of strolling around Paris. And although Smyllie's reports are shot through with rumors and gossip about the machinations of the Sinn Féin diplomatic mission, this never amounted to much. A sympathetic recent account of their efforts sums them up as "relative failure," and this is more than fair: the problem for the *Irish Times*'s correspondent at the Paris Peace Conference was that there simply wasn't that much time devoted to Ireland at the meeting.[36] But Smyllie recognized that European affairs did affect Ireland—even, perhaps especially, when Ireland didn't seem to affect European affairs—and he used that to make a strong case that all of Ireland's people could benefit from a broader perspective.

In his reporting on the peace conference, Smyllie was fascinated by one country in particular: Czechoslovakia. Under the subtitle "An Ulster in Bohemia," he speculated about the possible Celtic origins of the area and noted that "I believe that there is even an 'Ulster' in Czecho-Slovakia. True, the inhabitants of this Bohemian 'Ulster' are mostly Germans, but they are strongly opposed to Home Rule, and tremble at the very idea of Czecho-Slovak Sinn Fein."[37]

Smyllie was not the first to see Czechoslovakia as a kind of Central European doppelganger for Ireland. But most of his predecessors had approached the topic from the opposite end of the political spectrum. In the late 1800s and early 1900s, nationalists in both countries had performed a neat pas de deux. Initially, Czech political nationalists had found Ireland a useful model for their political aspirations. In turn, Irish cultural nationalists had looked to the Czech revival as an example for how to save their own endangered language. In the summer of 1905, the liberal editor of the *Tuam Herald*, Richard John Kelly, visited Prague. To judge from Kelly's editorials, Bohemia was what Ireland might hope to be in a few years. The two areas were similar in their religious makeup, close in population, and likewise subject to "foreign domination." Yet, in Czechoslovakia, agriculture was "perfection," there was "little or no emigration," and the country was "today as progressive and as prosperous as any country in Europe." Best of all, the Czech language and culture had "survived every form of oppression."[38] For Kelly, and for other Irish Catholics and nationalists, Czechoslovakia pointed the way to Ireland's future.

The link between Czech and Irish nationalism grew even stronger with the end of the war and the establishment of Czechoslovakia as an independent nation. In Sinn Féin propaganda, Czechoslovakian comparisons became practically their own genre. "Cannot you be as true to Ireland as the Czechoslovaks are to Czecho-Slovakia?" asked one poster.[39] Another featured a kind of imaginary postwar ballot, with X's next to "Independence" for "Czecho-Slovaks" and "Jugo-Slavs" but with the Irish section blank. "Ireland's mark is not yet made," the caption read. "The Czecho-Slovaks and the Jugo-Slavs are younger than this ancient country by a thousand years. They have voted for independence, and are now free."[40] "The Czecho-Slovaks . . . were refused Home Rule, too, by their masters," announced another poster. "They ignored their masters and asked the world for Independence. THEY GOT IT."[41] Another taunted its readers with the fact that "The Czecho-Slovaks are to-day as free as the English. Is it because you are Irish you are less worthy of freedom than the Czecho-Slovaks or the English?"[42] Finally, another made a probably accurate although rather ungracious assertion:

> The Czecho-Slovaks are Demanding Independence.
> Nobody is quite sure who the Czecho-Slovaks are.
> But the Whole World Knows Who the Irish Are.
> And Would Wonder if that Ancient Race did not Demand Independence.[43]

For Sinn Féin, Czechoslovakian independence was a great rhetorical opportunity and one that they exploited to the utmost. (Rather awkwardly for Sinn Féin, that debt was repaid over the next two decades by Czech Germans, who started comparing themselves to the Irish almost immediately, creating some unfortunate implications during the Sudetenland crisis.)[44]

Although Irish Catholics and nationalists tended to dominate the discussion about Czechoslovakia, southern Protestants also got in on the act. One of Kelly's fellow travelers on that 1905 trip was the reformist Unionist Horace Plunkett. Artistic and literary links between the two nations also often involved southern Irish Protestants. Karel Mušek was the first continental European translator of Synge to have the Irish author's plays produced, and he visited Ireland in 1906. He was somewhat surprised to find his Irish Protestant contacts relatively downbeat about their country's future. After meeting with Yeats and Edward Martyn at Coole Park, he came away with the sense that by comparison, the Czechoslovaks were doing rather well after all. According to Yeats and Martyn, they had better representation in their parliament than the Irish did in theirs, and at least their monarch was subsidizing their national theater, which was more than one could say for the Abbey.[45]

There were political links between Czechoslovak and Irish Protestants as well. The connection was natural: as in Ireland, Czech Protestants made up a small portion of the population (just over 2 percent, in Czechoslovakia's case) but played an outsize role in the political life of the nation.[46] In a survey of Czechoslovakia's history, a writer for the *Irish Times* noted mischievously, "as has happened elsewhere, the leaders of the revolution were mostly either Protestants or Catholics who had repudiated the authority of the Church."[47] Czechs, like Irish Protestants, had a complicated relationship with their home country's history. Scholars such as Frantisek Palacký—whose wife's family was of Irish origin—echoed the tone of nationalist Irish historians but reversed their confessional allegiances. Palacký's histories, like Irish nationalist versions, feature a nation crushed under the heel of foreign heretics, but his villain is Catholic Austria rather than Protestant England.[48] Tomas Masaryk, the first president of Czechoslovakia and a convert to Protestantism, had an even greater profile in Ireland. As a convert to Protestantism and one who had married a descendant of both Huguenots and Pilgrims, he was particularly suited to idealization by the southern minority.

After 1918, Czechoslovakia was more directly represented in Ireland by official diplomats and visitors. In 1929, Pavel Růžička, a Protestant and a former officer in both the czarist and Czechoslovak armies, was appointed Czechoslovak consul in Dublin. He promoted Czech music on Irish radio and gave lectures on Czechoslovak history to local groups such as the Rotary Club and Dublin Literary society.[49] His successor, Karel Košťál, an accomplished musician, was just as successful in integrating himself into Irish life, founding his own string quartet and often appearing on the radio. By the outbreak of war, he was so entrenched in Dublin society that he was allowed to maintain the Czechoslovak consulate throughout the war, even though the tolerance of such an office was a direct violation of the policy of Irish neutrality—in most other foreign capitals, Czechoslovak diplomats were replaced by representatives of the Third Reich. (The Irish government finessed this by continuing to officially acknowledge the existence of the consulate while carefully censoring references to it in print.)[50] Even when censored, Růžička and Košťál succeeded in bringing Czech culture to Ireland, perhaps most impressively when Růžička convinced the Free State Army to include Sokol—the Pan-Slavic gymnastics education method—into their training regimen. A first lieutenant from the Czechoslovak Ministry of Defense was brought over in the summer of 1934 and immediately began introducing Irish recruits to the benefits of Sokol. At first, despite the strong endorsement of Irish minister of defense Frank Aiken (who pointed

out, with some justification, "that an almost perfect analogy existed between the Sokol movement in Czecho-Slovakia and the Gaelic Athletic
movement"), the sight of Irish troops exercising to Bohemian rhythms elic-
ited some ridicule.[51] In the nationalist *Irish Press*, the columnist "Roddy the
Rover" asked "why is sokol so-kolled?" and suggested that Irish traditional
airs would be preferable to Czech music.[52] But by the late 1930s, Sokol exer-
cises were being performed in schools as far away as Donegal, and the 1939
Rathmines Feis even featured its own Sokol competition.[53]

As a friend of both Růžička and Košťál, Smyllie could have been expected to have gained some knowledge of Czechoslovakia over the course of
the 1920s and 1930s, but his involvement in the country went far beyond po-
lite interest. He made two visits to the country during the 1930s, each time
writing a series of articles for the *Irish Times* that were eventually published
in book form.[54] He first visited Prague in 1932, during the Sokol Congress.

As he had in his reports from the peace conference, Smyllie again used
a European comparison to simultaneously criticize, exalt, and urge Ireland
to learn from a continental example. As he had in Paris, he implies that the
minority has as much a responsibility for reconciliation as the majority: "It
would be untrue to say that the Germans and Magyars of the generation
that lived through the War have thrown in their lot whole-heartedly with
the Czecho-Slovak majority—human nature is the same the world over—
but they realize that they are getting a square deal from the Government,
that citizenship of the Republic entitles them to benefits that they would
enjoy in few other countries, and that Czecho-Slovakia to-day is a country
of which anybody might be proud."[55] He makes the same argument that the
Irish do not have it as bad as they think they do. "The differences between
the Irish Free State and Northern Ireland are negligible in comparison with
those between the several peoples of Central Europe," he notes; "as unintel-
ligent as has been the handling of the Anglo-Irish situation, the handling
of the Danubian situation has been very much worse."[56] As in Paris, he
discovered that the people of Europe had much to teach the Irish. At the
Sokol competition, he was impressed not only by the performances—"no
other people in the world has achieved a comparable expression of national
ideals"—but also by the absence of "aggressive nationalism." "I found a spirit
which, although intensely individualistic and race-conscious, seemed, at
any rate to me, to be free from any trace of national arrogance or intolerance." Smyllie notes a tolerance for minority languages and religions and
credits official policy for this: "the Czecho-Slovak Government has tried to

create a homogenous nation, in which Germans, Magyars, Poles and Ruthenians, while retaining their own languages and their own cultures, will become patriotic citizens of the Republic." This, one would assume, could potentially serve as a model for the Irish government. Finally, unlike in some countries, the Czechs have managed to avoid the tendency of peoples in newly independent nations to develop an "inferiority complex, [and] to become intensely suspicious, not only of one another, but of all the world, and to brood over their grievances, real or imaginary, to the neglect of their work as civilised nations."[57]

But for the most part, during this first visit, Smyllie followed the path that Richard John Kelly had blazed twenty-five years earlier: praising the strength of the Czechoslovak economy, exploring its agriculture, and highlighting the efforts of the government to provide social services.

During Smyllie's second visit to Czechoslovakia in 1937, when he traveled much farther east in the country, he made more direct comparisons to Ireland—and his view was darker. The series starts with him arriving by train. Whereas earlier nationalist visitors had highlighted Czechoslovakian unity, Smyllie now sees sharp distinctions: "The Dresden-Prague express had drawn up at the frontier station, known either as Podmokly or as Bodenbach, a choice which depends on your nationalist affiliations. If you are a Czech, it is Podmokly; if you are a German, it is Bodenbach. If you are a foreigner, you pay your money and take your choice. The difference is even more pronounced than that between the respective partisans of Dun Laoghaire and Kingstown, and the visitor to Czechoslovakia is not five seconds in the country before he discovers that the problem of the German minority is a really live issue."[58]

Whereas earlier visitors had highlighted the success of the Czech and Slovak language revival movements, Smyllie now sees them as an indictment of Ireland. He heads east, into Slovak territory, and compares the position of Slovaks with the Irish. "The big Hungarian landowners . . . were far worse than ever the poor Irish landlords," he writes; "the Slovaks were far closer to Hungary than the Irish were to England. The Hungarian methods of repression were far more brutal, as well as more subtle, than the English methods were in this country." Even so, he notes, the Slovak language survived and even thrived. "How did the Slovaks succeed where the Irish failed? Some abler man than I must solve the problem."[59]

Throughout this journey he was accompanied by an (unnamed) Irish tourist, who provided Smyllie with the perspective of what his employee

Brian O'Nolan would later immortalize as "The Plain People of Ireland." The tourist was from Cork, and Smyllie took the opportunity to describe him in terms that his largely Dublin-based audience would have appreciated: "Most Corkmen knew a lot, but this one knew everything. I tried many times to catch him out on some bit of esoteric information; but it was no use. Invariably he was ready for me, and whether it was some abstruse point in Canon Law, the history of Babylonian civilisation, the multifarious uses of the Soya bean, or even how to make drisheens, he could hold forth for a couple of hours and never became boring. I have changed my opinion of Corkmen because of him."[60]

Throughout Smyllie's account of his travels, the "Corkman" makes observations that Smyllie might not feel entirely comfortable expressing. When the travelers observe that throughout Slovakia and Ruthenia women seem to be doing most of the work in the fields, the "Corkman" notes: "'If we had women like that, at home . . . we could make things hum in Ireland.'"[61] When they visit Zakopane in Poland, which Smyllie describes as "a total loss . . . a miserable-looking town, which would be dubbed a 'joint' in the United States, lacking any kind of attraction, and filling us all with an urgent desire to get out of it as quickly as possible," it is the "Corkman" who makes the comparison to Ireland: "'Too much like one of our own country towns,'" he says.[62]

At other times, however, Smyllie seems entirely willing to make direct comparisons with Ireland. Travelling east of Chop, in what is now western Ukraine, he notes that "all around us there seemed to be just bleakness . . . we were in a country that reminded us only too vividly of parts of our own dear land—parts of Mayo, for example, or Leitrim or—but I had better go no farther."[63] In Uzhorod, Smyllie was struck by the power and influence of a local government official: "When I heard of the amount of patronage that is dispensed in Uzhorod, I was sorely tempted to draw an analogy with Cork."[64] He compares the poor roads in eastern Czechoslovakia and western Poland to those in the west of Ireland and, in a desperately poor town, meets a woman "who looked exactly like a Connemara peasant."[65] If, at its best, Czechoslovakia could show Ireland what it could be, Smyllie seems be suggesting, at its worst it can show Ireland what it is—or even what it has successfully avoided becoming. "Conditions in the north of Podkarpatska Rus are similar to those that exist even to-day in parts of the West of Ireland; but, of course, they are infinitely worse," he observes. "There is no such thing as real poverty in Ireland when one considers the standard of Ruthenia."[66]

Even the better-off inhabitants seem to be suffering. Smyllie encounters an aging aristocrat living in Uzhorod, a "remnant" of Magyar culture, now living among "a few books, a few fading photographs and her memories ... she ekes out her existence by letting rooms to lodgers—she who thirty years ago might have been the bell of the ball in the Castle of Budapesth [sic]."[67] Encountering poverty in the Podkarpatska Rus, he clearly blames the Hungarians, rather than the Czechoslovakian government, for the situation: "the distress had its roots deep in history ... aristocratic Hungary had created it centuries ago."[68] Although he does not make an explicit link here to the "Anglo-Irish," the implication is clear.

Other minorities play an important part in Smyllie's second visit to Czechoslovakia, and in those cases he is much more willing to make a direct link. In Uzhorod, Smyllie spends a great deal of time exploring the position of one minority in particular: the Jews. His companion the "Corkman" is surprised to find that many of the Jews in the area live in dire poverty—"he was under the impression that all Jews, if not rich to-day, certainly would be comfortably off tomorrow"—which reminds Smyllie of a story: "I [once] managed to get a job as an apprentice grave-digger in Mount Jerome Cemetery for a boy whose mother used to do odd jobs for us in Dublin. He was about seventeen years of age at the time, and one of his first tasks was to assist at a pauper's funeral. That evening he came home in a state of much excitement. 'Mother,' he burst out when he entered the house, 'there's poor Protestants!'"[69] Again, however, as he had in his earlier reports, Smyllie suggests that it is the duty of minorities to make an effort at integration. He encounters a poor college student who "would study his text-books or play his fiddle in a room that would disgrace a Dublin slum— and that is saying something. But the Jews seem to be able to lift themselves above their surroundings."[70]

Although in this second visit, Smyllie is much more willing to use Czechoslovakia to criticize Ireland, he makes it clear that this is the criticism of an Irishman of his own people rather than that of some foreign interloper. In fact, the least sympathetic characters he encounters are English:

As we were dawdling over our meal we were astonished to hear an unmistakable English voice calling for "Zwei Beah bittah." A large burly individual with his wife, both got up in regulation hiking kit, had stamped into the room after a day on the hills. They were the first English speaking people that we had seen since we left Prague. We were hundreds of miles from anywhere, and even the Cockney accent would have been as sweet music to our ears after weeks of Yiddish, Ruthenian, Czech, Slovak and all the rest of it. But, alas, there was nobody to introduce us. So, although those English folk were in the hotel for two whole days with us, we never exchanged a word. Towards the end it got rather on my nerves, and it took all the Corkman's blandishments to prevent me from going up to the hikers and breaking the ice with "Dr. Livingstone, I presume!" I like the English, but there are limits to exclusiveness.[71]

At the end of the second series, Smyllie concludes with two articles summing up his views. The first understandably, considering the situation in Czechoslovakia at the time, deals mainly with its strategic options and with the role of the German minority in the state. The last, however, makes much more explicit comparisons between the two states. Both countries had been dominated by foreign rulers since the 1600s: "nearly all the aristocracy in Bohemia consisted of German-speaking nobles. The Czechs were the hewers of wood and drawers of water."[72] In both countries, the native language declined as a result of this occupation: "during the eighteenth century the Czech language almost disappeared as a literary medium of expression."[73] Because of this legacy, and because of their relationship to their larger, more powerful neighbors, the people of both Ireland and Czechoslovakia display a host of pathologies: "There are many who argue that the Czechs are suffering from an inferiority complex—that they are nationally aggressive, self-opinionated, and all the rest of it; and, above all, that they are treating their minorities badly. It is only natural that, after so many generations of bondage, they should be inclined to be rather self-conscious and 'touchy'—have we not had a like experience in our own country?"[74] Both countries have to deal with poverty; both countries have to balance the desire for national unity with a respect for the rights of minorities; both countries have to find a balance between government power and individual responsibility.

The difference was, for Smyllie, that the Czechs simply seemed to be more invested in their country than the Irish were in theirs. Whereas both countries traded aristocratic for middle-class governance, the reason that the Czech language survived and Irish did not was because the people themselves took the initiative to save it. "To draw an analogy with Ireland would be easy, but futile. There really is no analogy; because whereas the Irish language ceased to be the general tongue of the people, the Czech language never did." Czech language, music, and literature succeeded because the people wanted it to rather than because the government required it. While the people of Czechoslovakia and the people of Ireland share what Smyllie calls "an exaggerated sense of nationality," Czechs have found a way to combine that with a respect for minority rights: "they are the only real democrats in Europe to-day, outside France and the Scandinavian countries," and their education policy, which provides schooling in all major minority languages, "speaks for itself."[75] Even the Czechoslovak economy works better than the Irish equivalent—again, not so much because of government policy but because of individual characteristics:

> Wages are not high. Judged by Irish standards, indeed, they are extremely low; but I should say that, taken all round, the standard of life in Czechoslovakia is substantially higher than it is here at home.
> That statement calls for some little explanation. An Irish worker probably eats more meat and good farm produce in a week than the average Czech or Slovak sees in a year; but how does he eat them? Every Czechoslovak woman is a finished housewife. She knows not only how to cook, but how to buy to the best advantage; and I have known women with University degrees in Prague to get up at the crack of dawn and go down to the market with their baskets. The Czechs are the thriftiest people I have met; and probably the cleanest. They dress plainly but comfortably, and their homes are models of efficiency. There is no waste, no luxury, no extravagance; and I will wager that a Prague woman with the equivalent of thirty shillings a week will make a better fist of things than a Dublin woman with twice that amount.[76]

Smyllie's second report from Czechoslovakia paints both Czechoslovakia and Ireland in a pessimistic light. Whereas earlier visitors (as well as Smyllie himself in the early 1930s) had used comparisons with Europe to highlight what Ireland could be, now he uses Europe to reveal Ireland's worst qualities. At the same time, however, in both of his reports from Czechoslovakia from the early 1930s, Smyllie is a good deal more invested in his critique than he had been in Paris in 1919. When reporting from Paris, he had come fairly close at times to using Europe to ridicule Ireland. His European comparisons then suggested that Ireland's people had no reason to complain, that Ireland's political situation was far less complicated than it seemed, that Sinn Féin was a shadow of its more successful continental equivalents. But in his tours of Czechoslovakia, he is determined to show Ireland that Europe can serve as both an example and a cautionary tale. Before, he made the case that the Irish people should pay more attention to Europe because Europe is more sophisticated and more civilized and often better organized and better run than Ireland. By the late 1930s, he is telling his Irish readers that they should pay attention to Europe because it can reveal what is most worth saving in Ireland. He is using an international frame to make—for lack of a better word—a nationalist case. Although

Smyllie earned the honor of the Order of the White Lion for his contributions to "the wider knowledge of Czechoslovakia and her people," it was Ireland he was most interested in.[77]

Notes

1. Seanad Debates, June 11, 1925, col. 443.
2. R. F. Foster, *W. B. Yeats: A Life II: The Arch-Poet* (Oxford: Oxford University Press, 2003), 296, 298.
3. "Anglo-Irish People," Wikipedia, accessed 17 July 2017, https://en.wikipedia.org/wiki/Anglo-Irish_people.
4. Gordon Forth, "'No Petty People': The Anglo-Irish Identity in Colonial Australia," in *The Irish World Wide*, vol. 2, ed. P. O'Sullivan (Leicester: Leicester University Press, 1992), 128–42; Donald H. Akenson, "No Petty People: Pakeha History and the Historiography of the Irish Diaspora," in *A Distant Shore: Irish Migration and New Zealand Settlement*, ed. Lyndon Fraser (Dunedin, New Zealand: Otago University Press, 2000), 13–24.
5. Foster, *Arch-Poet*, 298.
6. Seanad Debates, col. 436.
7. Ibid., 439.
8. Ibid., 441.
9. Ibid., 442.
10. See Charles C. Ludington, "Between Myth and Margin: The Huguenots in Irish History," *Historical Research* 73, no. 180 (2000): 1–19; Ruth Whelan, "The Huguenots and the Imaginative Geography of Ireland: A Planned Immigration Scheme in the 1680s," *Irish Historical Studies* 35, no. 140 (2007): 477–95; and Raymond Hylton, *Ireland's Huguenots and Their Refuge, 1662–1745: An Unlikely Haven* (Brighton: Sussex Academic Press, 2005).
11. See John Coakley, "A Political Profile of Protestant Minorities in Europe," *National Identities* Vol. 11 (2009): 9–30; and David Martin, "Notes for a General Theory of Secularisation," *European Journal of Sociology/Archives Européennes de Sociologie* 10, no. 2 (1969): 192–201.
12. Andrew Sinclair, *The Last of the Best: The Aristocracy of Europe in the Twentieth Century.* (London: Macmillan Company, 1969), 95.
13. Matthew Kelly, "Languages of Radicalism, Race, and Religion in Irish Nationalism: The French Affinity, 1848–1871," *Journal of British Studies* 49, no. 4 (2010): 801–25; Colin Barr, "Giusseppe Mazzini and Irish Nationalism, 1845–70," *Proceedings of the British Academy* 152 (2008): 125–44.
14. Dermot Keogh, *Ireland and the Vatican: The Politics and Diplomacy of Church-State Relations, 1922–1960* (Cork University Press, 1995).
15. Dermot Keogh, *Ireland and Europe, 1919–1948* (Dublin: Gill & MacMillan, Limited, 1988); Michael Hopkinson, "President Woodrow Wilson and the Irish Question," *Studia Hibernica*, no. 27 (1993): 89–111.
16. *Irish Times*, October 27, 1916, 6.
17. *Irish Times*, January 18, 1916, 6.
18. *Irish Times*, November 25, 1916, 6.

19. Ibid., 8.
20. Brian Inglis, *West Briton* (London: Faber & Faber, 1962), 26.
21. Terence de Vere White, *The Anglo-Irish* (London: Victor Gollancz Ltd, 1972), 40.
22. Stephen Brown, *The Press in Ireland: A Survey and a Guide* (New York: Lemma Publishing Corporation, 1971), 34.
23. Inglis, *West Briton*, 38.
24. Lionel Fleming, *Head or Harp* (London: Barrie and Rockcliff, 1965), 160–61.
25. Ibid., 161.
26. *Irish Times*, January 20, 1919, 5.
27. *Irish Times*, January 27, 1919, 5.
28. *Irish Times*, January 28, 1919, 3.
29. *Irish Times*, March 29, 1919, 7.
30. *Irish Times*, May 23, 1919, 5.
31. *Irish Times*, April 24, 1919, 6.
32. *Irish Times*, January 28, 1919, 3.
33. *Irish Times*, January 30, 1919, 5.
34. *Irish Times*, March 6, 1919, 5.
35. *Irish Times*, February 3, 1919, 5.
36. Pierre Ranger, "The World in Paris and Ireland Too: The French Diplomacy of Sinn Féin," *Études Irlandaises* 36, no. 2 (2011): 39–57.
37. *Irish Times*, February 7, 1919, 3.
38. *Freemans Journal*, July 1, 1905.
39. "Election poster for Sinn Féin," National Library of Ireland, Ephemera Collection, EPH F230, accessed July 1, 2017, http://catalogue.nli.ie/Record/vtls000509131.
40. "Czecho-Slovaks Independence," Irish Large Books (ILB) 300, 1, Item 80, National Library of Ireland.
41. "'No Home Rule'. The Czecho-Slovaks knew the line to take. Why not do as they did?" ILB 300 p 1, National Library of Ireland.
42. "The Czecho-Slovaks are to-day as free as the English: Be Men and vote for freedom!" ILB 300, 1, National Library of Ireland.
43. "Election poster for Sinn Féin," National Library of Ireland, Ephemera Collection, EPH F230, accessed March 1, 2016, http://catalogue.nli.ie/Record/vtls000509131.
44. Daniel Samek, *Czech-Irish Cultural Relations 1900–1950* (Prague: Centre for Irish Studies, Charles University, 2009), 38.
45. See Karel Mušek, "V zapadlém kraji—Črty z Erina, ostrova hoře" [In a remote country—Sketches from Erin, the Isle of Sorrow], *Zvon* 7, no. 23 (1907): 362–65; 7, no. 24 (1907): 378–81; 7, no. 25 (1907): 388–92, quoted in Samek, *Czech-Irish*, 33.
46. Patrick Cabanel, "Protestantism in the Czech Historical Narrative and Czech Nationalism in the Nineteenth Century," *National Identities* 11, no. 1 (March 2009): 32.
47. *Irish Times*, November 11, 1944, 4.
48. Monica Baár, *Historians and Nationalism: East Central Europe in the Nineteenth Century* (Oxford: Oxford University Press, 2010), 29–35; see also Cabanel, "Protestantism," 34.
49. *Irish Times*, June 17, 1930, 3.
50. Samek, *Czech-Irish*, 51.
51. *Irish Press*, June 20, 1934, 7.
52. *Irish Press*, May 10, 1934, 6.

53. *Strabane Chronicle*, May 23, 1937, 1; *Irish Press*, May 25, 1939, 2.

54. R. M. Smyllie ("Nichevo"), *Carpathian Contrasts* (Dublin: Irish Times, 1938); R. M. Smyllie ("Nichevo"), *Carpathian Days—and Nights* (Dublin: Irish Times, 1942).

55. *Irish Times*, August 11, 1932, 4.

56. *Irish Times*, September 6, 1932, 4.

57. *Irish Times*, September 6, 1932, 4.

58. *Irish Times*, November 15, 1937, 4.

59. *Irish Times*, November 19, 1937, 6.

60. *Irish Times*, November 17, 1937, 4.

61. Ibid.

62. *Irish Times*, November 22, 1937, 4.

63. *Irish Times*, November 24, 1937, 4.

64. *Irish Times*, November 26, 1937, 4.

65. *Irish Times*, December 8, 1937, 4.

66. *Irish Times*, December 10, 1937, 4.

67. *Irish Times*, December 1, 1937, 4.

68. *Irish Times*, December 10, 1937, 4.

69. *Irish Times*, November 29, 1937, 4.

70. Ibid.

71. *Irish Times*, December 13, 1937, 4.

72. *Irish Times*, December 22, 1937, 4.

73. Ibid.

74. Ibid.

75. Ibid.

76. Ibid.

77. Department of the Taoiseach S/9805, National Archives, Dublin.

4

PATRONS

Southern Irish Protestants played an outsize role in the intellectual, cultural, and artistic life of independent Ireland. This is perhaps one of the least surprising characteristics of the group, considering its long association with the "Anglo-Irish": ask most people familiar with Ireland to name some famous southern Irish Protestants, and they will list Yeats, Synge, and Lady Gregory rather than, say, successful business families such as the Findlaters or Arnotts. On the other hand, it is striking how many southern Irish Protestants made a mark on Irish culture not just through original creative work but through a kind of patronage that was often practical as well as cultural. In addition to Lady Gregory herself, Hugh Lane and Sarah Purser might serve as the archetypal examples here, although there were dozens of others. For instance, while Hugh Lane is understandably celebrated, it is worth remembering that it was Sir Denis Mahon, Frank Pakenham, and Bryan Guinness who finally brokered the deal that brought some of the Lane pictures "home" to Dublin.[1] And although Sarah Purser set the pace for a whole host of would-be south Dublin chatelaines, she was only one of many.

One of these was Beatrice, Lady Glenavy. Beatrice's father was an Elvery, of the sporting goods dynasty, and her mother was a scion of the Moss family, which could boast not only a polar explorer and the first woman elected to the Royal Scottish Academy but also one of the founders of the Irish Radium Institute.[2] Beatrice attended the Dublin Metropolitan School of Art—she also considered the South Kensington School of Art in London but only briefly, as her parents had heard terrifying stories about a relative of the family who had attended the school and had converted to Catholicism. She learned her trade, both artistic and social, at Sarah Purser's "At Homes," where on any given day the guests could include George Bernard Shaw, G. K. Chesterton, or Sara Allgood and where the young Miss Elvery's job was to "hand tea and cake to the visitors and to talk to the old ladies seated round the outskirts of the storm of conversation."[3]

Although Beatrice went on to become a distinguished stained-glass artist and painter, perhaps her greatest talent was for society. Despite the self-deprecating title of her memoir, *Today We Will Only Gossip*, her social network encompassed a virtual who's who of Irish and English artistic and literary life; after she married Charles Henry Gordon Campbell, Second Baron Glenavy, secretary of the Department of Industry and Commerce, and a director of the Bank of Ireland, her circle expanded to include those in business and politics as well. This continued during and after the upheaval of the late 1910s and early 1920s. Beatrice remembers nationalist heroes not as icons but as real people one meets at parties. Padraig Pearse was a "rather bulky, pale, shy young man" who stopped by Sarah Purser's art studio to translate captions in a children's book that Beatrice was illustrating; Constance Markiewicz was "a gay, adventurous young woman, whom no one at that time took very seriously either as a painter or a politician."[4] Although her father's house was raided and her own house was burned, during the period she emerged more influential than ever.[5] The Glenavys' house became a locus for cultural and intellectual life: frequent visitors included Paul Robeson, D. H. Lawrence, and Thornton Wilder.

It is difficult to trace the influence of figures such as Beatrice Glenavy. In part this is because they are often as discreet in writing as they are voluble in life. Glenavy ends her book with the image of her burning her letters to and from her great friend S. S. Koteliansky, the literary translator who was nearly as connected as Glenavy herself.[6] But it is also because their contributions are so important yet also so ephemeral: introducing a mentor to a teacher; helping raise funds for a great artist at a crucial moment; helping a friend find a job working for another friend. These are the people who often leave little historical trace beyond the "To:" sections of literary archives; the kinds of people who don't often write books but instead have books dedicated to them. Southern Irish Protestants such as Beatrice Glenavy—apparent outsiders in independent Ireland who actually earned the status of "insiders"—were particularly well suited to this position. Although R. M. Smyllie shared neither Lady Glenavy's family connections nor her resources, he too was able to fill the role of Protestant-as-patron.

As Smyllie settled into life at the *Irish Times*, he increasingly began to remake the paper in his own image. He even created his own column, a conglomeration of jokes, humorous observations, and trivia that despite its title—"The Irishman's Diary"—presented a distinctly Anglo-Irish view of the New Ireland.[7] Daily, in several short paragraphs, "Quidnunc" commented on the minutia of daily life in Dublin, described the activities of Dublin's Anglo-Irish establishment, and gently ridiculed most of the government's efforts to run the country—particularly its attempts to promote the Irish language. Although as the years went on the column became increasingly idiosyncratic (many of "Quidnunc's" artistic and literary "friends" must have seemed rather "clever" to many of the *Irish Times's* most loyal readers), the column fit in well with the paper's general tone: dozens of real "Quidnuncs" could be found in the Shelbourne Bar every Saturday afternoon, lingering over their whisky-and-splashes. When Healy retired as editor in 1934, Smyllie was the obvious man for the job.

But if on paper Smyllie was solidly Protestant and solidly Establishment, in person he was anything but. Brian Inglis remembered meeting him for the first time at the Island Golf Club:

> Among the new members was a short, burly man who wore his disreputable clothes with an air of someone who has nothing better to wear—not, as other members did, because they kept shabby old clothes in the club house to change into. Robert Maire Smyllie was not, to look at, a man who could normally have expected to become a member of the Island, but it would have been difficult to exclude him; he was the editor of the *Irish Times*. . . . Smyllie's companions, too, when he came down to the Island were usually the French Minister and the Czech Consul-General, and this was some guarantee of respectability (the diplomatic service ranked high in the Dublin social register).[8]

Inglis' emphasis on Smyllie's "companions" and "friends" is telling—to a large extent the editor's genius was his ability to maintain a delicate social equilibrium between respectability and something considerably less so. His circle included diplomats and high government officials but also lowly civil servants and businessmen. Even his golf was eccentric: as Tony Gray succinctly puts it, he was the kind of man who made his tee shots with a nine-iron.[9]

And if on the golf course he moved in what to Inglis's set seemed suspiciously cosmopolitan circles, his work environment was even more diverse. Despite the paper's solid reputation, the *Irish Times* attracted a motley group to its offices on Westmoreland Street. When Smyllie arrived at work at 4:30 p.m., he was immediately assailed by a bevy of hangers-on. Many of these existed in a kind of journalistic gray area: Inglis remembers how a network of independent informants would phone the paper to alert it about fires or arrests or murders and then show up the next day to collect payment for the "information." (And the *Irish Times* paid them—not because their information was particularly useful but as a form of "insurance" against being scooped on a really big story.) The main difference between staff members and beggars was that the beggars showed more initiative, as Patrick Campbell, who also worked for Smyllie, remembers:

> [Smyllie] spent most of his time on the run from the importunities of such characters as Chloral O'Kelly and Twitchy Doyle. They lay in wait for him every evening in their chosen lairs in the front office and threw themselves in his path, as though to halt a rushing locomotive, as soon as he appeared at the door. Chloral O'Kelly was a deeply melancholic youth who drank disinfectant, and was in constant need of 3s. 9d. for another bottle. Twitchy Doyle was a little old man with a straggly, jumping moustache who lived by reviewing reprints of Zane Grey.[10] The moment the Editor burst through the front door they closed on him with urgent appeals, battling for position with Dierdre of the Sorrows, an elderly woman who believed for twelve years that she was being underpaid for her contributions to the Woman's Page. The Editor shot through them, weaving and jinking, crying: "No—not tonight—tomorrow—goodbye"—and put on an extra burst of speed which carried him up the stairs to the safety of his own room, there to deliver his unforgettable cry: "Pismires! Warlocks! Stand aside!"[11]

But Smyllie himself got something out of this solidly unrespectable strata of Dublin life; his constant contact with such characters kept him in touch with parts of Ireland that the old *Irish Times* would have had no time for. As Inglis remembers, "however deeply he resented the spongers and sycophants, grumblers and bores who abused his accessibility, he did not like to think that some day, by shutting out someone, he might deprive the *Irish Times* of a good story."[12]

From 4:30 to 6:00 p.m., Smyllie met with advertisers and management in his office amid the labyrinthine warren that was the *Irish Times* building. By all accounts it was an unimpressive place. Patrick Campbell remembers the office as "high, dusty . . . there were no outside windows, so that the lights burned day and night."[13] (Because of the office's need for constant light, the *Irish Times* produced its own fuel from anthracite.) If the paper itself stood as a symbol of wealth and privilege, the office bespoke at best genteel poverty and at worst sheer squalor. This was a paper run on the cheap, particularly by British standards. An article Patrick Campbell wrote for the *Sunday Dispatch* after the war paid five times his weekly wage on the *Irish Times*. During the war, shortages reduced the length of the paper (and therefore advertising space and therefore profits). Raising the price of the paper to three pence in 1942 made little difference, and printing a front-page notice encouraging readers to share the paper only acknowledged an unprofitable reality. Certainly the editor himself would have been no help: these 4:30 to 6:00 meetings with management were a trying time for Smyllie, who, as "one of the last of the old-style editors," believed that "the business of the proprietors of a newspaper was to appoint a man whom they felt they could trust and leave him to get on with the job."[14] However advanced his ideas about art, literature, or politics, Smyllie was left cold by the modern belief that a newspaper should be a profitable enterprise: he heartily resented the few attempts by the paper's owners to improve efficiency and increase profits.

It was probably for this reason that if one wanted to find the editor of the *Irish Times* between 6:00 and 9:30 or 10:00 (when most of the reporters arrived,) the last place to look for him was at the *Irish Times* office itself. Instead one crossed Westmoreland Street and turned into the oak-fronted Palace Bar. Passing the snug (where reporters who had displeased the editor liked to hide), and moving through the narrow front room, one entered the lounge, where from behind a square table Smyllie held court. This was known as "family time," because around Smyllie in concentric circles sat, talked, drank, talked, and talked the social circle in which he felt most comfortable: Dublin's intelligentsia as well as assorted civil servants, politicians, lawyers, bankers, talkers, hangers-on, and anyone else who hoped one day to tell people that he had once been a member of the "Palace Bar Set." Tony Gray describes the subtle diplomacy that underlay the seemingly chaotic scene:

> The drill was well established, as invariable as an Aboriginal tribal ritual, and was always impeccably executed, without rehearsal and without any bungling on anybody's part, though it was never discussed or even mentioned. The supplicant, whoever he happened to be, would wait around on the fringes of Smyllie's circle, drinking with others far lower down the pecking scale, but keeping a wary eye on the centre table until he could see that the seat beside Smyllie was empty. He would then take his drink, slip into the seat and, as soon as there was an appropriate gap in the conversation which Smyllie was conducting with his intimates, seize his opportunity. As often as not the newcomer would offer Smyllie a drink, which might or might not be accepted, according to his status and the desirability of the project he was proposing. After occupying a reasonable amount of Smyllie's time and attention, it was tacitly

expected that he would withdraw discreetly and allow a similar supplicant to take his place.[15]

If it was a "poet's pub," it was hardly a lawless bohemia.

Dublin has had dozens of "poet's pubs": before the Palace's heyday in the late 1930s and early '40s, there had been the Bailey and Davy Byrne's, after it would come the Pearl and McDaid's. But none of these pubs drew such a wide swath of Dublin intellectual, literary, artistic, and public life as the Palace—largely thanks to Smyllie's patronage. His editorial influence attracted not only impoverished poets looking for reviewing jobs but also portrait painters wanting to discuss the Irish Exhibition of Living Art, civil servants interested in the paper's position on bread rationing, and ex-republicans intrigued by the possibility of a coalition government.

Certainly the Palace Bar was a gathering point for that generation of artists that found itself in the unique position of having to follow Joyce, Yeats, and Shaw. On any given night you could find many of Ireland's leading painters: William Conor, Harry Kernoff, Jerome Connor, Seán O'Sullivan, and Paul Henry. The world of drama was well represented by the playwright Brinsley MacNamara, director of the Abbey Theatre Roibeard Ó Faracháin, the actor Liam Redmond, and *Irish Independent* drama critic David Sears. Novelists and writers came to the Palace, especially Leslie Montgomery ("Lynn Doyle"), Brian O'Nolan, and even occasionally Oliver St. John Gogarty. There were, of course, plenty of poets, including F. R. Higgins, Patrick Kavanagh, Séamus O'Sullivan, and Ewart Milne. Finally, there was always a seasoning of journalists, civil servants, politicians, and assorted others, including *Irish Times* staffers Alec Newman, Alan Montgomery, Jack White, and John Robinson; the literary editor of the *Irish Press* M. J. MacManus; the public relations specialist Desmond Rushton; the labor leader Cathal O'Shannon; Roger Casement's brother Tom; the book collector John Chichester; and the legendary *Irish Times* advertising manager (and father of TV star Dave Allen) "Pussy" O'Mahony. Visitors interested in wartime intellectual life were automatically taken to the Palace Bar; John Betjeman, Louis MacNeice, and Cyril Connolly counted themselves among the "irregulars." It was, on balance, a slightly less respectable group than the one that gathered around Sarah Purser or even Beatrice Glenavy, but, like those, it was one brought together by the liberating environment created by its Protestant overseer.

To call this group a cross section is an understatement; it almost forms a definitive survey of intellectual Dublin life, remarkable not only for its political and ideological but also its generational diversity. It was less exceptional in its gender variety—most reminiscences of the Palace Bar during this period describe the "set" as exclusively male, as were most Irish pubs during this period. Tony Gray does recall once seeing "a girl with a cloak (I think she was a student at Trinity)" and Peggy Gough, then Arthur Duff's mistress and later a successful PR representative for Gannex raincoats.[16] The rise in female pub-going that occurred in Dublin during the war—it became a minor moral panic around the time of the debates over the Intoxicating Liquor Bill in 1942—seemed not to reach the Palace. But for its time and place, the Palace Bar hosted a wildly mixed gathering—RHAs and modernists, Fianna Fáil TDs and Fine Gael senators, reactionaries and nationalists all met over what Brian O'Nolan (writing as Myles na gCopaleen) immortalized as the pub's famous "balls of malt."[17]

What brought the Palace Bar set together was not just the drink, however. The place became notable most of all for its constant stream of conversation that even by Dublin standards was particularly inspired and particularly vicious. Brian Inglis remembers it in glowing terms, as "Irish culture on permanent exhibition—valuable evidence that the cultural renaissance in Ireland had not died with Yeats."[18] Not everyone was so impressed. Cyril Connolly, describing the scene in the 1942 Irish issue of *Horizon*, called it "as warm and friendly as an alligator tank."[19] Tony Gray found it exhausting—"all that endless talk," he sighs in his memoir.[20]

In his posthumously published autobiographical novel, *By Night Unstarred*, sections of which are set in a thinly disguised Palace Bar, Patrick Kavanagh describes the Palace Bar set as "a poisonous element, bitter, clever, good at making hurtful witticisms about their neighbours. But they had nothing creative to their name."[21] Kavanagh's objection to this "poet's pub" was that there were not enough poets in it—and too many businessmen. Worst of all even the poets often acted like businessmen, marketing themselves for public consumption: For Kavanagh, the Palace represented a step too far in the direction of materialism and "jobbery." And "The Editor" was the worst of them. Kavanagh's novelistic depiction of Smyllie demonstrates his own mixed feelings of resentment and admiration but also reveals (perhaps unintentionally) the way Smyllie, a Protestant insider, was able to act as a bridge between the artistic, commercial, and political worlds.

Kavanagh's description also demonstrates how the Palace Bar differed from later Irish literary pubs, such as McDaid's, which would usurp the Palace's standing in the 1950s, or even from contemporary British pubs, such as the haunts of Fitzrovia. Certainly what is true of all literary pubs was true of the Palace: they are good places to see writers not doing any writing. The two most prolific writers living in Dublin during the war—Sean O'Faoláin and Frank O'Connor—were rarely seen at the Palace. But what is often over-looked is how influential many members of the Palace Bar set were in Irish public life, not only as critics and intellectuals but also in the less visible realms of government and business. Today Séamus O'Sullivan is remem-bered less for his poetry than for his editorship of the influential *Dublin Magazine*, whose diverse portrayal of Irishness paved the way for *The Bell*. M. J. MacManus shaped the literary tastes of the conservative readership of the *Irish Press* and helped expose young writers to a much wider audi-ence than they otherwise would have had access to. Brinsley MacNamara was not just a playwright but was also the curator of the National Gallery of Art. And the Palace set included a disproportionately high number of what Brian Inglis called "Protestants and Protestant-minded Catholics." [22] Alan Montgomery and Alec Newman would both succeed Smyllie as edi-tors of the *Irish Times*; Jack White and John Robinson would go on to hold executive positions at RTE (Radio Telifís Éireann, Ireland's public service broadcaster) and the BBC, respectively; Brian Inglis would become editor of *The Spectator*. Patrick Campbell would make his name as a TV personal-ity in Britain. Finally, it is important to remember that Smyllie, too, was no poet, nor did he want to be. Like so many of the Palace Bar set, he combined a love of art with a practical eye.

This was immediately apparent even in the time Smyllie actually spent at the *Irish Times* office (9:30 or 10:00 p.m. to 3:00 or 4:00 a.m., Sunday through Friday, depending on whether he went to the private *Irish Times* club in Abbey Street for a few more drinks after finishing the day's lead articles or how early he repaired to the United Services Club for a few more drinks in the morning). He filled the office with a presence that is alternately described as either "Hemingwayesque"[23] or "Chestertonian."[24] Patrick Campbell, who started working for the paper during the war, has written the most famous description of Smyllie at the office: "When, in these trying times, it's possible to work on the lower slopes of a national newspaper for several weeks without discovering which of the scurrying executives is the editor, I count myself fortunate to have served under one who wore a green sombrero, weighed twenty-two stone, sang parts of his leading articles in operatic recitative, and grew the nail on his little finger into the shape of a pen nib, like Keats."[25]

Smyllie's speech was a blend of Dublin argot and pompous obscurity and often resembled the kind of English that non-Protestants believed Protestants spoke in private. Formalities held over from the earlier days of the newspaper remained but were subverted. "Mr. Smyllie, sir!" was the correct form of address, but it was likely to be met by a command to *"nemo me impune lacessit!"* or "prehensilize some Bosnian peasants!" ("Prehensile" had somehow came to refer to lucid prose—"Somerset Maugham was a prehensile writer, Henry James unprehensile in the extreme.")[26] Anyone from the king to the censor was liable to be deemed a "shudderer"; bicycles were "velocipedes"; a game of dominoes was termed "pimping" or "hooring."[27] Once, the IRA deemed the *Irish Times* overly concerned with English and Anglo-Irish affairs and threw stones through the windows of its Cork office. When Smyllie heard of this, he took a long pull from his noggin of brandy (filed under "B" in his correspondence cabinet) and told Patrick Campbell, "These shudderers cannot intimidate me by throwing half-bricks through the windows of the branch office while my lieutenants are taking a posset of stout in the shebeen next door."[28]

On the surface, it often appeared unlikely that any work at all took place at the *Irish Times* office. But Smyllie's personality could overwhelm the seriousness with which he took his role as editor of the *Irish Times*. If he acted like "The Editor," it's because he was. "The *Irish Times* was Smyllie," Brian Inglis remembers, "in a sense that no national newspaper today can be identified with its editor."[29] This was not out of a will to power or even a desire to be near the powerful. Smyllie's disagreements with the Arnott family, who managed the paper, arose not because he felt threatened but because he wanted to get back to his writing, and, as Inglis points out, "the eminence or influence of acquaintances meant little to him, except for its possible usefulness to his gossip column on Saturday morning."[30] (Certainly many of the members of the "Palace Bar Set" had little to offer but good conversation.) Rather it was because of Smyllie's real commitment to the craft of editing and to his sense of responsibility for the paper's role in Irish life.

Smyllie spent most of the time from 10:00 p.m. onward managing the business of writing: both supervising others' and honing his own. The first half of this job was made easy by the *Irish Times*'s chronic impoverishment and understaffing, which barred the luxury of indulging any stylistic excesses, and was helped along by Smyllie's own nose for talent. His hiring methods, like most of his administrative techniques, were ad hoc. Partly he relied on the paper's social and intellectual reputation to attract "good stock" and on its low pay to ensure that only the most dedicated report-ers would stay. Partly he just took chances—Gray, Inglis, and Campbell all got their jobs without having any previous experience and kept them be-cause Smyllie liked their "prehensility." Lionel Fleming got his not in spite of but because he had been fired as a schoolteacher. At the same time, this was not as mixed a company as Smyllie's administration would suggest. With a few notable exceptions, such as the ex-republican subeditor Larry de Lacy, most of the newspaper's staff were Protestants or "Protestant-minded Catholics."[31]

But they had a different perspective on Irish life than had the men of Healy's day. First, many were younger and thus did not carry with them the legacy of the Civil War and War of Independence. Like their fathers, these men had grown up with an ingrained sense of difference between "Us and Them,"[32] as Lionel Fleming puts it, among "people, who in their hearts, were disorientated . . . the future was seen to be not in Ireland, but in England."[33] But that emotional connection to England had been weakened by history. "In due course our political feelings were blunted by constant anxiety and fear, and the realization that the British army was falling down on the job," Fleming noticed. He resented "that any people who showed such little comprehension of Ireland had no right to have been trying to govern it for the last seven hundred years"[34] and could not relate to "the stability of people to whom history had been kind, who never had been harried or expropriated or made to feel as if they were outlaws."[35] Although several of Smyllie's editorial writers came from established families, many did not. Inglis recalls that his arrival at the paper reminded him of his ar-rival at school—but a school that, unlike his alma mater, was full of "men-acing lower-class boys of the kind that at Shrewsbury we would have called oicks."[36] Finally, they were more literary-minded than the older group had been. Their ideas had been shaped by a reaction against Victorian certain-ties: "all the values of one's parents had become vulnerable since the Great War . . . Lytton Strachey had conclusively debunked Queen Victoria and the public school system, and now here came the Irish loyalists, riding for a similar fall."[37]

Smyllie's secret was not only surrounding himself with younger and better writers, however. His great achievement was finding and encourag-ing writers who shared his perspective on Irish life, a view that Lionel Flem-ing has termed "Protestant Nationalism." The paper's distinctive editorial stance was as much the work of these writers and editors—a group that included Fleming, Inglis, Campbell, Gray, Alec Newman, Alan Montgomery, Jack White, Bruce Williamson, and John Robinson, among others—as it was that of Smyllie. (Often literally—whenever Smyllie's muse left him it was these men who wrote the leading editorials.) Despite these various influences, the *Irish Times* maintained a characteristic ideology, informed by the different perspectives of its editorial staff. Fleming describes it as a belief that "Anglo-Ireland" should drop the first half of its hyphenation, without losing its identity.[38] The result of this reconciliation, for Fleming, would be the rebirth of a new, engaged class of liberal, Protestant intellectuals, able to see through the "prudery,"[39] "reverence for clerical authority," and "fanatical Gaelicism" of Catholic Ireland and finally provide a "critical . . . realistic view of life in Ireland . . . the mental health of Ireland would be the better for a general loosening up."[40] They could help build a country that was truly independent:

> The Anglo-Irish ought not only to accept their Irishness but assert it, and demand recognition for a point of view and a way of life which had done as much to mould Irish civilisation as the Gaelic influences that were being so much invoked. The liberal outlook, the critical and independent attitude, the readiness to examine new ideas on their merits—those were part of the legacy which England and Protestantism had left to Ireland, and they were worth pressing for. And although our section must accept the fact that Ireland is a Catholic country, they should support anything which did not concern religion. In this way, they could perhaps help to teach Ireland that true nationalism does not involve curling oneself up like a hedgehog, and, as for themselves, they should remember always that it is foolish to pretend to be part of an English garrison, an aboriginal Celt, or anything else which one obviously is not.[41]

For Fleming the *Irish Times*, as the expression of this new incarnation of "Anglo-Ireland," could provide a liberal, secular, alternative voice in Irish political and social life.

Brian Inglis also saw the *Irish Times* as the natural site for the kind of reconciliation necessary for the survival of Anglo-Ireland. Smyllie's great achievement, Inglis remembered long afterward, was that he was able to drag unwilling southern Protestants into the modern state:

> This was the man who had done more, probably, than anybody else to persuade the Irish Unionists, small in numbers, but disproportionately influential owing to their wealth and social standing, to come to terms with the Irish Free State. The Irish Times might easily have decided to go down, orange and blue colours nailed to its mast-head, with the Unionist ship. . . . Before Smyllie's

time, relatively little had been done by the paper to woo readers away from rigid Unionism; Smyllie himself had to teach them to accept Dun Laoghaire instead of Kingstown. He was at heart a Unionist, and indeed a royalist, himself; but he put the paper before personal feelings and, as a newspaperman, he could see that any attempt to cling to the old ways after the link with England had been severed would be to ensure his paper's eventual extinction.[42]

This approach meant helping Protestants to become a part of the nation that they felt had rejected them. If this would not be easy—the paper, like the people, would "[have] to be disloyal to its past if it [was] to survive"—it was necessary.[43]

Smyllie's editorship of the *Irish Times* is marked by many of the principles that Fleming and Inglis outlined. He believed that Protestants had contributed and would continue to contribute to Irish society and supported such causes as the setting up of an Irish version of the National Trust to preserve big houses. But his Scotch background, his experiences in Continental Europe, and his apparent obliviousness to social codes made him both less doctrinaire and less defensive about standing up for older traditions. Ireland's Protestants had to earn his respect like everyone else. He championed Irish intellectuals, promoting the foundation of the Writers, Artists, Actors, and Musician's Association, challenging censorship, and patronizing advanced artists in all mediums, yet he kept up a constant and steady attack on literary pretension—the "beards" and "corduroys," too, had to prove that they could do more than just talk. He was truly a Unionist at heart. But he accepted Ireland's independence from Britain, even justifying it in editorials, supported most other attempts at Irish cultural development, especially in the areas of film and music, and made space on the paper's editorial page for what was to become the most famous column ever written in Irish, "Cruiskeen Lawn."

The principle Smyllie was most committed to, however, was that the *Irish Times* should do more than just react to the contemporary political scene. It should be an active participant in it. For all his old-fashioned methods and reactionary instincts, he was a strenuous advocate for modernization, of everything from railways to agricultural production to trade relations with Britain. Smyllie heartily endorsed the activities of the Turf Development Board in the 1930s. C. S. Andrews, one of the Board's key members, has written one of the best summaries of Smyllie's version of "Protestant Nationalism": "Smyllie accepted that he was an Irishman owing unequivocal allegiance to Ireland. In this he differed from most of the

Anglo-Irish who remained in Ireland after the Treaty . . . he wrote from the standpoint of a free and independent Ireland rather than that of a province, regrettably and possibly temporarily separated from the motherland . . . Smyllie, in fact, integrated the *Irish Times* and what it stood for with the Irish nation."[44]

As a result of these activities, the paper's influence reached far beyond what its limited circulation would indicate. Brian O'Nolan's biographer, Anthony Cronin, who was a student at University College Dublin during the war, remembers how this unique editorial position represented freedom: "I bought the *Irish Times* whenever I could afford it because the *Irish Times* was a symbol of liberation from the values of one's *Irish Independent*–reading forebears."[45] This liberation was not only symbolic. John Garvin, Brian O'Nolan's supervisor at the Ministry of Local Government, remembers how "the very fact that the paper held a minority position gave it a degree of independence that Smyllie was able to exploit." Of the three major Dublin dailies the *Irish Times* was the "only organ free to be reformist, if not radical, in its social policies."[46] Andrews remembers how it appealed to the "rising lower middle classes" of clerks, merchants, and businessmen as the symbol of "ould dacency" and to the upper reaches of the civil service and the government as a stamp of approval. "When anyone in the civil service offices told you that he had seen such and such an item 'in the paper,' you knew that he was referring to the Irish Times," Andrews remembers. "Favourable comment from the *Irish Times* made a minister's day. Favourable comment from the other two Dublin dailies was of no importance to them.[47]

If this is an overstatement (certainly de Valera attached some value to the canonization he received in the pages of the *Irish Press*), it is not a great one. Ever since becoming editor of the paper in 1934, Smyllie had indicated his desire that the paper, and the people who read it, should play a greater role in Irish life. But becoming an insider—one who followed the older model of Protestant-as-patron but who also engaged with every aspect and every level of Irish life—allowed him to put those ideas into practice.

One Irish citizen Smyllie benefited more directly was Beatrice Glenavy's son Patrick, who, until he succeeded to the title of Baron Glenavy in the early 1960s, went by the more mundane Patrick Campbell, and who Smyllie hired in the 1930s. The connection? Glenavy's and Smyllie's mutual friend Tom Casement, whose older brother, Roger, Smyllie had chased out of Ruhleben twenty years before.[48]

Notes

1. See Anne Kelly, "The Lane Bequest: A British-Irish Cultural Conflict Revisited," *Journal of the History of Collections*, vol. 16, issue 1 (May 2004): 89–110.

2. Edward R. Moss, *Shores of the Polar Sea: A Narrative of the Arctic Expedition of 1875–6* (London: Marcus Ward & Co., 1878); and R. Charles Mollan, *Some People and Places in Irish Science and Technology* (Dublin: Royal Irish Academy, 1985), 103.

3. Beatrice Glenavy, *Today We Will Only Gossip* (London: Constable, 1964), 29.

4. Ibid., 90.

5. Ibid., 126.

6. Ibid., 194–95, and see also Galya Diment, *A Russian Jew of Bloomsbury: The Life and Times of Samuel Koteliansky* (Montreal: McGill-Queens University Press, 2011).

7. Although Smyllie began the column, he often drew on the contributions of other writers. Eventually "Irishman's Diary" was turned over to a single columnist, and Smyllie-exclusive columns were distinguished by the pen-name "Nichevo."

8. Brian Inglis, *West Briton* (London, Faber & Faber, 1962,) 39.

9. Tony Gray, *Mr. Smyllie, Sir* (Dublin: Gill and MacMillan Ltd, 1991), 71.

10. As Lionel Fleming remembers, Twitchy Doyle was also famous around the office for having written a conclusion to Dickens's *Edwin Drood*. At some point he had given the manuscript to Smyllie to read, and Smyllie had promptly misplaced it in the sea of papers that filled the *Irish Times's* editorial room. Hiring Doyle to write the Zane Grey reviews was his way of making up for losing the manuscript. Lionel Fleming, *Head or Harp* (London: Barrie and Rockcliff, 1965), 159–60.

11. Patrick Campbell, *My Life and Easy Times* (London: Blond, 1967), 72.

12. Inglis, *West Briton*, 55.

13. Campbell, *My Life*, 72.

14. Inglis, *West Briton*, 47.

15. Gray, *Mr. Smyllie*, 73.

16. Ibid., 74.

17. The Royal Hibernian Academy (RHA) is Ireland's leading artistic institution and as such was challenged during the Emergency by more innovative organizations such as the White Stag Group. TD (Teachta Dala) is a representative of the lower house of Parliament.

18. Inglis, *West Briton*, 50.

19. *Horizon* 5, no. 25, January 1942.

20. Gray, *Mr. Smyllie*, 75.

21. Patrick Kavanagh, *By Night Unstarred* (New York: The Peter Kavanagh Hand Press, 1978), 141.

22. Inglis, *West Briton*, 43.

23. *Horizon*, vol. 5 no. 25, January 1942.

24. Inglis, *West Briton*, 53.

25. Patrick Campbell, *The Campbell Companion* (London: Pavilion Books Limited, 1994), 71.

26. Ibid., 73.

27. Ibid., 75–77.

28. Ibid., 76.

29. Ibid., 48.

30. Ibid., 48.

31. Inglis, *West Briton*, 43.

32. Fleming, *Head or Harp*, 32.

33. Ibid., 45.

34. Ibid., 112.

35. Ibid., 114.

36. Brian Inglis, *Downstart* (London: Chatto & Windus), 81.

37. Ibid., 104.

38. Fleming, *Head or Harp*, 163.

39. Ibid., 164.

40. Ibid., 166.

41. Ibid., 167.

42. Inglis, *Downstart*, 54.

43. Ibid., 54.

44. C. S. Andrews, *Man of No Property* (Dublin: Lilliput Press), 137.

45. Anthony Cronin, *No Laughing Matter: The Life and Times of Flann O'Brien* (New York: Fromm International Publishing Corporation, 1989), 145.

46. John Garvin, "Sweetscented Manuscripts," in *Myles: Portraits of Brian O'Nolan*, ed. Timothy O'Keefe (London: Martin Brian and O'Keefe Ltd., 1973), 65.

47. Andrews, *Man of No Property*, 137–38.

48. Glenavy, *Today*, 135.

5

LIBERALS

IN 1950, A MINOR CONFLAGRATION AROSE IN THE correspondence columns of the *Irish Times* over a speech by Professor Felim Ó Briain, chair of philosophy at University College Galway. Ó Briain had given a talk warning against the "liberal ethic" that he believed was threatening Western civilization. Socialists behind the iron curtain and liberals on this side of it shared a belief in "a free morality—the ethics of free love," and unless Catholics stood up against it "the only freedom that would triumph . . . [would be] the freedom of the armed man to suppress the liberty of all who differed from his views."[1] Linking contraception to communism, and implying that Protestant clerics supported "mercy killing," Ó Briain's speech (or, perhaps more importantly, the report about that speech in the paper) was guaranteed to attract a response from southern Irish Protestants.

Although the first to write in was Owen Sheehy Skeffington—who, as an atheist, qualifies as "Protestant" only by the most generous definition of the term—he was followed by others who reversed Ó Briain's equation. Although the professors' respondents approached the issue from a number of different perspectives, the overall message was clear: if Catholics criticized the liberal ethic, then non-Catholics would defend it. Echoing Sheehy Skeffington's suggestion that in Ireland "a religion based on transcending love finds all too commonly its expression in uncharitable and misinformed attacks on any who dare to hold differing views,"[2] Brian Inglis suggested that, by Ó Briain's logic, "Protestantism must lead to Orangeism."[3] Hubert Butler, writing under his frequent pseudonym "Emilius," pointed out that "Most Liberals, even Protestant ones, are ready to acknowledge the almost invaluable kindness, selflessness and goodness of the Catholic clergy in Ireland, but they cannot allow this claim to superior wisdom, which is so often and arrogantly made. Does not dogmatic assertion always provoke its opposite? Was not Stalin a theological student?" [4] A host of other contributors followed, and for six weeks the correspondence columns were packed with full-throated defenses of "liberalism," broadly defined.

This was somewhat unusual for a group that could be as conservative as Irish society more broadly. Irish Catholics did not hold a monopoly on "respectability," and some Protestants "actually welcome[ed] the puritanical trend in family law and the discipline of the press" in independent Ireland.[5] It is true that Protestant faith leaders demonstrated a noted lack of enthusiasm for some of the more prominent attempts to legislate morality, such as the Committee on Evil Literature and the Censorship of Publications Board, and it is not unreasonable to infer disapproval from their silence.[6] On the other hand, it is also possible that they feared that speaking out on these issues might offend not only the Catholic majority but also some of their own parishioners.

Read from the perspective of more than half a century on, what became known as the "Liberal Ethic" controversy—the *Irish Times* even produced its own pamphlet collecting the correspondence in June 1950—was actually a much more even-handed conversation than it may have appeared at the time.[7] Ó Briain turned out to be a better debater than polemicist, and he went on to make a case for a kind of "Catholic Liberalism" that was much subtler and more thoughtful than his critics often gave him credit for. But what is striking about the discussion is how quickly it moved from Ó Briain's vehement but narrow denunciation of what he saw as "liberal and socialist" sexual and reproductive practices to a much broader and at times somewhat incoherent discussion about liberal political and social thought generally. (Ó Briain was uncharitable but not incorrect when he described his opponents' attacks as "a chaotic discordant amalgam.")[8] It was as though the paper's southern Irish Protestant readers were already on guard, ready at any moment to respond to any threat to liberalism—as though their faith committed them to a certain set of political and moral principles. In this sense, the "Liberal Ethic" controversy was an echo of another more focused debate over the relationship between Protestantism and liberalism, held in the Irish Senate eight years earlier.

Ireland was unusually aware of censorship during the war. But the most controversial censorship case of the period had nothing to do with protecting official secrets or with safeguarding neutrality. It was a debate in the Seanad (Irish senate) in November and December 1942 provoked by the Censorship Board's banning of three books: Halliday Sutherland's *Laws* of Life, Kate O'Brien's *The Land of Spices*, and Eric Cross's *The Tailor and Ansty*.[9] As a result of these bans, on November 18, 1942 Senator Sir John Keane moved "that, in the opinion of Seanad Éireann, the Censorship of Publications Board appointed by the Minister for Justice under the Censorship of Publications Act, 1929, has ceased to retain public confidence, and that steps should be taken by the Minister to reconstitute the board."[10] For twelve hours, spread out over four days, senators painstakingly compared texts, performed close readings, argued about theme and implication, and discussed the role of literature in Irish society. It was as if the Catholic Truth Society and WAAMA had accidentally booked the same meeting hall, and it seemed to have nothing to do with southern Irish Protestantism at all.[11]

At the same time, it is hard to imagine the debate taking the shape it did without southern Protestant voices. Some of these came from the sponsor of the motion, Sir John Keane, and from other Protestant senators. Another was the authorial voice of the writer whose work dominated the discussion: Eric Cross, although raised in England, had been born in Newry, County Down.[12] Most of all, the coverage of the affair provided by the *Irish Times*—which featured regularly on both the news and editorial pages—helped to frame this rather obscure discussion as a question of national importance. Keane, Cross, Smyllie, and the others were not making an argument just about censorship or morality or Catholic power but about what kind of nation Ireland was and what kind of nation it should be.

Of the three books that provoked the debate, *The Tailor and Ansty* was in many ways the least controversial and, as such, the least likely to have attracted the notice of the censors. *Laws of Life* includes information on birth control, which was explicitly proscribed. High-profile literary works such as *The Land of Spices* often come to the attention of the censors, especially if they were reviewed prominently in English or American publications. But *The Tailor and Ansty* is a quasi-anthropological account of the stories and sayings of the idiosyncratic *seanchai*, or traditional storyteller, Tim Buckley. Based on years of Cross's visits to the Buckleys', the book superficially resembles a sort of annotated transcript of the Tailor's conversation, and its plotless, rambling construction re-creates the experience of being in the Tailor's company.

As a result of the debate, it is difficult—probably impossible—to read the book from the perspective of its critics in 1942. Indeed, as it emerged over the course of the debate, to truly represent the perspective of many of the book's critics one must *not* have read the book. There is a good deal in the book that could offend more sensitive natures, as much for its offhand-edness as its content. "'Tis a small thing would put a man in good-humour again," the Tailor observes, "as the man said when he heard his wife was dead, and he went out into the yard and saw the cock mounting the hen."[13] His wife Anastasia's (Ansty's) interest in the sexual life of friends, acquain-tances, animals, and virtually everything else is inexhaustible, and in a pas-sage that the debates would make famous, she is shocked by a story of a young woman who does not know the difference between a bull and a cow.[14]

There is some very mild political and social commentary in the book. Although his physical world extends only about the distance his cow can graze, the Tailor has much to say about national affairs. Despite his flu-ency in Irish, he disparages the government's attempts to revive and main-tain the language, referring to the bilingual movement as "'the boiling programme.'"[15] He suspects that Fianna Fail is in trouble when the *Irish Press* stops lighting his pipe as well as it used to—"I must change my pol-itics."[16] Nor does he have much respect for religious authority, although the Buckleys' closest friend is a priest and they say the Rosary together in Irish daily. He remembers a trip to Belfast during which a group of Orangemen threatened to throw him into the Lagan unless he said "to hell with the Pope"—"I did a bit of quick thinking. I thought—well, they can always get another pope, but there is only one me!"[17]

While the book's attackers would seize on these isolated examples of "blasphemy and corruption" during the debate, the real issue for many of the book's critics was its author's intentions. In the course of the debate, sev-eral senators worried that "this Englishman's" depiction of the Tailor and Ansty would harm Ireland's image by making the pair appear to be repre-sentative rather than exceptional types. Even defenders of the book noticed aspects of stage-Irishness in the portrayal of the title characters. Patrick Kavanagh—whose opinion of the book changed considerably, sometimes over the course of a single review—suspected that Cross was playing up the pair's eccentricities to appeal to an English audience: although the book was "a gorgeous evening's entertainment . . . one mustn't deduce anything about Ireland from the reading."[18] Kavanagh was certainly right on the first count and probably right on the second, but his dismissal reveals something im-portant about the book: in its modest way, it does represent an attempt to present a more liberal picture of Irish rural life. Cross depicts a world in which the timeless rhythms of Irish folklore coexist with international news and gossip columns, in which the ascetic virtues of the farming life run up against the Tailor's philosophy that one should "take the world fine and aisy and the world will take you fine and aisy," in which a puritanical version of Catholicism thrives alongside an obsessive interest in the racier side of human existence.[19] It was a world that many of the book's severest critics, who had come from rural Ireland, knew well. But this only angered them further. It was one thing for a son of the soil to paint a complex picture of Irish rural life, quite another for an "Englishman" to attempt the same. It was not just the Irish people's decency that was threatened—what was at stake was their very identity.

Frank O'Connor, for one, recognized the broader significance of the book when he wrote to the *Irish Times* on October 9, 1942. "The Tailor and Anstey [*sic*] are the last of their kind; they represent dead generations of Irishmen and women, and we of the new Ireland should show them at the end something of their own great charity and courtesy."[20] O'Connor's defense of *The Tailor and Ansty* provoked a storm of correspondence. "The members of the Censorship Board have, possibly unwittingly, struck a grievous and staggering blow not only against this grand old couple, but also against the spirit and tradition of Ireland itself," wrote the composer (and Dublin Protestant) Frederick May.[21] "Is [censorship] open war against all culture—and Irish culture in particular?" asked Dermot Foley.[22]

The *Irish Times* was not going to let this controversy be restricted to its editorial pages. In "An Irishman's Diary" column on October 15, "Quidnunc" suggested that the banning of *The Tailor and Ansty* is "an opportunely sent argument for Dail changes in our censorship code . . . the action against the poor 'Tailor' will, as I say, be the best ammunition against the stupid front of our glorious censors."[23] Two days later, Sean O'Faolain wrote in to the paper to point out that as an example of the censors' incompetence, the *Tailor and Ansty* ban was not an isolated case: in 1941 the board had banned Halliday Sutherland's health primer *Laws of Life*, despite the book having received the *permissu superiorum* from the Westminster Diocesan Council. The Censorship Act, wrote O'Faolain, was not only being worked improperly but was "quite incapable of being worked properly;" the "five addle-pates" who made up the board had proven again that the censorship was "an embarrassment to the Government and a humiliation to the people."[24] Wave after wave of letters followed, and on October 23, the *Irish Times* reported that "Sir John Keane has given notice to move at next sitting of the Senate that the Board 'has ceased to retain public confidence.'"[25]

Keane proved to be an indefatigable opponent of the censorship. He was also, in some ways, the worst friend that more quietist Protestants could have possibly wished for. Keane was a baronet, educated at Clifton College in Bristol and the Royal Military Academy (RMA) in Woolwich. He served with distinction in the Boer War and the First World War and in between had played a leading role in moderate political organizations ranging from the All-Ireland League to the Co-operative Movement. When he returned to Ireland after World War I, he had attained the rank of lieutenant colonel and had received the Queen's South Africa Medal, the Distinguished Service Order (DSO), and the French Legion of Honor: exactly the kind of figure who, the new government hoped, could be safely ensconced in the newly formed Senate of the Irish Free State, where he would no longer cause any trouble. But Keane refused to be sidelined. Although his house in Waterford, Cappoquin, was burned in 1923, he spent the rest of the 1920s restoring it—along with the help of his wife, Eleanor Hicks Beach, the daughter of a former chief secretary—as a symbol of resistance against the "Shinners." Unlike some Protestant members of the senate, who respected the implicitly honorary nature of their appointment, Keane took the job seriously, racking up an impressive attendance record and rarely holding his tongue during debates, both in and out of Leinster House.[26] When he was asked to contribute to the Patrician Conference in 1932, he chose to speak on the subject of "tolerance." An anodyne enough topic, it would seem, until Keane explained that his interpretation of the term was anything but. "Toleration is not an attitude of insipidity or indifference," he told his audience, but "implies disagreement and opposition allied with a belief that fallacy must be exposed and truth must triumph under conditions of free expression."[27] The National Portrait Gallery's collection contains several portraits of Keane from the early 1920s; with his distinguished gray hair, his three-piece suit, and his general air of someone about to dress down an adjutant caught smoking on duty, he looks like a nationalist's worst nightmare of what the Irish senate might become.[28]

Keane first attacked the Censorship Act from a practical perspective. He stressed that a few "racy" passages of a book do not make it "in general tendency indecent": "'a book to be condemned must *ex professo* be immoral; it cannot be condemned if it is immoral merely *obiter*,'" he explained, quoting from the 1929 debate on the bill (and perhaps unwittingly opening the door to what was to become as much a battle of Latin idioms as a debate.)[29] Using Kate O'Brien's *Land of Spices* as an example, he pointed out just how much the "marked passage" system—by which readers could bring offensive literature to the attention of the censors by simply marking a passage in the book and sending it in—can mislead readers as to the intent of the book. He read the single-sentence reference to sodomy that had provoked the book's banning and suggested that not only was it "commendably short" but also acted in the book as a plot device leading to an outcome even the most pious censor could approve of—it "made this lady enter the convent life and ultimately rise to be the Mother-General of this Order—an international Order."[30] In his third case study, Keane suggested that the ban on Halliday Sutherland's *Laws of Life* was simply a mistake: any book granted the *permissu superiorum* by the Archdiocese of Westminster could hardly be said to "advocate unnatural methods and unnatural prevention of conception."[31]

But most of Keane's argument depended not on presenting a practical or even an ideological case against censorship—he defended the books on the basis of their Irishness. To ban *The Tailor and Ansty*, Keane argued, was to deny the public an authentic picture of rural Irish life: "[the book's] banning has aroused more indignation, I think, on the part of those interested in the domestic literature and genius of our people than on the part of those interested in that of the wider world," he pointed out, adding that "I understand—many people know this better than I do—that country folk, talking around the fireside, are somewhat frank and, perhaps, coarse in their expressions."[32] He quoted from the book, provoking the most ridiculed moment of the debate, when Senator Magennis requested that the quoted passages be stricken from the record—"otherwise, we shall have some of the vilest obscenity in our records, and the Official Reports can be . . . bought and read by members of the public."[33] (They were omitted and still are—it is possible to restore most of the passages Keane quoted by comparing the page numbers Keane gives with the 1942 edition of the book.) Keane's examples, intentionally or not, revealed that aspect of the book identified by Patrick Kavanagh as "stage-Irish."[34] As examples of the "frank and coarse" talk recorded in *The Tailor and Ansty*, Keane read a passage in which the Tailor goes to the movies (during a love scene, he complains about the hero's diffidence, shouting "Hould her! Hould her!" at the screen and declaring that "man, if I was twenty years younger, I'd come up there and give you lessons.")[35] When Keane referred to another passage in the book, in which the Tailor and Ansty discuss the failure of modern education—as demonstrated by the young married woman who cannot tell the difference between a bull and a cow—Magennis objected to Keane's method of citation, arguing that his failure to quote the passage in its entirety "omits the gravamen of the offence . . . some fig-leaf language can be used to describe it, but it must not be referred to merely as a piece of harmless, if coarse, jocosity."[36] Keane read the passage (Ansty: "that was the queer kind of marriage. What was she married to? They must have had the strange carry-on. Didn't know the difference between a bull and a cow, and married!"[37]) After a final passage (for which Keane did not give the page number), the *cathaoirleach* (chairperson) declared that "the House has heard sufficient quotations."[38]

Keane concluded with a list of more "general" problems with censorship, including the limitations inherent in the "marked passage" system;[39] the "Victorian" perspective of the board, unable to realize that "the standard of judgment on these moral questions have changed"; the loss to booksellers and libraries when newly banned books have to be removed from circulation; and the cost to Irish writers who lose the majority of their market.[40] He concluded by alluding to "the hidden forces at work in this matter" (a phrase that would haunt him later) and by declaring, "I want clean, fresh air on the facts of life. I want a sense of proportion applied to human values and temptations, and, if I read my history a right, I feel that, under this censorship continued in its present form, the seeds are being sown now of a movement which, though we may not see it in our time, will sweep away the authority that is striving to repress us in these matters."[41] Senator The McGillycuddy of the Reeks (aka Ross Kinloch, also an RMA graduate and a DSO recipient) somewhat reluctantly seconded Keane's motion.

It is revealing that almost the first words spoken against the motion, by Senator Goulding, a former Fianna Fáil TD, did not defend the "marked passages" system or question Keane's distinction between *ex professo* and *obiter* immorality but rather attacked *The Tailor and Ansty* for making an "utter travesty of the Irish country." "I know the Irish people," he declared, "and I know the people of the Irish country districts a bit better than Senator Sir John Keane. . . . Any man who dared to sit at an Irish country fireside and use the language used by these two characters would be forbidden to enter the house again."[42] He went on:

> I will just say quite a number of Irishmen have written books within the past few years at least unfair to Irish people. They take certain types—and we have, unfortunately, types that people would not care to associate with—they take these types of people and they hold them up as representative of us Irish

people. Apart from the moral point of view it is a thing we should object to and do everything in our power to suppress. The writers to whom I have referred have a name abroad of being wonderful writers of English prose. Perhaps they are. But the more famous they are and the greater their name abroad the more damage they can do. These men have written plays and books that are damaging to us Irish people all over the world. I wonder what sort of opinion people who do not know us very well form of us, people in European countries to whom Ireland is but a name? At one time we were told we were a nation of drunkards. If our character is to be taken from the writers of these books we are not alone drunkards but we are immoral. Apart from the moral censorship I think there should be a censorship of books that portray us Irish people in the way I have indicated.[43]

He went on to suggest that "perhaps the standards of [Senator Sir John Keane] are not ours" by linking him to England, where "only one out of 20 ever went in a church. Thank God our standards are not those, anyway." Although Goulding concluded by declaring that "the Censorship board is quite justified in banning a book if it contains one passage subversive of Christianity or morality," most of his speech was taken up with the board's responsibility to guard against the subversion of Irish identity.[44]

After a rather abstract defense of the motion by Joseph Johnston, Senator Kehoe rose to argue that "the only standards with which we are concerned are the standards of ordinary public decency—the standards that the ordinary man in the street recognises even in his wildest moments."[45] First comparing indecent literature to typhoid, Kehoe promptly moved on to discuss literature's effect on Irishness, declaring that "our reputation is built on other things than on literature which is indecent in its tendency . . . the fact of having fathered George Moore and others of his ilk—I do not know if that added one jot to our national reputation."[46] "Censorship should be doubled," he argued, adding somewhat illogically that "there is absolutely no demand for this stuff."[47] After all, "the moral standards in the Ireland of to-day and in the Ireland of the past, whether people like it or not, are based on one particular standard, that is the religion we profess." Censorship is the "will of the majority" that "in this as in every other democratic country, must prevail."[48] Next came Kehoe's coup de grace: "I challenge anyone to read [*The Tailor and Ansty*] and to lay it down without a profound depression that any man posing as a litterateur, coming here from England, should go along to collect garbage and father it on somebody as evidence that the Irish people are depraved. Perhaps they are depraved— so are people in all countries—but why should a man from England come over to portray them and make capital out of it? Have we no spirit that we do not rise up in revolt against this kind of thing?"[49]

In its blend of anti-intellectualism with anti-Englishness, Kehoe captures the spirit of the book's severest critics.

After an interesting but somewhat confused contribution from Desmond FitzGerald and a short interlude during which Senator O Máille lamented Irish writers who "feed the English public . . . if they belittle their own country or if they belittle the religion of the people they become heroes overnight,"[50] Minister for Justice Frederick Boland vigorously defended the work of the board. For him indecency was temptation: "these are people who can write freely and who could sell their books without putting in these bits of filth which do not add to the books at all. . . . They are not worthy of themselves. . . . They think that they will get extra sale by pandering to the lowest instincts of human nature."[51] But not just Irish human nature: "I have a feeling that some of them are not concerned with this country, that they are glad to have their books banned so as to get a sale. . . . I have a feeling about some of them that they are really writing for an English clientele."[52]

Finally Senator William Magennis, chair of metaphysics at UCD and Sir John Keane's most formidable interlocutor, rose. He immediately condemned the "array of noisy agitators" who had unduly influenced Senator Sir John Keane's "angle of view,"[53] observing that Keane "used to speak for 'the wealth, respectability and intelligence of Ireland' as contrasted with us, the People, degraded and depressed." He called *The Tailor and Ansty* "a low, vulgar, blasphemous work. It is true, according to the Act, that we are not entitled to take its vulgarity or its blasphemy into account. I mention them as a further illustration of what English papers recommend to English readers."[54] Quoting only from the book jacket and the foreword, from which he concluded that the Tailor is "sex-obsessed" and Ansty a "moron," he declared:

> *Voilá L'Irlande!* There is Ireland! This sex-ridden, sex-besotted Tailor speaks of no subject whatsoever without spewing the foulness of his mind concerning sexual relations. The author, Mr. Cross, leaves our Tailor and Ansty to speak out of his own personality, and what do you get? They arrive in Paradise and Ansty does not like the whiskers of St. Peter. Eventually, they are tired of Heaven, because they miss the cow and the neighbours, and 'sweet Saint Francis of Assisi' goes down from the joy of the Beatific Vision in Heaven and shares hell with them by preference. I suggest that it is a blasphemous book.[55]

But blasphemy is not the worst of it: "it is propaganda, to show the English-speaking world what manner of man the Irish peasant is who is the citizen of Eire. It is propaganda, naked and unashamed."[56] This deliberate elision of blasphemy and anti-Irish propaganda was echoed when Magennis went on to suggest that to attack censorship was really to attack Catholicism. "What does this conspiracy—this conspiracy against Irish morality—seek to make out? That we take our orders from the Church, that we are merely hirelings and tools of the Church whose 'power' Senator Sir John Keane says 'will be swept away.'"[57]

The reaction outside Leinster House was immediate. The Government Publications Office in College Street sold out of the official report, and clerks advised customers to reserve copies of the next debate in advance.[58] The *Irish Press* praised the board.[59] But in the *Irish Times*, Smyllie's leader suggested that "there are two prevailing schools of thought in this country":

> One, an outlawed class, maintains that mankind possesses a fundamental sense of decency, and that the Irish people are not worse than the rest. This is the class which insists that virtue sooner or later finds its own level, that the naturally decent mind remains uncorrupted even by the dirtiest book, and that a nation which is prone to sin will not be distracted therefrom by Act of Parliament or by any process of constraint. There is the other class—the class in power, if not, thank Heaven, in the majority—which, while professing the belief that Irishmen exceed all other races in virtue, spoils the whole argument by a paradoxical insistence that every possible occasion of sin shall be removed as far as possible from them. The second class was in the ascendancy at yesterday's debate, exuding unction from every pore.[60]

"It is less against the Board's existence that we protest," it concluded, "than against its illegalities and its capacity for national insult."[61] While it is impossible to definitively identify Smyllie as the author of this editorial, the argument—that the Irish people should be trusted to decide what is best for them—was one that he would have heartily approved of.

On December 2 the motion was resumed. Senator Magennis—who, at times like this, almost seemed to be daring the *Irish Times* to attack him—started by requesting that it be made clear in the official report that he had read only from the blurb and foreword of *The Tailor and Ansty* and had not debased himself by reading from the book itself: "I feel myself left open to the misinterpretation by readers of the Official Report, either now or by and by, that I, too, read out objectionable matter."[62] Having cleared himself of the taint of quotation, he went on to describe recent obscenity prosecutions in England—"the spiritual home of the Senator [Keane], where all is perfect and all is well, as contrasted with this wretched, miserable country, with its literary Gestapo of which he speaks."[63] He quoted a letter from Sean O'Faolain opposing the censorship in the October 20 *Irish Times*, suggesting that it was remarkable that he and Keane had been "thinking the same thoughts at the same time" and noting that "it is rather a coincidence that the writer of this and the framer of the resolution were reported in the public Press as being together at a public meeting."[64] "Apparently they do not take [*The Irish Times*] in at the Kildare Street Club," Magennis suggested, twisting the knife.[65]

Then Magennis let loose. Not only were these conspirators scheming to let "the fornicator's *vade mecum*,"[66] "the sodomy book,"[67] and "this low, vulgar, obscene, blasphemous book" that will "gratify the English mind by seeing what the Irish peasant really is when shown up by 'one who knows him'"[68] do the "work of hell in Ireland,"[69] they were also part of "a campaign going on in England to undermine Christianity."[70] "It is a fight between Christianity, on the one hand, and the forces of paganism on the other," he declared, "and there is no use trying to disguise it."[71] More immediately, they aim to undermine the family and the state: "The corrupting and depraving influences of the works that have been turned out hour after hour by the press in Great Britain . . . the very people that are radically in opposition to the censorship idea are people who want to overthrow the State altogether."[72] It would have been impossible to follow Magennis's tour de force, and no one tried. The debate was mercifully adjourned until the next day.

The *Irish Press*'s headline on the morning of December 3 read "Prof. Magennis Hits Out at Critics: 'Attempt to Destroy All Censorship.'"[73] Smyllie's editorial in the *Irish Times*, on the other hand, adopted an ironic mode, declaring that "we are sorry for the members of the Censorship Board," who, despite being "good, honourable and educated men," have "made themselves objects of laughter." It suggested that the board be "paid, and paid highly," not only to reward them for playing the role as "determinant custodians of this country's morals" but also because if the public were aware of how much of their money was going to these efforts it would "amount to the wholesale rejection of the Censorship Board." Reminding Senator Magennis that his claim to "take his morals from Mount Sinai . . . has been at the root of half the rotten movements in history," the editorial concluded that censorship was "oppression." And if the censors have learned anything from Irish history, it is that oppression will "bear fruit—unless the Irish people has changed character within the last ten centuries—in a hundred years of violent reaction."[74] Smyllie—with the assistance of his subeditors and assistants, who almost certainly had a hand in crafting a jeremiad that was much more effective than anything the editor himself might have come up with—were not holding anything back.

The next day's debate opened with the seconder of the motion, The Mc-Gillicuddy of the Reeks, explaining his "sympathy" for the Board of Censors but making a generational argument against this particular ban. The problem was that the censors did not understand the point of view of "sensible young men and women with a genuine belief in the faith in which they have been brought up and which will sustain them when they do happen to come on a book calculated to deprave." "If we are going to guide them," he explained, "we must attempt to understand their point of view . . . I think it is generally a great deal more healthy than the outlook of past times when people sought to find some obscenity in almost every sentence." The "labours of the older men . . . require some reinforcement of sensible young men and women, if they can be got." [75]

Professor Tierney, professor of Greek at UCD, suggested that *The Tailor and Ansty* "was too unimportant to ban . . . it was a great pity to give it the advertisement it has got by censoring it."[76] He suggested that "I have sat by a good many country firesides, as a native, and I think it is absolutely absurd to say that the sort of language to be found in *The Tailor and Ansty* is not quite common in Irish country houses."[77] Statements such as Senator Goulding's only "add to the absurd calumny of the Irish people that has been spread about as a result of the debate on this question. Does not anybody who walks the streets of Dublin know that you will find children under 12 years of age using language both blasphemous and indecent, just as bad as anything in *The Tailor and Ansty*?"[78] Senator Goulding responded:

MR. GOULDING: What is the necessity for printing it?

PROFESSOR TIERNEY: I am not saying there is any necessity for it. What I am saying is that for Senator Goulding to say that this language is unheard of in Ireland, is the kind of pestiferous nonsense that is just as capable of injuring this country as the book itself could ever possibly be.

MR. GOULDING: I did not say that at all.

PROFESSOR TIERNEY: I read what the Senator said. I will read it again if he likes: "Any man who dared to use the language used by the character in the book referred to by Senator Sir John Keane would be thrown out from their firesides."

MR. GOULDING: And so he would—from any decent house in Ireland.

PROFESSOR TIERNEY: I can say nothing to that. I can only appeal to anyone who was born and brought up in the country as I was.

MR. GOULDING: And as I was.

PROFESSOR TIERNEY: It must be a very peculiar part of the country. That is all I can say about it. Another point that I dislike about the whole debate on this unfortunate book is the tendency to debate it from the standpoint that on our side is virtue and Erin and on the other side the Saxon and guilt, or something of that sort. There is a tendency to throw a white sheet over ourselves and pretend that we are the purest, finest, most lovely people in the world. I do not think, speaking as one person, that it shows a proper, Christian spirit to adopt that attitude of almost pharasaical pretence.[79]

Censorship could affect Ireland's international reputation, said Professor Tierney: "we are not so immune from the whole wide world as that we can afford lightly to indulge in actions like that and not expect to suffer for those actions."[80]

The *Irish Press* reported Professor Tierney's statement as "Censorship Board's Work Excellent"[81]; the *Irish Times*, as "Much Debated 'Tailor' Defended in Senate."[82] Its editorial noted that although "one may derive a crumb of comfort from the thought that, at a moment when most of the world is convulsed by the upheavals of a 'total' war, one of the Houses of the Irish Parliament should find time to discuss at considerable length a topic of literary interest," what was most important was that the debate "cannot but create the most lamentable impression abroad."[83]

The final day of debate was given over almost entirely to Keane. He spent most of his time responding to specific attacks. He began (somewhat unwisely) by questioning the charge that the public did not care about censorship at all. It depended on *which* public: "I do say that the views of educated people are important. You cannot say that changes or public movements are brought about by the large inert masses. They are brought about by the intellectual minority." He questioned the argument that Irish people's standards were different from others': "If there is no demand what is the object of preventing [these books'] circulation?"[84] He denied a conspiracy: "I acted solely on my own responsibility in putting down this motion."[85] He suggested that PEN, the Catholic Truth Society, the Royal Dublin Society, and the universities should have a role in the operation of the board. And then, clearly realizing that he was fighting a losing battle, Keane attempted to withdraw the motion. This was rejected, and the main motion was put to a vote. The result: thirty-four senators against ("*Níl*"), only two—Keane and Joseph Johnston, who was professor of economics at Trinity—in favor ("*Tá*").

"Only Two Votes for Censorship Censure,"[86] reported the *Press*. "Methods Defended and Criticised: Suggested Committee of Inquiry,"[87] reported the *Times*. The debate was over. For the next few weeks, occasional reminders bubbled up: Patrick Kavanagh recommended a book by warning that "a page of Nihil Obstats and Imprimaturs must not put readers off";[88] "Quidnunc" suggested that if one was opposed to objectionable content, one should ban ancient Gaelic literature;[89] and Myles na gCopaleen's fictional Cruiskeen Court of Voluntary Jurisdiction considered what to do with the case of an "immoral" book that turned out to be the Christian Brothers' *An Outline of Irish Grammar* in a *Madame Bovary* dust jacket.[90]

But the most visible event in what Michael Adams has called "the highwater mark of criticism of the Board" was over.[91] What is most striking, considering the intensity of the debate, is how quickly criticism of literary censorship faded from public view. The most salient legislative result of the debate was that in 1944, when an amendment initiated by Keane persuaded the Censorship Board to allow a three-person appeal board. The memory of the debate understandably lived on in the imaginations of writers, as censorship came to be considered merely another aspect of an oppressively conservative society. As Julia Carlson has suggested, the next literary generation "looked upon censorship as an anachronism; they were to become so disillusioned with the political process in Ireland that, with few exceptions, they removed themselves from public affairs as a matter of principle."[92] The monolithic vision of Irishness presented by Senator Magennis and his supporters in the debate came to be taken for granted: there was no more convincing proof of this than the treatment the nonfictional Tailor and Ansty suffered in West Cork, boycotted by their neighbors and in one instance forced to burn the book in their own hearth. The Níls won.

But it was not a total victory. Although the appeal board did not have any great practical effect on the mechanics of censorship, it did symbolize a change: as Michael Adams notes, it "destroyed the utter permanence which had hitherto been the most irksome characteristic of the decisions of the board."[93] The fierce denunciations of imported filth and warm evocations of pure Irish hearts that littered the speeches of Senator Magennis were not just the usual "Puritan whines,"[94] they were also more than slightly ridiculous. Reading them, it is often easy to forget that you're not enjoying the minutes of a particularly absurd meeting of Myles na gCopaleen's Cruiskeen Court. It was not only prurient interest that made the official reports best sellers, and it is difficult to deny that the effect of reading them is to lessen one's respect for at least some forms of authority. The Níls won, but at great price—never again would censorship go unquestioned.

And, in many cases, it would be southern Protestants who would be doing the questioning. The *Tailor and Ansty* debates comprise perhaps the most colorful example of how southern Protestants found themselves thrust into the position of defending liberal ideals. The book's attackers treated the Tailor and Ansty as unwitting fifth columnists, used by the English (and their fellow travelers on this side of the Irish Sea) to undermine Ireland. Southern Irish Protestants made the case that this quirky, original, occasionally unseemly, and almost always unorthodox couple represented all those aspects of Ireland that most needed defending. The debate, whether it took place in the Seanad chamber or the pages of the daily newspapers, was vicious and often personal. But perhaps what is most striking to the contemporary reader is how both sides had the same goal: preserving the Ireland that they loved.

Notes

1. *Irish Times*, January 24, 1950.
2. *Irish Times*, January 26, 1950.
3. *Irish Times*, February 2, 1950.
4. *Irish Times*, February 14, 1950.
5. Andrew R. Holmes and Eugenio F. Biagini, "Protestants," in *The Cambridge Social History of Modern Ireland*, ed. Eugenio F. Biagini and Mary E. Daly (Cambridge: Cambridge University Press, 2017), 105.
6. John Horgan, "Saving Us from Ourselves: Contraception, Censorship and the 'Evil Literature' Controversy of 1926," *Irish Communication Review* 5, no. 1 (January 1995): 61–67; Anthony Keating, "Censorship: The Cornerstone of Catholic Ireland," *Journal of Church and State* 57, no. 2: 289–309.
7. Terence Brown, *The Irish Times: Fifty Years of Influence* (London: Bloomsbury, 2015), 205–7; Mark O'Brien, *The Irish Times: A History* (Dublin: Four Courts Press, 2008), 133–37.
8. *Irish Times*, March 15, 1950.
9. Under the terms of the Censorship of Publications Act of 1929, a book could be banned for "indecency" (defined as "suggestive of, or inciting to sexual immorality or unnatural vice or likely in any other similar way to corrupt or deprave") if it was "in its general tendency indecent or obscene" or if it advocated "the unnatural prevention of conception or the procurement of abortion or miscarriage." *The Land of Spices* and *The Tailor and Ansty* were thought to exhibit the first flaw; *Laws of Life* the second. See *Censorship of Publications Act 1929*, Part I, Section 6.

10. Seanad Debates, vol. 27, November 18, 1942, col. 16.

11. WAAMA was the Writers, Artists, Actors and Musicians Association, a lobbying group founded in 1941. Contrary to popular belief, it was not invented by Myles na gCopaleen in his column "Cruiskeen Lawn" in the *Irish Times*.

12. He later became a well-known figure in and around Westport, County Mayo, working as a tutor for a local family; publishing works on mathematics, Canadian history, and music; and appearing often on RTÉ's *Sunday Miscellany*. He is buried in the Church of Ireland cemetery in Knappagh. See http://www.ouririshheritage.org/page/eric_cross, accessed May 12, 2016. A local historian even claims that Cross spent time in Los Alamos, working on the Manhattan Project: see Michael Mullen, *Mayo: The Waters and the Wild* (Donaghadee: Cottage Publications, 2004), 34.

13. Eric Cross, *The Tailor and Ansty* (Cork: Mercier Press, 1999), 53.

14. Ibid., 71.

15. Ibid., 18.

16. Ibid., 143.

17. Ibid., 125.

18. *Irish Times*, August 8, 1942, 2.

19. Cross, *Tailor and Ansty*, 14.

20. *Irish Times*, October 9, 1942, 3.

21. *Irish Times*, October 10, 1942, 3.

22. *Irish Times*, October 14, 1942, 3.

23. *Irish Times*, October 15, 1942, 3.

24. *Irish Times*, October 19, 1942, 3.

25. *Irish Times*, October 23, 1942, 1.

26. Glascott, J. R. M. Symes, *Sir John Keane and Cappoquin House in Time of War and Revolution* (Dublin: Four Courts Press, 2016).

27. Bell and Emerson, *Church of Ireland*, 181.

28. "Sir John Keane," NPT x120415, Photographs Collection, National Portrait Gallery, available at http://www.npg.org.uk/collections/search/portrait/mw59449/Sir-John-Keane?search=ss&sText=Sir+John+Keane&LinkID=mp60624&role=sit&rNo=0, accessed December 12, 2016.

29. Seanad Debates, vol. 27, November 18, 1942, col. 18.

30. Ibid., col. 24.

31. Ibid., col. 25.

32. Ibid., col. 19.

33. Ibid., cols. 20, 23.

34. *Irish Times*, October 24, 1942, 2.

35. Eric Cross, *The Tailor and Ansty* (Gateshead on Tyne: Northumberland Press Ltd., 1942), 54.

36. Seanad Debates, November 18, 1942, col. 20.

37. Cross, *Tailor and Ansty* (1942), 66.

38. Seanad Debates, November 18, 1942, col. 23.

39. Ibid., col. 26.

40. Ibid., col. 27.

41. Ibid., col. 30.

42. Ibid., cols. 30–31.

43. Ibid., col. 32.
44. Ibid.
45. Seanad Debates, November 18, 1942, cols. 36–37.
46. Ibid., col. 38.
47. Ibid., col. 39.
48. Ibid., col. 40.
49. Ibid.
50. Ibid., col. 51.
51. Ibid., col. 56.
52. Ibid., col. 57.
53. Ibid., col. 60.
54. Ibid., col. 63.
55. Ibid., col. 65.
56. Ibid., col. 66.
57. Ibid., col. 67.
58. *Irish Times*, December 4, 1942, 1.
59. *Irish Press*, November 20, 1942, 1–2.
60. *Irish Times*, November 19, 1942, 3.
61. Ibid.
62. Seanad Debates, vol. 27, December 2, 1942, col. 122.
63. Ibid., col. 125.
64. Ibid., cols. 151, 156.
65. Seanad Debates, December 2, 1942, col. 170.
66. Ibid., col. 149.
67. Ibid., col. 162.
68. Ibid., col. 158.
69. Ibid., col. 165.
70. Ibid., col. 171.
71. Ibid., col. 172.
72. Ibid.
73. *Irish Press*, December 3, 1942, 1.
74. *Irish Times*, December 3, 1942, 3.
75. Seanad Debates, December 4, 1942, col. 258.
76. Ibid., cols. 262–63.
77. Ibid., col. 262.
78. Ibid.
79. Ibid., col. 263.
80. Ibid., col. 265.
81. *Irish Press*, December 4, 1942, 3.
82. *Irish Times*, December 4, 1942, 1.
83. *Irish Times*, December 5, 1942, 3.
84. Seanad Debates, vol. 27, December 9, 1942, col. 307
85. Ibid., col. 311.
86. *Irish Press*, December 10, 1942, 3.
87. *Irish Times*, December 10, 1942, 1.
88. *Irish Times*, December 17, 1942, 2.

89. *Irish Times*, December 16, 1942, 3.

90. *Irish Times*, December 11, 1942, 3.

91. Michael Adams, *Censorship: The Irish Experience*. (Dublin: Scepter Books, 1968,) 98.

92. Julia Carlson, *Censorship and the Irish Writer* (London: Routledge, 1990), 16.

93. Adams, *Censorship*, 115.

94. Cross, *Tailor and Ansty* (1999), 10.

6

PATRIOTS

ON St. Patrick's Day 1943, at the height of the Battle of the Atlantic, two days after the Germans temporarily retook Kharkov, a week before Montgomery's Eighth Army broke through the Mareth Line in North Africa, and a month before the first Warsaw uprising, Eamon de Valera, the prime minister of Éire, addressed his country on the radio:

> Acutely conscious though we all are of the misery and desolation in which the greater part of the world is plunged, let us turn aside for a moment to that ideal Ireland that we would have. That Ireland which we dreamed of would be the home of a people who valued material wealth only as the basis of right living, of a people who were satisfied with frugal comfort and devoted their leisure to the things of the spirit—a land whose countryside would be bright with cosy homesteads, whose fields and villages would be joyous with the sounds of industry, with the romping of sturdy children, the contests of athletic youths and the laughter of comely maidens, whose firesides would be forums for the wisdom of serene old age. It would, in a word, be the home of a people living the life that God desires that man should live.[1]

This was de Valera at his most eloquent, at his most lyrical, and—to some listeners—at his most self-important, pompous, and narrow minded. But with a few exceptions—in the pages of the *Irish Times* the following day, Smyllie vowed that he, for one, would never "see our country sacrificed before the idols of a dead doctrine"[2]—little notice was paid to what modern readers would now consider to be the most striking characteristic of de Valera's speech—the almost total absence of the war.

In some ways Ireland was just as removed from the war as de Valera's speech suggests. When World War Two began, Ireland declared itself to be in a state of emergency: the period 1939 to 1945 would become officially known by this title. De Valera and his government maintained relationships with both combatants that were scrupulously correct—most notoriously in 1945, when de Valera visited the German Diplomatic Mission to express condolences upon Hitler's death. And there was, officially anyway, a tendency to view the war with Olympian disapproval. "How much easier must it have been during the war," Robert Fisk observes, " to regard the outside world as evil, a universe gone mad in which Éire and a few other non-belligerent nations were able—or lucky enough—to retain their sanity."[3] Ireland would set an example.

At the same time, the Emergency was exactly that. Frank Aiken, the minister for the Co-ordination of Defensive Measures, had early on announced that neutrality was "not a condition of peace with both belligerents, but rather a condition of limited warfare with both."[4] Shortages were worse than in belligerent countries in some cases, transportation was severely restricted, and although the lights never went out in Dublin, they dimmed considerably. The country was even bombed; although the South saw nothing like the scale of destruction England did, Belfast suffered serious damage.

When war came to Britain, and Emergency to Ireland, the alienation of southern Protestants became palpable. In some ways they were in an even more precarious position than they had been at the outbreak of the First World War. After seventeen years of uneasily hiding in plain sight, southern Protestants were suddenly thrown back into a world in which their choices became very public. Maintaining any sort of dual allegiance to Ireland and Britain had never been easy; now it appeared impossible.

On the other hand, however, southern Protestants were in a very different position in 1939 than in 1914. Mark Bence-Jones has argued that "whereas 1914 was as fateful a year for the Ascendancy as 1789 was for the old nobility of France, the same cannot be said of 1939," and this is true for the wider group as well as for the "Anglo-Irish" minority within the minority.[5] Whereas Irish volunteers in the First World War—Protestant and otherwise—had been ostracized upon their return home and officially forgotten for long afterward, their counterparts in the Second World War were treated differently. By the late 1930s, as John A. Murphy explains, the country "could afford to accept the option exercised by individuals to serve in the British forces"; this was now possible in a community that had reached "some kind of consensus."[6]

Murphy's qualification is important here, however: this was a kind of consensus, rather than a consensus, full stop. Smyllie would later describe the country as "nonbelligerent" rather than "neutral in the generally accepted sense of the term."[7] If southern Irish Protestants were not entirely sure how to feel about Irish neutrality, this put them in line with millions of their non-Protestant countrymen. The majority of Irish people who supported the policy of neutrality, many of whom also served in British uniforms, did so for a variety of different reasons. The scholar attempting to establish a unified "southern Irish Protestant opinion" on neutrality might reasonably look to two debates in the fall of 1939: one taking place in the *Irish Times* correspondence page and the other in the Seanad. But this scholar would discover that these were in fact debates, featuring a diversity of opinion. In the *Irish Times*, H. J. L. Armstrong wrote from Howth Rectory to suggest that Ireland should "use all our powers of sympathy and natural friendliness to preserve contact with both warring sides in the hope that we may yet be able to serve the cause of a just, merciful and enduring peace," only to be met by Canon Dudley Fletcher writing from St. Laserian's, who argued that "unjust violence must be opposed by force used in the defence of right and justice."[8] And although Sir John Keane's attack on neutrality in the Seanad was described by his opponents as the views of "a very small minority in the country,"[9] in that same debate other members of that minority declared, "I do not believe that any purpose of any kind can be gained . . . by saying our country is not going to be neutral,"[10] "I think we ought to give the Government all the powers and all the encouragement they require,"[11] and "I am not offering any alternative policy to that which the Taoiseach has declared to be the policy of his Government."[12]

Younger southern Irish Protestant men and women found themselves in a particularly confusing situation. They had to make two decisions: first, whether to fight, and second, whether to join the British or Irish forces. Brian Inglis remembers how at the beginning of the war most young Anglo-Irishmen felt pressure to join "the *real* army":

> The "Free State Army," as we still thought of it, had won some reputation for its equestrian capabilities at the horse show; but otherwise none of us took it seriously, and our aunts and cousins thought of anybody who joined it in terms of white feathers. They actually felt less resentful about a man of fighting age who stayed in his civilian occupation in Ireland, looking after the family firm or holding on to his job; this was understood, because a soldier from the wars returning would have no guarantees in Ireland, of the kind he had in England, that he would get his job back. But if a man decided to join up, the aunts' argument ran, he ought to join the *real* army.[13]

Inglis joined the RAF. But there he felt like a foreigner:

> [We had] to defend, in mess arguments, the right of the Irish to go their
> own way; for as time went on, however little we might care for the ideals and
> policies of Ireland's rulers, we adopted a kind of protective chauvinism, half-
> serious, half-exasperated, in their defence. . . . We might concede that Cham-
> berlain had been foolish to hand [the Treaty Ports] back . . . but we realized
> that there could be no question of de Valera agreeing to return them. To do so
> would have been to abandon neutrality: a principle we had come grudgingly
> to respect.[14]

"By the Second World War Ireland had almost come of age as a nation,"
Inglis recalls. "Many of the Irish volunteers in the English forces had never
known what it was like to regard themselves as British."[15] Once, while on a
training course in Rhodesia, Inglis nearly found himself transformed into
an enemy when a rumor went around that Ireland had been invaded by
the British. "The two of us who were Irish on the course conferred on what
we ought to do," he remembers. "We had decided to present ourselves for,
presumably, internment, when the rumour was killed by a revised trans-
mission of the message."[16] Although many like Inglis wholeheartedly supported the Allied cause, they increasingly did so from the perspective of a
sort of born-again Irishman: "By the time the war ended I was more Irish—
in the sense of thinking of myself as Irish—than when it began."[17] Choosing
to fight for Britain would seem to indicate a definitive rejection of Ireland.
But for many, the reality was more complicated.

Another Protestant response to the challenge of the war was to try to
act as an emissary between the two countries. Many of the most detailed
reports to the British government on Ireland in the early years of the war
came from southern Protestants. Their opinions were often unsolicited.
They were also mostly prescriptive, describing how a particular policy or
attitude toward Ireland would best serve Britain's war effort. Some observers attempted an objective, careful examination of Irish opinion and Irish
life while others provided exactly what they thought the British government wanted to hear.

A good example of the latter, which nevertheless found its way to the
desk of Anthony Eden, then secretary of state for Dominion Affairs, was
sent by an anonymous "ex-soldier in the Leinster Regiment" in early 1940.
He warned of an imminent invasion of Ulster by American-funded, Ger-
man-trained "factions of De Valera-ites,"[18] assuring the War Office that
"this is no cry of 'wolf' and I might add that I was the first to warn General

Sir William Marshall in Malabar in 1920 re the pending outbreak of the Moplah Rebellion, having on shikari seen Moplahs sharpening knives, pikes and sickles, in outlying forges in the jungle."[19] The former Unionist MP Herbert Shaw also struck a critical note—albeit with a less feverish tone—when he wrote the Foreign Office in 1941 to share his own impressions of Ireland. According to Shaw, the Irish seemed determined to ignore the war—even, perhaps especially, if its events threatened to implicate Ireland.[20]

But other Irish Protestants submitted reports that were more hopeful about the prospect of some sort of collaboration between the two countries. In 1939, Shane Leslie—the poet, writer, Home Guard volunteer, and cousin of Winston Churchill—wrote the Ministry of Information to suggest that it might want to tamp down the strongly antineutrality editorial line taken by the English Catholic newspaper *The Tablet*:[21] Later the same month he intervened on behalf of two IRA men sentenced to death for their roles in a bombing in Coventry, fearing that executions would turn the men into martyrs.[22] Although the Foreign Office recommended against carrying out the death sentences, Leslie's attempt at opening up intergovernment cooperation ultimately failed; the men were hanged. But his letters demonstrated how, like many southern Irish Protestants, he saw himself acting as an intermediary between Britain and Ireland.

Perhaps the most extensive report on Ireland in the early years of the war was provided by Frank Pakenham in late 1939. Frank and his brother, Edward, represented one of the clearest examples of how southern Irish Protestant families often had to balance dual, occasionally contradictory identities as a result of the war. The Pakenhams, members of "the writingest family in Dublin" and both eventually earls of Longford, personified divided loyalties.[23] Edward Pakenham, who inherited his father's earldom while still at Eton, had been converted to Irish nationalism via the grooms at the family's home in Westmeath. Eventually founding a theater company with his wife, Christine, he remained a "loyal neutral" during the war, provoking the German minister when his company's production of de Maupassant's play *Boule de Suif* updated the setting from the Franco-Prussian War to the current conflict. Edward's brother, Frank, made his career in England, first as an education policy analyst for the Conservative Party and then as a Labour politician in the early 1930s. After several years of teaching economics at Christ Church, he served in the British army during the war.

As Christine Longford remembered, the two brothers represented opposite ends of the spectrum of southern Irish Protestant identity:

> Frank did a brave thing, he joined the British Army. Strange as it seemed and heroic, his action was more than brave, it was logical. His home and his life and career were in England; he lectured in economics at Oxford and was needed in English politics. As he wrote in *Born to Believe* and *Five Lives*, he was an Irish republican and an English socialist in one person; and with perfect consistency he could say 'there was never a time when I have not been proud to call myself an Englishman.' Edward's life was quite different. He owed no duty to England; he wasn't 'Irish and proud of it,' but Irish and thankful for it, Irish without reservation, he had no choice.[24]

Nevertheless, it was Frank who most clearly saw himself as an intermediary, contacting the Ministry of Information in late 1939.

Pakenham claimed that although eight out of ten Irish people supported the policy of neutrality, they also favored the Allied cause, for a variety of economic and religious reasons. But he stressed that this preference was in no way strong enough to justify any attempt to try to bring Ireland into the war on the Allied side. Only a deliberate violation of Irish neutrality by one combatant could bring Ireland in on the side of the other.[25] Pakenham warned against explicit propaganda directed at Ireland, but he did have one recommendation: Rather than attempting to change Irish opinion, Pakenham argued, the British government's first priority should be to show its support for neutrality. He proposed that Britain immediately provide de Valera antisubmarine vessels, guns for coastal defense, and airplanes.[26] Pakenham seems quite convinced of the value of his suggestions, although his report must have bemused its readers at the MOI. His report reads more like a brief for the Irish government on how to best protect Irish neutrality than a guide to bolstering the British war effort.

The best-known example of a southern Irish Protestant working with the British government during the war is the writer Elizabeth Bowen. She contacted the MOI in June 1940 with a request for a travel permit to finish a historical novel. According to Harry Hodson, head of the MOI's Empire Division, Bowen made the case that the novel would help facilitate Anglo-Irish understanding—an argument which failed to convince Hodson.[27]

No permit was forthcoming. But Hodson wrote again on June 25 to reveal that Bowen's case had been taken up by the writer (and Bowen relation) Stephen Gwynn and by John Dulanty, Irish high commissioner in London.

Based on their recommendations, the MOI decided that Bowen's request for a travel permit should be granted.[28]

There is much that is surprising about these revelations, not least that the Irish high commissioner was recruiting British spies (Churchill wasn't just being diplomatic, apparently, when he described Dulanty, who had worked with him in the Department of Munitions in the First World War, as "thoroughly friendly to England").[29] But Dulanty was no traitor—he had been an important—and, for the British, frustrating—player in negotiations about neutrality in late 1938, and he surely realized that known spies were better than unknown ones.[30] On the other hand, there is no reason to believe that Dulanty's decision was purely cynical—he may have seen in Bowen a sympathetic observer of the Irish scene. The circumstances surrounding Bowen's attempt to get a permit suggest that she was not just "posing" as Irish, as some writers have suggested—or at least that, if she was, she was doing so with the blessing of Ireland's most senior diplomat in Britain.[31]

Indeed, in the extensive reports that Bowen ended up sending back to Britain, she spent more time making the case for Ireland's neutrality than trying to undermine it. While she could occasionally manifest some stereotypes about southern Irish Protestants, much more often she urges her readers to respect Ireland's position.[32] Neutrality was not just about avoiding a fight: Ireland regarded it as an act of national assertion, and as such the British should take it seriously.[33] Irish planning and preparation for "Emergency," sometimes ridiculed in the British press, was in fact impressive: witnessing a mock invasion exercise by the Irish Army, Bowen was impressed.[34] Even Bowen's choice of pronouns was significant: while she would occasionally refer to "the Irish," she more often explained their actions using "we."[35] As the reports went on, far from "spying on" Ireland, she ended up defending it.[36] Bowen, like many southern Irish Protestants, supported the British war effort. But as the war went on, she found herself becoming more sympathetic to Ireland than ever. Far from dissociating southern Protestants from their country, the war, and the Emergency, actually strengthened their connection to it.

One reason that Irish Protestant supporters of the British war effort felt the need to contact the British government privately was that at home, a public expression of their views in print would almost certainly have been censored. As Donal Ó Drisceoil, Robert Cole, and others have shown, Ireland had been planning for wartime censorship since the establishment of the Free State.[37] In September 1938 a censorship committee set up by then minister of defence Frank Aiken proposed a system that borrowed much of its structure and design from the British model. It would be overseen by Aiken, who would take up the post of minister for the Co-ordination of Defensive Measures in 1939. (De Valera created this ministry specifically for the Emergency; it was primarily concerned with censorship.) The rest of the department would consist of Joseph Connolly, a former senator and the chairman of the Commissioners of Public Works, as controller of censorship and Thomas J. Coyne as assistant controller.[38] The organization also provided for divisions of postal, telegraph, and press censorship (with Michael Knightly acting as chief press censor).

Censorship guidelines were set up according to the requirements of the Emergency Powers Act of 1939. The act outlined a practical set of guidelines for newspapers—specifying the topics that must, by law, be submitted to the censors before being published—but also attempted to instill a broader sense of responsibility in Ireland's journalists and editors. References to the activities of Defence Forces would be censored, as would any comment "calculated to prejudice recruiting for, or to cause disaffection in, any of the Defence Forces."[39] References to the activities of foreign forces in Ireland, commercial shipping, and weather reports were censorable, as was "matter reflecting adversely on the solvency of the Exchequer and other public financial institutions or bodies," suggestions of shortages, and "matter likely to provoke discontent amongst servants of the State."[40] Most controversial were the act's restrictions on comment on the policy of neutrality:

SAFEGUARDING NEUTRALITY
Matter which would or might be calculated to endanger the policy of strict neutrality of the state and in particular:
  (a) Statements or suggestions casting doubt on the reality of such neutrality or on the wisdom or practicability of maintaining neutrality,
  (b) Epithets or terms of a nature liable to cause offence to governments of friendly states or members thereof,
  (c) Expressions likely to cause offence to the peoples of friendly states whether applied to individuals or to the method or system of governments or to the culture of the people of such states.[41]

Later addenda contained more specific details, including restrictions on referring to the presence of Irish in foreign service (or obituaries of those Irish), censoring stories about "hostilities or acts of war directed or which appear to have been directed against the State," and prohibitions on advertisements for war charities. It also attempted to prevent criticism of censorship itself, either directly (references to the activity of censors was banned) or indirectly through omission ("matter consisting of any reference to or purported explanation of the omission of any matter from the issue of a newspaper").[42]

The censors had a nearly impossible job. Foreign newspapers could not be censored, and obviously "unneutral" British papers were as visible (and in some cases more visible) as Irish ones on Dublin's newsstands. The deck was stacked against the censors, who always had to act prohibitively and in secret; even for those who sincerely believed in neutrality, their contribution could only be hinted at.[43] Perhaps the greatest weakness of all was the inadequate size of the censorship's staff—at the beginning, the entire department consisted of only about two hundred people. Many of these were eventually loaned to the equally understaffed Department of Defence or assigned to the even more time-consuming task of postal censorship. The Press Censorship Office, tasked with surveying every newspaper, magazine, and journal in Ireland, consisted of nine people (in addition to Knightly and Coyne).

The censors' eyes were peeled for any violation of the Emergency Powers Act by any periodical but especially by those run by or associated with Protestants. The censors warned the *Irish Tatler and Sketch* when it blamed "Hitler and his hounds" for the cancellation of the Irish Ladies' Golfing Championship in 1940,[44] and it took the *Irish Field* to task for identifying sportsmen killed serving in the British forces.[45] When the *Church of Ireland Gazette* published a letter from a correspondent suggesting that "the ideals and axioms of the Church of Ireland are far better represented by that which is suggested by The King than that which is suggested by The President" and insisting that "we have to make our choice—Eire or Empire," Coyne called a meeting with the paper's editor. Telling Reverend Greening that "for historical and other reasons, the Protestant community here exercised a disproportionate influence in the State," he insisted that the *Church of Ireland Gazette* had to be especially careful in what it printed: what "might be regarded as no more than verbal excess if it emanated from some less responsible source" had serious implications in a Protestant publication.[46]

Knightly was on guard against Smyllie and the *Irish Times* from the first days of the war. In one of his first reports to Aiken, he explained that this position was entirely justified, since "it seemed to be the studied policy of this paper to undermine our neutrality. Running through all its editions was a suggestion that our neutrality was unreal and of a temporary nature."[47] In early September 1939, the Office of the Controller of Censorship noted the paper's tendency to refer to British organizations merely with the definite article (i.e., "The Army" for "The British Army.")[48] An early communiqué from Connolly to Aiken proposed that clearer grammatical restrictions be put in place. "When referring to the President, the Taoiseach, Ministers, Departments, the Army," he wrote, "the definite article will be used and the adjective 'Irish' or 'Ireland' or 'na hEireann' will not be used, unless an official document is being quoted." The censors also instructed Smyllie that the adjective "British" *must* be used when referring to that state's forces and officials.[49] In January 1940 Chief Press Censor Michael Knightly objected to the *Irish Times*'s listing obituaries of Irishmen in the British armed forces under the heading "Roll of Honour" and began deleting the heading in the newspaper's submissions. In response, Smyllie proposed the alternative, seemingly more controversial heading of "Killed While Serving with His Britannic Majesty's Forces," and this, remarkably, was allowed—for a while.[50]

In January 1940 the *Irish Times* reported on a speech by Senator Frank MacDermot at a meeting of University College's Literary and Historical Society. The newspaper had not submitted the text of this speech, in which MacDermot criticized Hitler and suggested turning the so-called Treaty Ports over to England for the duration of the war. (Berehaven, Cobh, and Lough Swilly, which the British Navy had retained under the terms of the Anglo-Irish Treaty, had been restored to Ireland just before the outbreak of war.) As a result of this report and what he called "a series of contraventions of our Directions by this newspaper," Knightly ordered the *Irish Times* to submit each issue to the censors in entirety before publication.[51] This was, in Smyllie's view, unendurable, not only for ideological reasons but also for practical ones: the paper's layout would have to be completed much earlier than other Dublin papers, thus opening the door for scoops.

He decided that only the Taoiseach could properly address the problem and wrote him on January 15. Smyllie reminded de Valera of the *Irish Times*'s support for his government's policies, even when that support endangered the support of the newspaper's most loyal readers: "[the paper] has certain traditions, of which, rightly or wrongly, it is proud; and often at the risk of a serious breach of those traditions, it has gone out of its way to uphold the authority and the dignity of your administration."[52] Unfortunately for Smyllie, de Valera was unyielding (or uninterested). And Smyllie, for the most part, abided by the new restrictions.

The order had one unintended consequence for the censors, however: it meant they had to spend much more time dealing with Smyllie, who now contacted them about every possible violation. "Is it too much to ask you, in these circumstances, to let me know at your convenience what I am allowed to say about Russia?" he wrote Knightly in February 1943. "I think that the working journalist is entitled to some measure of guidance, however irrational and wayward it may be, so that he may be able to temper the wind of his lucubrations to the shorn lamp of ministerial susceptibilities."[53] "You will agree, I am sure," he wrote in 1944, "that the task of a leader-writer becomes almost impossible when he is forced to submit his work to a Chief Press Censor who is prepared to insist over the telephone, that Hungary is situated in the Balkan Peninsula."[54] A disagreement over the paper's policy regarding charity appeals ended with an exasperated Coyne asking Smyllie, "Must you always forget that you have a country of your own?"[55] In April 1944 the censor's refusal to allow an advertisement for the Kingstown Presbyterian Church to appear in the *Irish Times*—they insisted that the Irish name of the town, Dun Laoghaire, be substituted— was dragged into the public view. In a debate in the Dáil (Lower House of Parliament) that nominally concerned additional expenditure for the army, James Dillon questioned Aiken about how he could possibly believe that the proper name of Dun Laoghaire/Kingstown was a matter of Irish national security. "We are frankly at daggers drawn" with the newspaper, Aiken explained.[56] Not only did the *Irish Times* refuse to adopt the Irish name for the town, it also listed the president's activities in the "Social and Personal" column "after every hyphenated person in the country . . . the only precedence he gets is over an advertisement for corsets in one of the down-town shops."[57]

Even when under a "submit-before-publication" order, the *Irish Times* was hardly the organ of "neutral-mindedness" envisioned by J. P. Walshe. Smyllie's relationship with the censors often resembled a cat-and-mouse game. In 1941 John Robinson, formerly of the *Irish Times*'s editorial staff, was serving on the *Prince of Wales* when the ship was torpedoed near Singapore. When news arrived that he had survived, Smyllie printed his picture on page three, along with the notice that "the many friends in Dublin of Mr. John A. Robinson, who was involved in a recent boating accident, will be glad to learn that he is alive and well."[58] One of Smyllie's most famous victories over the censors occurred on February 11, 1941, when the following item appeared in "Irishman's Diary":

Nippon Go Brath!
In his broadcast on Sunday night, Mr. Winston Churchill, the British Prime Minister (N.B.—Britain is an island to the east of Eire), mentioned by name nine military and naval commanders who had gained fame recently in North Africa and the Mediterranean.

I append the names and origins of the gallant nine:—
General Wavell, English.
General Mackie, Australian.
General Wilson, Japanese
(North Island).
General O'Connor, Japanese.
General O'Moore Creagh, Japanese.
General Dill, Japanese
(North Island).
General Brooke, Japanese
(North Island).
Admiral Cunningham, Japanese.
Admiral Somerville, Japanese.[59]

Knightly was not amused and warned Smyllie against future offences. Smyllie's response was conciliatory: he defended the item on the grounds of giving "a few people a much needed laugh in the gloomy times" and asked if he could "plead guilty, and throw myself on your mercy as well as your sense of humour? . . . Honestly, with the exception of that paragraph, I have been doing my dead best to keep the I.T. well inside the reasonable limits, and I think that I have not been too bad!"[60]

It was true that the *Irish Times* was rarely as critical of Britain as it was of Germany. The censors' complaint that the paper often treated Ireland as if it were one of Britain's western provinces was often hard to refute. But at the same time, its pro-British leanings (and, more importantly, the public's perception of those pro-British leanings) meant that it could also be *more* critical of Britain than other Irish newspapers. A 1940 editorial favorably compared Ireland's interest in Europe with what it saw as Britain's traditional insularity: "[the Irish people] show an interest in continental affairs, in foreign languages and foreign travel which is, possibly, rather more intelligent and widespread than anything of a corresponding type to be found across the channel."[61] If the wartime *Irish Times* could fairly be described as Anglophile, its love was hardly blind.

Often the paper's tone toward Britain was tongue-in-cheek. When Leslie Hore-Belisha, Britain's former secretary of State for War, visited Ireland in 1941 and pronounced it "rather like Athens" and "very civilised," an editorial chided him for falling into the usual trap of English visitors who try to say "nice—and meaningless—things" about Ireland:

> He must be the first visitor to Dublin, however, who found our ancient city "very civilised"; or is he the first who has had the courage to make such a challenging statement? One cannot but wonder what Mr. Hore-Belisha expected. When he arrived in Dun Laoghaire harbour did he, like stout Cortez, gaze upon our island with a wild surmise, anticipating the discovery of antres vast and deserts idle, and dreading his first encounter with the Antropophagi, and men whose heads do grow beneath their shoulders, with accounts of whom the Moor of Venice beguiled the gentle Desdemona?[62]

Smyllie was also particularly hard on Britain's propaganda efforts, especially in the early days of the war. Declaring German propaganda "much ahead that of any other country . . . an even more efficient weapon than the mammoth tanks which were used in France," he condemned Britain's efforts as "almost crude."[63]

Occasionally the paper's criticism of Britain was more serious. Although the *Irish Times* was consistently critical of the IRA's methods, it was also consistently sympathetic to IRA members sentenced to die in Britain and the North. The paper made its position clear when it pled for the lives of Peter Barnes and James Richards, the two men sentenced to death for the Coventry bombings of August 1939. Declaring "we look forward to the day when a free, united, and contented Ireland will take her place proudly among the sister nations of that Commonwealth in the creation of which her sons and daughters have taken such a glorious part," Smyllie also explained that mercy would serve both countries' interests: "if in 1916 the lives of the Easter Week leaders had been spared, what a difference there might have been in the subsequent course of Anglo-Irish history!"[64] The paper covered the story in detail until the day after the execution:

TWO IRISHMEN EXECUTED

———

Theatres Close; Flags at Half Mast

———

MEETINGS AND SPORTS ABANDONED

———

THEY DIED TOGETHER[65]

The *Irish Times*'s treatment of the Coventry executions represented a sincere effort by an Irish newspaper to make Ireland's case.

As the war went on, the paper became critical of many of its traditional associations. In May 1941, when the general synod of the Church of Ireland rejected a proposal to include a prayer for the president of Eire in the Book of Common Prayer, an editorial took the group to task. The synod was being impractical, Smyllie suggested, and, worse, it was ruining the image of Protestants generally: "[The additional prayers will] deprive its critics of any excuse for the charge that members of the Church of Ireland are clinging desperately to memories of the *ancien régime*, having forgotten nothing and learned nothing during the last twenty years. . . . The decision will be likely to give a totally false impression of the attitude of Irish Protestants towards the President and Government of Eire."[66] The paper's editorial position remained consistent on this issue, even during the "State Prayers" controversy later that decade. In 1949, after Ireland had left the Commonwealth, the question was not about the inclusion of the president of Eire but about the exclusion of the king. The *Irish Times* remained firm, condemning the "obscurantist attitude" that insisted on retaining the king's name in the prayers of a republic and declaring that "Irish Protestants in the south must make up their minds that they can have only one political allegiance; they must be unconditionally loyal to the Republic."[67]

The paper also criticized its supposed core readership, the "Anglo-Irish." An article titled "Big Houses" began in traditional mode—"the stately homes of Ireland—the 'big houses'—are lamentably fewer than they were thirty years ago"—but went on to advocate turning these houses over to the state when they came up for sale, for use as schools or hospitals.[68] The argument here was typical of the *Irish Times*'s ability to offend everyone at once—nationalists didn't want to conserve symbols of oppression; conservatives didn't like the idea of surrendering private property to the state—and demonstrated the delicate balance that the paper tried to maintain.

The paper also challenged its readership's traditional reluctance to acknowledge Northern Ireland. The bombings of Belfast on April 15 and 16, 1941, provoked a lyrical evocation of Irish unity that even de Valera would have admired. Praising the efforts of the southern Irish firefighters and ambulance drivers who went to help, Smyllie noted that "the Constitution of Eire claims all Ireland's thirty-two counties as the national territory; and yesterday's events proved the basic justice of that claim": "The men, women and children of Belfast, whether they live in the Falls or the Shankill, are as Irish as those of Dublin, whether they live in Gloucester Street or Carrickmines. We all are of the same stock, flesh of one another's flesh and bone of one another's bone . . . the heart and soul of North and South are as one."[69] The bombs "did something that they hardly could have been intended to do. They blasted a hole in the border," another editorial observed the following week.[70] The *Irish Times* even set up its own relief fund for northern bomb victims.

As the war went on, it became clear that the *Irish Times*'s principle loyalty was to Ireland. Smyllie and his staff made sure that the paper highlighted and promoted Ireland's emergency and defense preparations, necessities that they believed superseded politics. "Our Government is alive to the perils that lie about us, and, in spite of the critics and a large amount of hostile public opinion, it has commanded the country, secure as we are now, to prepare for the worst," an editorial proclaimed in early 1940, going on to praise the work of the St. John Ambulance Brigade and Ireland's nascent Air Raid Precaution (ARP) program.[71] It supported the foundation of an interparty National Defence Council in 1940. It proposed the establishment of community kitchens to complement rationing in early 1942. It thoroughly supported all Irish national defense activities, even calling for volunteers among its traditional base:

> This newspaper has been associated popularly with the Protestants and the so-called ex-Unionists of Ireland. To them we would make a special appeal. . . . To the Protestants and ex-Unionists of the twenty-six counties we say: "Join up, in one or another arm of the Irish Defence Force; give the lie to the nonsense that has been talked of you; show, by your conduct, that your sense of nationality has been at least as true and as sincere, as deeply-rooted and as highly aspiring, as that of the many who have traduced you. Your traditions are among the strongest on earth. Show yourselves worthy of them."[72]

A few months later an editorial praised the Local Security Force not only for its effectiveness but for its contribution to national unity. "We regard the Local Security Force as a moral factor of the first magnitude," it proclaimed: "It has brought into being among Irishmen a new sense, not only of patriotism, but of unity. Every class and condition of citizen has found a place within its ranks. Protestant and Catholic, Republican and 'ex-Unionist,' rich and poor, rub shoulders with one another, give commands to one another, and take one another's orders. It is a strange commentary on human nature that the mere noise of war should be able to create a result which common-sense failed to produce in twenty years of peace; but let us be thankful that the thing has happened."[73] There is a good deal of wishful thinking here—certainly the experiences of *Irish Times* writer Patrick Campbell in the Marine and Coastwatching Service (the forerunner of the Irish Navy) and Brian Inglis's account of the attitudes of his section of Anglo-Ireland to Ireland's defense forces undermine some of Smyllie's rhetoric. But this is not the *Irish Times* of previous generations, either.

On the morning of May 11, 1945, an editorial hoped for the end of censorship; later that day its wish came true. Of all the newspapers that had been subject to censorship, the *Irish Times* was the quickest to take advantage of the new freedoms. The May 12 issue published recently released Allied reports of German plans to invade Britain, reported that German soldiers were to be shown films of concentration camps, and published the names of Irish VCs (a later report proudly noted that Eire had won seven such awards, more than either Canada or South Africa). It also printed the first of a series of photographs entitled "They Can Be Published Now: Pictures That Were Stopped by the Censor during the War."

Beginning on May 17 Smyllie finally got the opportunity to state what he really thought about neutrality. After Churchill's May 13 speech accused de Valera of "frolicking" with the German and Japanese representatives in Dublin while Ireland's sons and daughters fought for the Allies overseas, Smyllie joined in the criticism—of Churchill. "We have an uneasy feeling that possibly he went just a little too far," he began in a series of editorials titled "Aftermath." Reminding his readers that "this newspaper has never been neutral," he also declared that it "must pay a tribute to de Valera"[74]:

> Let us be fair to Mr. de Valera. He gave an undertaking that this country's territory never would be used as a basis of operations, military or political, against Great Britain and her Allies. It never was so used. On the contrary, it is an open secret that the Irish Army throughout the war worked in fairly close co-operation with the British General Staff. All the arms and munitions that were needed to transform our Army from a negligible quantity into a highly efficient fighting force, small as it may have been, were supplied from British sources. The representatives of the Axis Powers in Dublin might as well have been in an internment camp; and we have a shrewd idea that this is not unsuspected in London and Washington.[75]

Smyllie was one of the first Irish journalists (and thus one of the first journalists anywhere) to recognize that de Valera's evenhanded diplomacy concealed economic and intelligence policies that clearly favored the Allies. If Smyllie's final words struck an ambiguous note—"Ireland must forego any claim to credit for an achievement which many a belligerent State might envy"—it is the ambiguity of an Irishman finding fault with Ireland, not of a West Briton attacking a disloyal province.[76]

Early the following year, he made the case for Irish neutrality to an international audience. In "Unneutral Neutral Eire," published in *Foreign Affairs* in January 1946, Smyllie attacked the "widespread, and sometimes even vindictive, misrepresentation in all the Allied countries" that Ireland had suffered during the war. In fact, neutrality had been a positive assertion of Irish independence, whose roots lay deep in Irish history, proof "that, after more than seven hundred years of subjection to England, the 26 counties of Southern Ireland at last were really free."[77] He praised de Valera's decision to continue to allow the Irish to volunteer for British forces—"the fact that they did so in comparatively large numbers provides almost a complete answer to those who have been holding Eire up as a hate-ridden nation, eager for Britain's humiliation and defeat"—and highlighted the country's contributions to the Allied war effort.[78] He even foreshadowed an argument that historians of the period would later make when he suggested that "it may be argued that Eire was of greater assistance to the Allies as an official neutral than she could have been as an active belligerent."[79]

He even made peace with the censors. In "An Irishman's Diary," Smyllie reminisced about the censors as though memorializing old boys at a school reunion. Although Frank Aiken treated Smyllie as if he were "a scoundrelly-looking moron with a red whisker, and a dagger between his teeth, in the pay of the Kremlin, and planted in this country in order to organise the Bolshevist Revolution," he was also "one of the most charming and courteous of men." Coyne, who "was about as tough as they are made!" was also "a most charming and entertaining fellow" and one who, Smyllie couldn't help but point out, fought in the RAF during the last war. Another "An Irishman's Diary" on June 2 fondly recalled the "battle" over Dun Laoghaire/Kingstown: "what a wonderful game it all is!"[80]

Perhaps Smyllie's genial tone was the result of a party he had attended a few days earlier, after receiving the following invitation from Frank Aiken:

> The Minister for the Co-ordination of Defensive Measures will celebrate the "Liberation of the Press Censors of the Castle" in Room no. 108, Gresham Hotel, from 7:30 pm Saturday, 12th May, 1945, and humbly presenting his compliments to Mr. R.M. Smyllie craves the pleasure of his company for the evening—without prejudice to the morrow.

Dinner jacket optional.
Rapier de rigueur.
Dagger verboten.[81]

By all accounts the party was a great success, despite the absence of the *Irish Independent* Acting Editor F. J. Keane, who had declined the invitation, telling Aiken that "you are, of course, fully aware of the views this paper has held concerning the censorship and the manner of its operation, and I feel that, under the circumstances, it would be unfair and embarrassing not only to myself but to you . . . to attend the dinner."[82]

Smyllie, on the other hand, regaled his hosts with stories of his attempts to undermine their efforts. Like many southern Protestants, his confidence came from his knowledge that he had responded to the war as a citizen— with all the contradictions, discomforts, and critical self-examination that true citizenship requires.

Notes

1. "The Ireland That We Dreamed Of," radio broadcast, March 17, 1943, in *Speeches and Statements by Eamon de Valera 1917–73*, ed. Maurice Moynihan (Dublin: Gill and Macmillan, 1980), 466.

2. *Irish Times*, March 18, 1943, 3.

3. Robert Fisk, *In Time of War: Ireland, Ulster and the Price of Neutrality 1939–45* (London: André Deutsch Limited, 1983), 474.

4. "Neutrality, Censorship and Democracy," memorandum produced by Frank Aiken, January 23, 1940, S 11586A, Department of the Taoiseach, National Archives, Dublin. Reprinted in Donal Ó Drisceoil, *Censorship in Ireland, 1939–1945: Neutrality, Politics and Society* (Cork: Cork University Press, 1996), 307–11.

5. Mark Bence-Jones, *Twilight of the Ascendancy* (London: Constable, 1987), 266.

6. John A. Murphy, "Irish Neutrality in Historical Perspective," in *Ireland and the Second World War: Politics, Society and Remembrance*, ed. Brian Girvin and Geoffrey Roberts (Dublin: Four Courts Press, 2000), 16.

7. R. M. Smyllie, "Unneutral Neutral Eire," *Foreign Affairs* 324 (January 1, 1946): 317–26.

8. *Irish Times*, September 14, 1939, 6; *Irish Times*, September 16 1939, 5.

9. "First Amendment of the Constitution Bill, 1939—Second Stage," Seanad Debates, September 2, 1939, col. 1026.

10. Ibid., col. 1024.

11. Ibid., col. 1037.

12. Ibid., col. 1036.

13. Inglis, *West Briton*, 59–60.

14. Ibid., 60–61.

15. Ibid., 63.

16. Ibid., 64.

17. Ibid., 67–68.

18. Sent by General Beaumont-Nesbitt to Anthony Eden, January 9, 1940, 5. Cabinet Papers 63/147, National Archives, Kew (NA).

19. Ibid., 6.

20. "Notes on a Visit to Ireland," Herbert Shaw to Foreign Office, 2, Foreign Office Papers 371/29108, NA.

21. P. R. Cowell to Prof. Basil Matthews, October 27, 1939, Foreign Office Papers 371/23966, NA.

22. Cavendish-Bentinck to J. E. Stephenson, October 26, 1939, Foreign Office Papers 371/29108, NA.

23. Herbert A. Kenny, *Literary Dublin: A History* (Dublin: Gill and Macmillan Ltd, 1974), 252. Frank inherited the title after Edward's death in 1961.

24. John Cowell, *No Profit but the Name: The Longfords and the Gate Theatre* (Dublin: O'Brien Press, 1988), 133.

25. Frank Pakenham, "Irish Opinion and the War: Written After a Visit to Northern and Southern Ireland," October 23, 1939, 1, Dominions Office Papers 35/1005/10, NA.

26. Pakenham, "Irish Opinion," 4–5.

27. Hodson to Stephenson, June 10, 1940, Dominions Office Papers 35/1011/3, NA.

28. Hodson to Stephenson, June 25, 1940, Dominions Office Papers 35/1011/3, NA.

29. Winston S. Churchill, *The Second World War: The Gathering Storm* (Boston: Houghton Mifflin Company, 1948), 728.

30. See Fisk, *In Time of War*, 71–82.

31. For a critical view, see the editorial notes in Jack Lane and Brendan Clifford, eds., *Elizabeth Bowen: "Notes on Eire": Espionage Reports to Winston Churchill, 1940–2; with a Review of Irish Neutrality in World War 2* (Cork: Aubane Historical Society, 1999). For less critical treatments, see Brian Girvin, *The Emergency: Neutral Ireland 1939–45* (London: Macmillan UK, 2007); Heather Bryant Jordan, *How Will the Heart Endure? Elizabeth Bowen and the Landscape of War* (Ann Arbor: University of Michigan Press, 1992); and Anna Teekell, "Elizabeth Bowen and Language at War," *New Hibernia Review/Iris Éireannach Nua* 15, no. 3 (fómhar/autumn 2011): 61–79.

32. Elizabeth Bowen, "Notes on Eire," November 9, 1940, 3, Dominions Office Papers 35/1011/3, NA.

33. Bowen, "Notes," July 13, 1940, 2.

34. Bowen, "Notes," August 14, 1940, 4.

35. Bowen, "Notes," August 14, 1940, 8.

36. Bowen, "Notes," November 9, 1940, 4.

37. Ó Drisceoil, *Censorship in Ireland*; and Robert Cole, *Propaganda, Censorship and Neutrality in the Second World War* (Edinburgh: Edinburgh University Press, 2006).

38. Coyne would become controller when Connolly was transferred in September 1941.

39. Emergency Powers (No. 5) Order, 1939, National Archives, Dublin, reprinted in Ó Drisceoil, *Censorship in Ireland*, 315–24.

40. Ibid.

41. Ibid.

42. Ibid.

43. Ó Drisceoil, *Censorship in Ireland*, 23–25.

44. The *Irish Tatler and Sketch* to Chief Press Censor, OCC 4/63 no. 76, 93/1/91, Records of the Office of the Controller of Censorship, Department of Justice, National Archives, Dublin.

45. Harold Brown to Knightly, OCC 4/63 no. 175 93/1/188, Records of the Office of the Controller of Censorship, Department of Justice, National Archives, Dublin.

46. DJ/OCC 4/63 93/1/11, Records of the Office of the Controller of Censorship, Department of Justice, National Archives Dublin.

47. Knightly to Aiken, October 4, 1939, 2, P104/3462, Frank Aiken Papers, University College Dublin Special Collections.

48. JUS/OCC/3 September 8, 1939, Records of the Office of the Controller of Censorship, Department of Justice, National Archives, Dublin.

49. Connolly to Minister, December 23, 1939, 2, DJ/OCC no. 3, pt. 1, NAD.

50. Knightly to Aiken, January 1940, 2, P104/3466, Frank Aiken Papers, University College Dublin Special Collections.

51. Smyllie to Taoiseach, January 15, 1940, 1, DJ/OCC no. 3, pt. 1, NAD.

52. Smyllie to Taoiseach, 1.

53. Smyllie to Knightly, February 16, 1943, DJ/OCC 4/63, NAD.

54. Smyllie to Controller, August 29, 1944, DJ/OCC 4/63, NAD.

55. Coyne to Smyllie, April 13, 1944, DJ/OCC no. 3, pt. 5, NAD.

56. Dáil Debates, vol. 93, April 25, 1944, col. 1535.

57. Dáil Debates, vol. 93, April 25, 1944, col. 1536.

58. *Irish Times*, December 17, 1941, 3.

59. *Irish Times*, February 11, 1939, 4.

60. Smyllie to Knightly, February 14, 1941, 1. DJ/OCC no. 3, pt. 2, NAD.

61. *Irish Times*, November 11, 1940, 4.

62. *Irish Times*, September 5, 1941, 4.

63. *Irish Times*, July 16, 1940, 4.

64. *Irish Times*, February 6, 1940, 4.

65. *Irish Times*, February 8, 1940, 5.

66. *Irish Times*, May 30, 1941, 4.

67. *Irish Times*, February 14, 1949, 7.

68. *Irish Times*, February 6, 1943, 3.

69. *Irish Times*, April 17, 1941, 2.

70. *Irish Times*, April 26, 1941, 4.

71. *Irish Times*, January 16, 1940, 4.

72. *Irish Times*, June 8, 1940, 6.

73. *Irish Times*, August 29, 1940, 4.

74. *Irish Times* May 15, 1945, 3.

75. Ibid.

76. Ibid.

77. R. M. Smyllie, "Unneutral Neutral Eire," *Foreign Affairs*, January 1, 1946, 317–26.

78. Ibid., 320.

79. Ibid., 325. See Trevor C. Salmon, *Unneutral Ireland* (Oxford: Oxford University Press, 1989); and Karen Devine, "A Comparative Critique of the Practice of Irish Neutrality in the 'Unneutral' Discourse," *Irish Studies in International Affairs* 19 (2008): 73–97.

80. *Irish Times*, June 2, 1945, 3.

81. Aiken to Smyllie, n.d., P104/3747, Aiken Papers, UCD.

82. Keane to Aiken, May 12, 1945, P104/3747, Aiken Papers, UCD.

7

GAELS

PERHAPS THE MOST CONTROVERSIAL CLAIM ONE CAN MAKE about southern Irish Protestants is that they are not all that different from southern Irish Catholics.

In 1988, the historian D. H. Akenson made exactly this argument. In *Small Differences: Irish Catholics and Irish Protestants, 1815–1922: An International Perspective*, he argued that the two groups were more alike than they were similar, and he marshaled an impressive amount of statistical data to make his case. "Either [the data] indicate no significant differences (and thus, should be taken as *positive* indications of fundamental *similarities* [italics in text] between the two religious groups,) or they yield no decipherable results at all," Akenson wrote, in an uncharacteristically awkward but typically insightful formulation.[1] The book ends in 1922, at a time when Akenson admits "the two major Irish cosmologies . . . collided disastrously"; but Akenson suggests that even this conflict was proof of how similar the structure, if not the content, of each group's belief system was.[2] Catholics and Protestants did not necessarily believe the same things, but they believed in the same ways.

One could easily extend Akenson's analysis to the post-1922 period. More recent analyses of Irish attitudes toward a variety of different aspects of identity suggest that southern Protestants and southern Catholics actually grew closer together as the century wore on. A large-scale comparative survey sponsored by the Economic and Social Policy Research Institute demonstrated that by the first decade of the twenty-first century, southern Irish Protestants and Catholics shared similar views on a host of issues, ranging from political loyalty to sexual morality.[3] This includes topics that had appeared to divide the two groups earlier in the twentieth century: in his study of attitudes toward the Irish language, Pádraig Ó Riagáin found that, while differences remain in Northern Ireland, southern Irish Protestants and southern Irish Catholics appeared to share many of the same views about the Irish language and its role in modern Irish life.[4] Irish Catholics may have "become Protestant," but, just as importantly, both groups became Irish as the century wore on.

Did southern Irish Protestants resent the promotion of the Irish language? This was not a question just for enthusiasts. It had practical economic implications: since the civil service required fluency in Irish, Protestant children educated in Irish schools that did not emphasize the language or in England were at an enormous disadvantage. But the Irish language made southern Protestants uncomfortable for other reasons as well. It seemed to many to be an attempt to highlight and deepen the gap between Ireland and Britain. Others objected because they thought it was a waste of time and money, an eccentric enthusiasm shoehorned into national policy: Irish children would be better served learning a modern European language. And some saw it as an attempt to marginalize anyone who did not fit the government's definition of what it meant to be Irish. Some felt the appointment of Douglas Hyde, a southern Irish Protestant and the first president of the Gaelic League, to the Irish presidency to be less an ecumenical gesture than a subtle jab, telling southern Irish Protestants that they too would be welcomed into the new Ireland, but only if they learned to speak "our" language.

On the other hand, southern Irish Protestants had played a key role in the Irish revival of the turn of the century, Trinity College Dublin remained a center for the study of the language, and many in the group saw the language as part of the rich tapestry of Irish culture that made them patriots, if not necessarily nationalists. At the same patrician conference in 1932 where the Warden of St. Columba's praised Ireland's "British heritage," many speakers praised the government's efforts to promote the Irish language—and two sessions at the conference were held entirely in Irish.[5]

Smyllie's attitude toward Irish culture generally was quite positive. He was a strong proponent of collecting Irish folklore: at a meeting of the Writers' Club in 1929, he praised the preservationist work of Douglas Hyde and rhapsodized that "if [we] had any virtue as a nation and any charm as individuals, that virtue and charm were due to the native folklore."[6] He never missed the chance to praise Irish as one of Europe's great languages. In an article nominally on the topic of learning languages by gramophone, he segued into a memory of his attempts to learn and even to teach Irish while in Ruhleben. Although he includes a few Smyllie-esque jibes—he notes "at least one Englishman [who] became so enamored of it that he is now a first-class Irish scholar, and, I rather suspect, has taken to wearing a kilt"[7]—he concludes the article on a lyrical note:

> Some of the most beautiful poetry has been written in Irish, and nobody who has listened to a Connemara woman crooning its soft tones over a turf fire can question its melodious qualities. From the linguistic view, of course, it is one of the most important languages in Europe. The mere fact that there has been a Celtic seminar in Berlin for many years indicates the value that is laid upon Irish in Germany; and, although there may be many who think that other languages of greater material value are being neglected in its favour, nobody who ever has given Gaelic an hour's study can deny its undoubted charm.[8]

On the other hand, while he approved of Irish in the abstract, he heartily opposed any attempt to force it on the Irish people. One tradition that Smyllie carried over from the paper's earlier days was a deep aversion to compulsory Irish language education. While it is not true that "the only Irish known to Smyllie was whiskey," the exaggeration does reveal an important stereotype about the paper.[9] Opposition to the government's language policy was perhaps the characteristic that, along with Anglophilia, the public had most associated with the *Irish Times*. After an article critical of life in the Meath Gaeltacht appeared in the paper, its author was physically attacked in Dawson Street. "*Tusa an reporter a bhi í Conndae na Midhe!*" ("You are that reporter who was in County Meath!") his assaulters shouted.[10]

The paper usually made its argument against Irish and against Gaelicism in pragmatic terms. For one thing, commitment to a dead language and intolerance of "foreign" culture would alienate the North, making reunification less likely: "The prospect of being compelled to speak nothing but Gaelic in a State where everything is 'foreign' that is suspected of being English; where reels, jigs and hornpipes are the only dances 'permitted' by 'sporting' organisations that spy on their members for offences against their narrow code of nationalism; where Bernard Shaw's works have been publicly burned, and films may be rationed—how alluring it must be to our fellow-countrymen over the border!"[11] For another, the paper argued, compulsory Irish education put Irish children at a disadvantage. A clause in the 1942 School Attendance Bill that appeared to penalize parents who wanted to send their children to schools abroad was harshly criticized. Reminding readers that "before the foundation of Maynooth College, almost all Irish priests were educated abroad," it went on: "If Irish culture is so delicate a plant that it must be guarded from any breezes from the outside world, it must be questioned whether it is worth retaining at all. It survived the persecution of centuries; it seems likely to die under the cultivation of twenty years. A strong and healthy native culture would be able to profit abroad of a few citizens, and would not be injured by it. If the native culture is feeble, only a fool would think to save it by the immolation of a few."[12] The paper strongly opposed using Irish fluency in consideration for civil service or administrative positions. "Does not this imply that the most ignorant native speaker of Irish is better qualified to lecture, for instance, in mathematics, than Professor Erwin Schrödinger?" a leading editorial asked. "Surely no university graduate would claim that it does not matter if a man talks nonsense, so long as he talks it in the right language."[13]

Occasionally the paper's criticism of Irish language education spilled over into broader political affairs. After de Valera's 1943 St. Patrick's Day broadcast, which urged his audience to "do their part" by speaking Irish, the paper attacked him for his "other-worldliness." "From men and women and children who are crying aloud for food he demands an additional effort to learn a language which is foreign to nine-tenths of them, in the name of a nebulous ideal," it thundered. De Valera's attempt to link a distinct national identity with a national language "means nothing: if evidence is needed, it is furnished by the United States of America." In fact, this commitment to such "a nebulous ideal"[14] threatened Ireland's nationalism, the editorial pointed out (in terms that came as close as Smyllie ever did to expressing a manifesto):

> For ourselves, we hate to see our country sacrificed before the ideals of a dead doctrine. The spirit of Irish nationalism reached its peak among men who knew no Irish; it will be maintained by men who know no Irish—by men, however, who believe in freedom, who hate compulsion, who keep their eyes fixed not merely upon their small country, but upon the whole round world. We believe that the bulk of the people of the twenty-six counties possess a wider outlook than that for which the more *doctrinaire* among their rulers give them credit—or discredit. We believe that a plebiscite, unfettered by appeals to the romanticism of false history, would result in a heavy vote against the continuance not merely of compulsory Irish, but of the revival of the Irish language by any means. Thousands of men throughout the world are fighting and dying for causes in which they have faith—for country for religion, for other real issues.[15]

"Here alone the Prime Minister can plead for a dying unreality against the will of a people that is dying with it," the editorial concluded.

Ironically this criticism of official attitudes toward the Irish language was something that the *Irish Times* shared with the man who, through his columns in the paper, became the Irish language's most popular exponent during the war. Smyllie's greatest literary discovery shared the editor's distaste for Celtic mysticism and official hypocrisy, but he was neither Protestant nor "Protestant Nationalist." Strictly speaking, he was not a discovery, either. Brian O'Nolan had been one of the most spectacular undergraduates of his time at University College, Dublin. After graduating he had managed to combine a respectable career as a civil servant with a promising literary start, working his way up the ranks of the Department of Local Government while still finding time to write and publish a wildly experimental novel in early 1939. The day *At-Swim-Two-Birds* was accepted by Longman's (thanks largely to the influence of one of its readers, Graham Greene), O'Nolan's supervisor, John Garvin, took him to the Palace Bar to celebrate.

As a Catholic, a nationalist, and a civil servant, Brian O'Nolan had little in common with R. M. Smyllie. But the two men shared more than just a common taste for the literary conversation and the whiskey available at the Palace Bar. Each believed that Ireland needed critical voices if it was to develop as a country. Each saw himself as uniquely qualified to provide that criticism—Smyllie for his extensive knowledge of Irish and international politics, O'Nolan as a native son whose religious, cultural, and intellectual bona fides were indisputable. Perhaps most importantly, each spoke for and also shaped the attitudes of the groups they represented. Smyllie was the most visible and active voice of southern Protestantism, but his liberal ideas also showed the more recalcitrant members of the group the way toward reconciliation with modern Ireland. O'Nolan was the best and brightest member of the first generation to come of age in independent Ireland, but his often ironic and satirical writing taught that generation that it should not take its inheritance for granted. As a result of their work together, Smyllie and O'Nolan changed the way that each of these groups thought about Ireland—and about each other.

In some ways even Smyllie and O'Nolan's upbringings reveal important connections between the two men: they existed on opposite sides of Irish culture in the early twentieth century but had much in common. O'Nolan's family was as nationalist as Smyllie's was Unionist—meaning that each believed strongly in its cause but had wildly unorthodox approaches to it.

O'Nolan's father, Michael Nolan, was a civil servant from Omagh, County Tyrone. The four Nolan brothers had been swept up in the cultural revival, and their enthusiasm was reflected in the fluidity of the Nolan name: at various times in his life, Brian's father was to be known as Michael Nolan, Michael O'Nolan, Micheál Ó Nualláin, and Miceál O Nualáin. His job in the Customs and Excise Service required constant relocation; the family spent time in Glasgow, Dublin, Strabane, and Tullamore. But although Michael Nolan schooled his children in the works of Mangan, Ferguson, Stephens, and Hyde, Michael did not see a contradiction between his professional allegiance to Britain and a higher loyalty to Ireland. When the family's house in Tullamore was searched during the War of Independence, "his attitude to these soldiers was clear. They were foreigners, 'the enemy,' and they should be sent back to their own country forthwith."[16] Brian would later inherit this ability—shared by Smyllie—to be a relentless critic of the Irish government while maintaining a strong belief in Ireland.

Michael Nolan enrolled his sons in the Christian Brothers School in Synge Street, but after two troubled years in the school he shifted them to the more genteel environment of Blackrock College: both Smyllie and O'Nolan would be shaped by a private school education. This helped O'Nolan gain entry to University College Dublin in 1929. Like Smyllie, O'Nolan would make his mark as a debater—in O'Nolan's case, at UCD's Literary and Historical Society, where twenty years earlier Joyce had famously spoken on "Drama and Life." But the atmosphere of the Literary and Historical Society and of the university had changed drastically since Joyce's day. If a staid bourgeoisie was still in charge, now it attended the Pro-Cathedral, not Christ Church, on Sundays. Cronin characterizes Brian's time at UCD as the dawn of "the first generation to be educated and to become possible critics of the society they confronted in an independent Ireland."[17] Smyllie and southern Irish Protestants of his generation had looked to Britain and Europe for answers—in part because they felt rejected by their own country—before returning to Ireland. As J. C. C. Mays points out, O'Nolan and his fellow Catholics took a similarly roundabout route before arriving home again: "Like most writers of his time, when early revolutionary hopes had waned and 'obscurantism had settled on the country like a fog,' he was not much inclined to be inspired by crude appeals to Catholic conscience or by over-indulgence in nostalgic nationalism. Even so, he did accept the basic ordinary values which those who had left Ireland felt they could not."[18] O'Nolan, like Smyllie, was caught between identities.

In 1935 O'Nolan sat for the civil service exam, and, due largely to his mastery of Irish, he earned a position in the Department of Local Government. He was a success at this new position, and he needed to be—in 1937 his father died, and with one of his elder brothers unemployed and the other writing a novel, O'Nolan was left to support his family. That he managed this responsibility as well as his job, while also finding enough time to write his first novel, *At Swim-Two-Birds*, is a tribute to just how well the young O'Nolan was able to manage his time in his early career. Like Smyllie, he was an effective multitasker.

Their similarities may have overcome any differences, then, when Smyllie hired O'Nolan to write the *Irish Times*'s first regular Irish-language column. O'Nolan's job was not—at least not primarily—the result of *At Swim-Two-Birds*. The book had received mixed reviews, although it had earned O'Nolan a portion of an award provided by the Bank of Ireland's AE Memorial Fund, it was hardly a best seller.[19] Part of this was due to an unfortunate circumstance: Longman's stocks of the book were destroyed by German bombs in 1940.[20] Coincidentally, the experience of having their literary work become innocent victims of a world at war may have been another thing that connected O'Nolan and Smyllie. According to the *Irish Times*'s golfing columnist, Dermot Gileece, Smyllie had sent a memoir about his time at Ruhleben, titled *By the Waters of Babylon*, to a London publisher in 1938, but "it never saw print, due to the restrictions placed on English publishing houses at the time."[21] But it is probably more likely that Smyllie's decision was based on O'Nolan's role in a spectacular set of literary controversies hosted by the correspondence section of the *Irish Times*.

After an unfavorable *Irish Times* review of Frank O'Connor's play *Time's Pocket*, O'Connor and Sean O'Faolain wrote letters to the paper defending the play. O'Nolan entered the debate under the pseudonym of "Flann O'Brien." "'Mr. Frank O'Connor and myself are artists,'" he wrote, "summarizing" O'Faolain's argument: "The plays we write are entirely faultless, because we write them and we are artists. We understand each other, but nobody else understands us, nor can anyone hope to, since our work is entirely esoteric."[22] An even more extensive controversy boiled up a year later. In a generally favorable review of Maurice Walsh's novel *The Hill Is Mine*, Patrick Kavanagh nonetheless managed to insult both *Gone with the Wind* and the Boy Scouts.[23] O'Nolan, writing as "Oscar Love," pointed out a few days later that "when Patrick Kavanagh wrote 'the boy scout may be said to represent civilisation at its lowest' he made a slight error. It would have been wiser to omit the word 'scout.'"[24] This response provoked another round of attacks from both real and imagined correspondents. The publication of Kavanagh's poem "Spraying the Potatoes" a week later only added fuel to the fire, with O'Nolan and his friends pushing themselves to new heights of fantasia. Many of the letters parodied well-recognized types of *Irish Times* letter writers, from the pretentious literary enthusiast to the doddering Anglo-Irish octogenarian. The controversy went on for two weeks straight, with several columns of letters a day.[25] At some point, Smyllie must have decided that the blend of absurdity, satire, and real criticism that Brian and his friends had invented was exactly what the *Irish Times* needed. On the strength of the phony correspondence as well as the recommendation of O'Nolan's friend and *Irish Times* staffer Alec Newman, Smyllie hired Brian that month.

Although O'Nolan's early columns were hardly what Irish-language enthusiasts would have liked, they demonstrated many of the qualities that would characterize the column. First, they often took as their jumping-off point an *Irish Times* editorial—ridiculing the paper's unique blend of old-fashioned conservatism with modern progressive instincts was to be a common theme. Second, they took a prosaic situation, one familiar to millions of Irishmen, to its logical—and then to its illogical—extreme. Finally, their primary preoccupation was language, in the broadest sense of the word. O'Nolan often wrote about the difficulty of translation into Irish and the greater difficulty of translating a world that seemed increasingly absurd into any language at all.

O'Nolan's October 4 column took issue with an editorial titled "Irish in the Home," published a week earlier. The editorial had been a typically *Irish Times*-style attack on the impracticality of making children learn Irish:

> Surely the Government has realised by this time that it is very far from an easy task to eliminate and extend the use of the Irish language in place of English. The task would be hard enough, even in normal years, unless conversation could be limited to requests for food and drink, and other expressions of the elementary wants of life; but at such a time as the present, when children all over the world are trying to keep pace with an influx of new words as a result of war news bulletins, it becomes well nigh impossible. Parents who confine the family meal-time discussions to conversations in Irish must find it very difficult to explain such words as air-raid warden, incendiary bomb, non-aggression pact, decontamination, and Molotoff bread-basket.[26]

This was exactly what the *Irish Times*'s worst enemies expected from it: as John Garvin notes, it represented the kind of "smug paternalism . . . securely based on ignorance, [that] would have brought the blood of any old-time Gaelic Leaguer to boiling point."[27]

But O'Nolan was no old-time Gaelic leaguer. The October 4 "Cruiskeen Lawn" envisioned one of the "stormy philological breakfasts that obtain in the households of the Gael," with a boy asking his mother the Irish term for "'Molotoff bread-basket.'" Eventually the embattled mother is so sick of her son's repeated requests that she resorts to assaulting the boy. "Of course, there is no necessity for such scenes, because the Irish for Molotoff bread-basket is easy," O'Nolan explains. "One can say it several ways—":

Cliabh ardin an duine-uasaíl Uí Mhuilitíbh
Manna Rúiseach
Ruiskeen Lawn
Feirin ó Staílin.
Brad-bhascoad Mhalatábh

[Translations:
"Breadbasket"—as in the English slang term—of Mr. Molotoff
Russian Manna
The full little shell
Gift of Stalin.
"Breadbasket"—as in the transliteration into Irish—of Molotoff]

He went on to suggest that even if Irish can be used only to discuss food and drink, "who wants conversation on any other subject?": "Why not admit that hardly anybody ever thinks of anything else? If on and after to-morrow the entire *Irish Times* should be printed in Irish, there would not be a word about anything but food and drink. Those who find that they cannot do without 'incendiary bombs,' 'decontamination,' and the like, would have to get some other paper to accompany their ghoul's breakfast."[28]

However humorous its expression, this first column was in its modest way a kind of mission statement. O'Nolan's apparent support for the *Irish Times*'s editorial position on Irish is almost immediately undermined by his own command of the language. But at the same time, he uses his mastery of the language to undermine the position of language enthusiasts, demonstrating that Irish can and in fact should be used to describe a world at war. O'Nolan's cynical tone conceals his sincere commitment to nationalism—his attack on the whole range of attitudes toward the language question only reinforces the very pride that the language is supposed to engender. One gets the sense that it is exactly the kind of column that Smyllie would have liked to have written himself.

The first few "Cruiskeen Lawn" columns were accompanied by another letter-writing campaign, both from real correspondents and from O'Nolan and his friends writing under pseudonyms. But unlike the O'Connor and Kavanagh "debates," this one raised serious issues. "West-Briton-Nationalist" wrote in to suggest that the new column was a case of an Irish enthusiast "fouling one's own nest . . . neither a dying tongue nor one struggling for life is a subject for irony."[29] "Far from poking fun at our native tongue, Myles has ably demonstrated its elasticity and adaptability," argued "Eamonn an Chnuic."[30] "At first you will shock the gentle susceptibilities of a good many Irish scholars by the audacity of your little horseman who appears to take for granted the assumption that Irish is neither dying nor dead, but is, in fact, a vigorous, contemporary European language," wrote "Lir O'Connor."[31] Although many of these early letters were probably the products of O'Nolan and his friends, soon after "Cruiskeen Lawn's" debut they did not need to make their own publicity; the column was an instant hit. Tony Gray remembers that "Myles became a Dublin talking-point almost overnight" and within days provided the *Irish Times* with a "barely perceptible but undeniable increase in circulation."[32] In some ways the early "Cruiskeen Lawn" was a sort of extended in-joke for Irish enthusiasts, although an equally good argument could be made that the later columns represented an in-joke for English speakers. (Myles himself, in one of his meticulous deconstructions of official jargon, proposed "to cheer up the Gaelic League by saying that nobody in this country knows English."[33]) But as much as the Irish columns were written for and could really be completely understood only by Irish experts, a good deal of the material in them was directed at the stereotypical southern Irish Protestant audience of the *Irish Times.* The obvious irony of the early "Cruiskeen Lawn" was that this was an Irish-language column in a newspaper whose readers didn't speak Irish. The less obvious irony—the one Smyllie would have appreciated—was that Myles used Irish so subversively that no newspaper with a large number of Irish-speaking readers would have dared publish his work.

Another column begins with an explanation, in English, of the difference between the two Irish verbs "to be" that, like his first column, manages to offend both sides of the language debate:

> The Irish language will probably become invaluable as an instrument of self-expression in these changing times, when most of us are sure of nothing. The Irish speaker, being the most equivocal of God's creatures, expresses his

ambiguous existence by two separate and dissimilar verbs "to be"—"is" and "ta." If he says "is fear me", he means that he is the eternal masculine, fundamentally and utterly a man; but if he says "tá mé mo fhear" he means that he is just man-like with trousers and looking as if he needed a shave as distinct from boy-of-twelve-like with pimples on his jaw and a sling in his pants pocket. . . . "Is" is really a god-word, unusable in its strict sense by mortals. Possibly Irish speakers are not mortals.[34]

Again a familiar trope to Irish speakers—the "to be" dilemma is one of the Irish student's first lessons—is spun out to absurd lengths; again Irish enthusiasts are both ridiculed and defended; again a serious message is buried beneath layers of irony. Most importantly, O'Nolan bridges the gulf dividing the two languages, a gulf sacred to *Irish Times* readers and Gaelic Leaguers alike.

Throughout O'Nolan's early columns, there is this interplay between languages and identities. "Cruiskeen Lawn" was often divided into sections, each with its own heading. Even when the sections were written in Irish, their headings were often in English and vice versa—one section of an entirely English-language column was headed "Mol an Oige" ("praise the youth," a famous *seanfhocail*, or saying.)[35] One of Myles's most common tropes was to Celticize English (and German and French and Japanese) names—John Ruskin became "Seán Ó Ruiscin,"[36] Chopin "Feargus Ó Cóipin,"[37] Cary Grant "Ciarán Mac Deontair."[38] In its first few months, the column often represented a pedantically correct but hugely misleading tutorial in Irish, with extensive sections dealing with the various uses of the prefixes "mac," "bean," and "fear," so that "mac Éireann" came to mean "a Tammany Hall man, a dawn-burster, a U.S. professional Irishman," "bean móna" meant "a female bringer of cans of hot tea to turf-cutting parties," and "fear smuilce" meant "a sewage-farmer, a writer of banned novels, a dustman, a man who suffers from catarrh, a nosey-parker, a W. C. Fields, a rocking-horse snout factor, one who peddles a *nostrum* claimed to be a cure for a sick *mare*, a mediterranean-dweller."[39] Another favorite technique was writing phonetic versions of Irish conversations. In these the character of "Mise" (myself), whose comments were written in Gaelic script, would be confronted by "Slánabhaile" ("safe home!"), who spoke in Latin script and said things like "Gurameelamahagut!" (from the Irish *go raibh míle maith agat*," "thank you very much.") He frequently translated Irish poems into English and vice versa and also provided Irish translations for English slang. "We had great gas at Tramore" became

"Bhi ard-gás againn ar an dTraigh Móir," and "Pipe Down!" became "Píob síos!"[40] There was even a crossword.[41]

Perhaps "Cruiskeen Lawn's" most famous recurring feature relating to Irish was Myles's transliterations into English. Early in October 1941, he translated this section of an Irish-language article titled "The Advantage of Irish":

> It is amazing how Irish fits the mind to a good understanding. As regards the sole-stop (in the full middle of the compass) and the sight-promontory (in the eastern direction) were it not that every movement is considered from the point of view of man and concerning man in only one direction—in relation to the common sight-promontory—there would only be confusion and disunity. Starting from the lowest sole-stop, the goodness of man is considered in relation to the goodness of the branch, or, if we wish to say, the goodness of man is seen in the goodness of the branch, the goodness of the branch in the goodness of human society, and the goodness of human society in the Goodness of God.[42]

This kind of exposé, by a native speaker, of the government's preferred medium would have delighted the *Irish Times's* core readership. But usually Myles's transliterations revealed a more complex interpretation. The following is an example from Tomás Ó Criomhthain's Irish-language autobiography, *An tOiléanach*:

> A time after that my brother Paddy moved towards me from being over there in Ameriky. There was great surprise on me he coming from being over there the second time, because the two sons who were at him were strong hefty ones at that time; and my opinion was that they were on the pig's back to be over there at all. On my seeing my brother on his arrival, there was no get up on him—as would appear to any person who threw an opinion with him—save that it was in the woods he had spent his years yonder. There was no cloth on him, there was no shape on his person itself, there was not a dun-coloured penny in his pocket, and it was two sisters to him yonder who had sent him across at their own expense.[43]

Like all of his writing on translation between Irish and English, this had the effect of seeming to criticize Irish—it made the language look unsophisticated, an easy object for ridicule—while on another level exposing the English language's own insufficiencies. The fact that English could make even a beautifully written book such as *An tOiléanach* seem unsophisticated and coarse, Myles suggests, is hardly to its credit.

Myles reserved his sharpest critiques for those who fancied themselves the staunchest defenders of linguistic purity. A frequent feature of the column in its early years was "Ag Féachaint Siar," ("A Look Back"), which attacked the Gaelic League's journal *An Claidheamh Soluis* (The Sword of Light) for its bad Irish—again, something that would have appealed to the *Irish Times*'s core readership. Ridiculous or incorrect quotations from the journal would be presented, often without comment. Similar quotations were taken from the variously nationalist and religious *Leader* and *Standard* (the latter newspaper, he claimed in terms that could have come straight out of one of Smyllie's lead editorials, "gave hostility to Russia a place between pig production and monetary reform as the three absorbing ecclesiastical issues of the day."[44]) When Myles discovered that the Gaelic Athletic Association held only one meeting in Irish a year, he imagined (in dramatic form) "this annual ordeal," with "FIRST GAEL" and "SECOND GAEL" trying to decipher the chairman's remarks.[45] Another column recounted Myles's "founding" of the Rathmines branch of the Gaelic League: "Having nothing to say, I thought at that time that it was important to revive a distant language in which absolutely nothing could be said."[46]

In fact, as with Smyllie, Myles's distaste for sentimental attitudes toward the Gaelic past concealed a sincere love for the language and for Irish culture. For Myles (and for Smyllie in his more optimistic moods) it represented a better world. "The talent for complex and recondite communication, with a great wealth of inflexion, does not belong to these times, as assuredly neither does the Irish language," he sighed—and Myles rarely sighed—in 1943.[47] An even more serious response was provoked by a series of editorials in the paper attacking Irish education, written by Smyllie and others in quintessential *Irish Times* style. Myles declared that "I feel I must speak out; otherwise there is the danger that the lying rumour will be spread by my enemies that I am silent because once again money has changed hands. (It cannot be too often repeated that I am not for sale. I was bought in 1921 and the transaction was final and conclusive.)"[48] This was followed by one of the most earnest passages Myles ever wrote:

> The horrible charge is made that Mr. de Valera is spending half a million a year on reviving Irish. I may be a wild paddy but I take the view that the free expenditure of public money on a cultural pursuit is one of the few boasts this country can make. Whether we get value for all the money spent on Irish, higher learning and on our university establishments is one question but that we spend liberally on these things is to our credit and when the great nations of the earth (whose civilisations we are so often asked to admire) are spending up to £100,000,000 (roughly) per day on destruction, it is surely no shame for our humble community of peasants to spend about £2,000 per day on trying to revive a language.[49]

He concluded this column with a portentous declaration delivered with "my hand upon my heart": "do not tamper with the Irishman. . . . For he is unique; if you kill him he cannot be replaced, and the world is poorer."[50] This was obviously facetious—Myles would never allow himself an unqualified defense of any cause. But real feeling lurks not far below the satirical surface. The world would be poorer without Irish.

In some ways, one of "Cruiskeen Lawn's" greatest influences was the Ireland associated with southern Irish Protestants. The pseudonym "Myles na gCopaleen" had "Anglo-Irish" origins: a character by that name had appeared in Gerald Griffin's nineteenth-century novel *The Collegians* and Dion Boucicault's play *The Colleen Bawn* and as a tenor in Sir Julius Benedict's opera *The Lily of Killarney*. O'Nolan's choice of the name reflects both stereotypical views held by southern Irish Protestants and stereotypical views held about southern Irish Protestants: although the Myles of *The Colleen Bawn* is a stage-Irish buffoon, in Myles of *The Collegians* he is a sympathetic—even a heroic—character. In the early "Cruiskeen Lawn," Myles is described as the heir to an Anglo-Irish estate. His father, "the da," was the fifty-eighth of one of the oldest baronetcies in Ireland (and a man who "never liked the so-called 'Free State' and consented to be 'loyal' only when he received a personal direction from the editor of the *Irish Times*."[51]) Myles's mother was "one of the Shaughrauns of Limerick," a master equestrian, and "one of Europe's foremost bottle-women."[52]

Myles also engaged southern Protestants directly by literally bringing Smyllie into his column on occasion. He would occasionally base entire columns on quotations (or misquotations) from Smyllie's editorials. In 1944, he noted that "the somewhat didactic Editor" had been railing against de Valera's "preposterous policy of a Gaelic-speaking, potato-digging Republic" and asked whether his preferred alternative would be "an English-speaking potato-digging monarchy."[53] One "Cruiskeen Lawn" began in the portentous tones of one of the editor's typical leading articles ("In that strange but distant land vast masses of men and metal are locked together in a battle-front which ranges from the Black Sea to the far-off Karelian isthmus") but then was interrupted by Myles, who explained that in fact he was the one who wrote the leading articles: "It's no trouble to me. . . . It is the same old stuff all the time. You just change it round a bit."[54] He frequently parodied Smyllie's tropes, such as his not-so-subtle attempts to build support for the Allied cause by identifying the Irish connections of its leaders: "General Chiang Kai-shek, who is visiting London at present, is a native of Sligo, Co. Leitrim."[55] "I formed the impression, many years ago in Ruhleben," began another Mylesian reverie about the "post-war world."[56]

Occasionally "The Editor" himself appeared in the column, such as when Myles was plugging *An Béal Bocht*—"a bitter, yet, a kindly book ... a chastening and salutory [*sic*] performance":

> **THE EDITOR:** Our advertising rates may be had gratis upon request.
>
> **MYSELF:** This is a high-class literary discussion.
>
> **THE EDITOR:** It is a blatant puff. Everybody has to pay for that kind of thing.
>
> **MYSELF:** Of course, if Art means nothing to you, if the lonely and god-like artist, fashioning and creating in solitude, is to be denounced as a commercial hack, a gobdaw on the make—
>
> **THE EDITOR:** This is more of it.
>
> **MYSELF:** Get back to your own page and play with your Panzerdivisionen![57]

Brian O'Nolan and R. M. Smyllie had always had a complicated relationship, rooted in their different backgrounds and their different views of what modern Ireland could be. But their almost daily juxtaposition in the pages of the *Irish Times* energized both writers.[58] And their differences should not overshadow how much they had in common: they shared a belief in Irish self-examination and self-criticism. O'Nolan expressed the opinions of the first generation to come to maturity in a free Ireland. Smyllie showed Protestant Ireland the way toward reconciliation, and something more than reconciliation, with the modern state.

In some ways, it is not easy to understand the bond between these two men, who—on paper, anyway—would seem to come from completely opposite ends of the spectrum of "Irishness." On the surface, Smyllie's motivations seem more explicable than O'Nolan's. The column was good business. "Cruiskeen Lawn" provided the *Irish Times* with an entirely new demographic—along with those who bought the paper only for its racing section or its social column, a whole new generation paid three cents daily primarily to keep up with Myles na gCopaleen. O'Nolan added to the paper's intellectual bona fides—although *At Swim-Two-Birds* had not been quite the success that he had hoped, O'Nolan was recognized as one of the fastest rising literary stars in Ireland. There was also a political motivation for Smyllie to let Myles have his say in the *Irish Times*, particularly in the early years, when the column was written in Irish: there was no better way to ridicule Gaelic enthusiasts and their political supporters than to do so in impeccable Irish. Declan Kiberd, for one, has suggested that O'Nolan often felt uncomfortable criticizing Ireland from the columns of an "Anglo-Irish" paper: "he had read Yeats's warning that every writer must express or exploit Ireland; and for him that choice lay between expressing the nation to itself (mainly in Irish) or exploiting it for the amusement of a 'superior' foreign audience (mainly in English.)" In Kiberd's view, O'Nolan squandered his talent by submitting to "the newspaper editor who had initially commissioned all this stage-Irish folly," only occasionally straining against the leash, such as when he dedicated *An Béal Bocht* to Smyllie (who, according to Kiberd, would never be able to read the book).[59]

Certainly O'Nolan was aware of this danger at the time; in the early years of "Cruiskeen Lawn," he made several references to selling his talent for "English gold." But this view is problematic for several reasons. First, it underestimates O'Nolan's comic gift—if "Cruiskeen Lawn's" "stage-Irish folly" was funny to the "English," it was even funnier to those of O'Nolan's generation, who were the only ones who could fully appreciate the column's language, its references, and its ironies. Second, it assumes that "Cruiskeen Lawn" was a diversion or a distraction from O'Nolan's "serious" literary work. In fact, many O'Nolan scholars would argue today that "Cruiskeen Lawn"—all three million or so words of it—represents O'Nolan's most important literary achievement, even if it is difficult to collect and anthologize.[60] Third, and most importantly, it too easily dismisses Smyllie as a patronizing opportunist. If he was aware of the practical benefits of having Myles on staff, he also sympathized with O'Nolan's satirical aims. It was not easy for Smyllie to represent the southern Protestant minority's perspective; it was no easier for O'Nolan to criticize the institutions of a country he believed in profoundly. "The very young will not readily understand this," the novelist Mervyn Wall wrote upon O'Nolan's death in 1966, "but those of Brian O'Nolan's generation know how very few have dared during the past forty years to express openly unpopular opinions either in speech or in writing."[61] The willingness to express openly unpopular opinions, perhaps above all else, connects R. M. Smyllie and Brian O'Nolan.

They did not agree on everything or, in fact, probably many things—it is important to remember that "Cruiskeen Lawn" ridiculed *Irish Times* editorials, attacked "Anglo-Irish" condescension, and defended Irish-language education. But the column also gave us an *Irish Times* editor who said "slawn lat," a native speaker ("the da") who was also a baronet, and a reminder that dissidence can provide a bond as strong as class, language, or that Ó in your last name.

Notes

1. Donald H. Akenson, *Small Differences: Irish Catholics and Irish Protestants, 1815–1922: An International Perspective* (Montreal: McGill-Queens University Press, 1988). 41.

2. Ibid., 148.

3. Tony Fahey, Bernadette C. Hayes, and Richard Sinnott, *Conflict and Consensus: A Study of Values and Attitudes in the Republic of Ireland and Northern Ireland* (Dublin: Institute of Public Administration, 2005).

4. Pádraig Ó Riagáin, "Relationships between Attitudes to Irish, Social Class, Religion and National Identity in the Republic of Ireland and Northern Ireland," *International Journal of Bilingual Education and Bilingualism* 10, no. 4 (2007): 369–93.

5. Ian d'Alton, "Religion as Identity: The Church of Ireland's 1932 Patrician Celebrations," in *Representing Irish Religious Histories: Historiography, Ideology and Practice*, ed. Jacqueline Hill and Mary Ann Lyons (Cham, Switzerland: Palgrave Macmillan, 2017), 197–210.

6. *Irish Times*, November 7, 1929, 10.

7. "Languages by Gramaphone" by "Nichevo," *Irish Times*, August 19, 1933, 5.

8. Ibid.

9. Declan Kiberd, "Flann O'Brien, Myles, and The Poor Mouth," in *Inventing Ireland* (Cambridge: Harvard University Press, 1995), 499.

10. The original article appeared in the October 20, 1943 issue. The Meath Gaeltacht was the result of a government plan from the mid-1930s to resettle families from Connemara, Donegal, Kerry, and Mayo in Meath, both to improve the families' own economic conditions and to bring Gaelic culture to the Midlands.

11. *Irish Times*, February 26, 1940, 6.

12. *Irish Times*, February 4, 1943, 3.

13. *Irish Times*, March 10, 1943, 3.

14. *Irish Times*, March 18, 1943, 3.

15. Ibid.

16. Cronin, *No Laughing Matter*, 19.

17. Ibid., 47.

18. J. C. C. Mays, "Brian O'Nolan: Literalist of the Imagination," in *Myles: Portraits of Brian O'Nolan*, ed. Timothy O'Keefe (London: Martin Brian and O'Keefe Ltd., 1973), 79.

19. In an unusual decision, the AE Memorial Award for 1939 was split between two authors. Patrick Kavanagh received £150 for *Ploughman and Other Poems* while "Flann O'Brien" received £30 for *At Swim-Two-Birds*.

20. Cronin, *No Laughing Matter*, 99.

21. *Irish Times*, November 11, 1986, 4.

22. *Irish Times*, January 11, 1939, 5.

23. *Irish Times*, January 20, 1940, 5.

24. *Irish Times*, July 23, 1940, 6.

25. *Irish Times*, August 7, 1940, 6.

26. *Irish Times*, September 28, 1940, 6.

27. John Garvin, "Sweetscented Manuscripts," in *Myles*, 63.

28. *Irish Times*, October 4, 1940, 4.

29. *Irish Times*, October 17, 1940; October 19, 1940.

30. *Irish Times*, October 19, 1940, 9. "Eamonn an Chnuic" is a well-known song.

31. *Irish Times* October 22, 1940, 5.

32. Tony Gray, *Mr. Smyllie, Sir* (Dublin: Gill and MacMillan, 1991), 173.

33. *Irish Times*, December 5, 1942, 3.

34. *Irish Times*, October 10, 1940, 5.

35. *Irish Times*, October 19, 1940, 6.

36. *Irish Times*, October 28, 1940, 4.

37. *Irish Times*, November 6, 1940, 4.

38. *Irish Times*, March 11, 1941, 6. "Deontair" comes from the verb *deonaigh*, "to grant."

39. *Irish Times*, November 12, 1940, 4; December 17, 1940, 6; October 4, 1940, 6. The literal translation of the terms is something like "Son of Ireland," "Woman of Turf," and "Man of Snout."

40. *Irish Times*, June 24, 1941, 5.

41. *Irish Times*, December 3, 1940, 4.

42. *Irish Times*, October 8, 1941, 3.

43. *Irish Times*, September 8, 1941, 3.

44. *Irish Times*, June 7, 1943, 3.

45. *Irish Times*, October 13, 1941, 2.

46. *Irish Times*, November 27, 1942, 3.

47. *Irish Times*, August 19, 1943, 3.

48. *Irish Times*, October 11, 1943, 3.

49. Ibid.

50. Ibid.

51. *Irish Times*, March 28, 1943, 3.

52. *Irish Times*, January 2, 1942, 3.

53. *Irish Times*, June 2, 1944, 3.

54. *Irish Times*, November 24, 1941, 2.

55. *Irish Times*, September 27, 1944, 3.

56. *Irish Times*, May 14, 1945, 3.

57. *Irish Times*, December 12, 1941, 4.

58. One of the most important analyses of this relationship is Steven Curran, "'Could Paddy Leave off from Copying Just for Five Minutes': Brian O'Nolan and Eire's Beveridge Plan." *Irish University Review* 31, no. 2 (2001): 353–75.

59. Kiberd, *Inventing Ireland*, 499.

60. See Jon Day, "Cuttings from Cruiskeen Lawn: Bibliographical Issues in the Republication of Myles na gCopaleen's Journalism," in *"Is It about a Bicycle?": Flann O'Brien in the Twenty-First Century*, ed. Jennika Baines (Dublin: Four Courts Press, 2011), 32–48.

61. *Irish Times*, April 2, 1966, 7.

8

ANGLO-IRISH

IF THERE WERE AN "ANGLO-IRELAND," SMYLLIE'S HOUSE IN Pembroke
Park could have been its capital. The street fell within the District Electoral Division (DED) of Pembroke West. Along with the Pembroke East
DED, Pembroke stretched across Ballsbridge, Sandymount, Donnybrook,
Irishtown, and Ringsend. The area would later become better known by another identifier: "Dublin 4," "the only Irish post code that became a term of
derision," a bastion of wealth and privilege and the satirical target of reverse
snobs throughout Ireland.[1]

In Smyllie's time, it was a kind of refugee camp for southern Irish Protestants. Even when you include only the major categories of non-Catholics
identified by the 1936 census—"Protestant Episcopalians," "Presbyterians"
and "Methodists"—Protestants made up approximately 18 percent of the
population of Pembroke, or about three times the national average.[2] Only
two DEDs in the entire country contained more Protestants than Pembroke: Rathmines and Rathgar, which bordered Pembroke on the east. In
1936, there were more Protestants living in the six or so square miles of
south Dublin encompassed by Pembroke, Rathmines, and Rathgar than in
the entire province of Connacht.[3] If the more than thirty-six thousand inhabitants of the Pembroke area had decided to incorporate themselves into
a town, it would have contained more Protestants than any other large town
in Ireland except Dun Laoghaire and Dublin itself, and it would have had a
higher percentage of Protestants per capita than any towns except Howth,
Greystones, and Ballybay.[4]

If Pembroke and its immediate surroundings seemed to stand out
against the rest of Dublin City, that was at least partly because until 1930
the area had not in fact been part of Dublin City. It was not until the Local
Government (Dublin) Act of 1930 that these areas—whose distance from

the city center, even in the 1920s, barely qualified them as suburbs—were incorporated into the city. This merger had been at least half a century in the making. Since the middle of the nineteenth century, the areas had been dominated by Unionist councils, in many cases made up of businessmen and professionals who had moved there to avoid the higher taxes imposed in the overcrowded inner city.

Until 1930, Pembroke's separation from the city proper benefited the residents of the area, who received all the advantages of suburban life while living within walking distance of the city center.[5] But for many Dubliners, incorporation of Pembroke and Rathmines became not just a municipal but a national issue. In an early manifestation of the populist critique of "Dublin 4" that would catch fire later in the century, critics accused residents of the area of being both insufficiently Irish and insufficiently committed to the city that saw them as insufficiently Irish. In the debate over the bill that would eventually add these districts to Dublin in early 1930, Sean T. O'Kelly explicitly compared their separation from the city to the partition of the island: "It is all one continuous city, and we believe it should be part and parcel of the city which is the capital of Ireland . . . this matter has been viewed with eyes that have no vision. [Critics of the additions] have not the courage to envisage the growth of Dublin or the growth even of their own amputated part of Ireland. . . . To my mind, the arrangement that is proposed is democratically and nationally grotesque."[6] But the area's separateness was not just a matter of demography or nationalism: it *felt* different. Although it was not as uniformly gentrified as it is today—boarding houses and ramshackle cottages were mixed in among mansions and diplomatic missions—it retained a rarified air. Even the electrical fixtures marked Pembroke as a place apart: whereas most of the city's lights featured elaborate shamrock filigrees, Pembroke's junction boxes displayed the Earl of Pembroke's coronet.[7]

This difference was reflected in the area's street names: the sheer number of aristocratic and imperial heroes commemorated by Pembroke's thoroughfares would have embarrassed the most demonstrative Unionist. Although it would have amazed those who knew Smyllie only as the mountainous presence in the back room of the Palace Bar, he occasionally walked or cycled to work. If one were to adapt Joyce's famous puzzle, changing "cross Dublin without passing a pub" to "get from Pembroke Park to the *Irish Times* without walking on a street named for a Protestant," it would have been a formidable challenge.[8]

The first problem would be leaving Smyllie's house. Pembroke Park, like the district itself, was named for the Earls of Pembroke. The title evoked not only the head of the family, whose original estate formed the foundation for the district, but also Richard de Clare, aka "Strongbow," the 2nd earl and the leader of the Anglo-Norman invasion of Ireland in the twelfth century—not a Protestant, of course, but a symbol of foreign occupation.[9]

There are two major routes into the city from Pembroke Park. The first, via Pembroke Road and Baggot Street, would have required Smyllie to choose between a murderer's row of Victorian imperial heroes. First would be Clyde Road, named for Colin Campbell, the 1st Baron Clyde, whose career highlights resemble a shelf of G. A. Henty novels: the Peninsular War, the War of 1812, the First and Second Opium Wars, commander of the "thin red line of Highlanders" at Balaclava, reliever of Lucknow, suppressor of the "white mutiny" among East India Company troops.[10] From there, Smyllie could have made his way via Wellington Road, named for the duke; Heytesbury Lane, named for the viceroy; or Raglan Road—which, in the 1930s, would have brought to mind "The Charge of the Light Brigade" rather than Patrick Kavanagh's poem or Luke Kelly's song. This route would also require passing Elgin Road, commemorating a viceroy of India.

Reaching Baggot Street would have provided a respite of a kind—Sir Robert Bagod was, if a Norman invader, at least also the first chief justice of the Irish Common Pleas.[11] But relief would end as soon as you crossed Macartney Bridge, named for the eminent diplomat who popularized the phrase "vast empire on which the sun never sets."[12] Next would be a barrage of reminders of the Pembroke family: Herbert Place, Pembroke Row, Herbert Street, Fitzwilliam Street, and Merrion Court, with Ely Place providing a brief but equally aristocratic break. Next Smyllie would have had to choose between a street named for an earl (Kildare), a chief secretary (Dawson), or a duke (Grafton.) Whichever he picked, he would pass—or perhaps pass through—Trinity. Then, in a final irony that Smyllie-era readers of the *Irish Times* would have appreciated, this *tour d'horizon* of Irish nationalism's enemies would end not with another Protestant conqueror but with a victim of Catholic bigotry. D'Olier Street, the home of the newspaper, was named for Jeremiah D'Olier, the grandson of a Huguenot exile who became one of the founders of the Bank of Ireland.[13]

The more direct route to the city center, via Leeson Street, would have been a less grand but just as evocative reminder of Dublin's Protestant past. Turning left out of Pembroke Park would have put Smyllie onto a major thoroughfare that actually loses its Irish accent as it passes through Pembroke. Entering from the south as Donnybrook Road, it disguises itself as Morehampton Road before emerging as Leeson Street, commemorating the family of brewers and eventually the earls of Milltown. From there Smyllie would have passed, on the east side of the street, a series of reminders of the Pembroke/Fitzwilliam/Herbert axis, including Wilton Terrace (named for the earl of Pembroke and Montgomery's seat in Salisbury), Fitzwilliam Place, and Pembroke Street. On the west side, he would see a kind of grab bag of Anglo-Irish semiluminaries, commemorating everyone from William IV's queen to John Hatch, the great-great grandfather of John Millington Synge and the developer of Harcourt Street, to John Scott, Baron Earlsfort and Earl of Clonmell.[14]

Upon reaching Stephen's Green, Smyllie, who often spent weekends walking in the country, would almost certainly have taken the shortcut through the park from its southeast to northeast corner. Today, the traveler heading in that direction passes the Three Fates Fountain, commemorating Irish help to Germany after the Second World War; monuments to Fianna Éireann and Constance Markievicz; the Haslam Memorial Seat (commemorating Thomas and Anna Haslam, the pioneering Quaker suffragists); and the Jeremiah O'Donovan Rossa memorial, before leaving through the Fusiliers Arch. In Smyllie's day, however, he would have passed only the Haslam Seat, a monument to moderate—and Protestant—feminism, and a tribute to the fallen heroes of the Boer War. And the most imposing feature would have been the enormous equestrian statue of George II, which dominated the center of the green until 1937.

Then Grafton Street, past King Street (now Clarendon Row), Anne Street, Chatham and Duke streets on his way to the "Old Lady of D'Olier Street."[15] Smyllie's walk would not have been entirely free of uneasy reminders of a troubled relationship with the past: after 1929, the statue of William of Orange in College Green would be gone, victim of an explosion. But he would have been spared the replacement of that history with the new nationalist present in evidence on Dublin's streets today. Thomas Davis would not appear in College Green until after Smyllie was gone.

If Smyllie's surroundings contained constant reminders of the area's aristocratic past, however, his neighbors largely came from upper-middle-class and professional backgrounds. A survey of the inhabitants of Pembroke Park provides a kind of microcosm of the area as a whole. Among the thirty-three inhabitants of Pembroke Park listed in *Thom's Street Guide* in

1939, there were two barristers, two solicitors, and an LLD (legum doctor, or doctor of law); three MDs; and two KCs (king's counsels). The street's residents boasted surnames that would not have been out of place in a Home Counties high street: Budd, Horsburgh, Anderson, Ball, Moorhead, Gatenby, Lloyd, Sherrard, Caulfield, Stanley.[16] As the scope expanded outward from Pembroke Park to the surrounding streets, you would find a wider range of jobs and surnames: the area was more diverse than it often appeared from the outside. But Pembroke as a whole was, as it had been for decades, the home of Dublin's business and professional class.

Perhaps because of these contrasts—Protestants surrounded by Catholics, an upper-middle-class outpost in a working-class city; hardworking professionals constantly confronted by reminders of a leisurely aristocratic past—the snobbery of the area's inhabitants was legendary. In *Untold Stories*, a compilation of brief memoirs of southern Irish Protestants, Colin Murphy and Lynn Adair uncovered a range of different attitudes about class. Almost all of their correspondents who lived in Dublin acknowledged the continuing existence of a thriving Protestant business community; there was, economically anyway, probably no better place to be a Protestant in Ireland. But many also mentioned that with that economic status came a tendency toward exclusivity. The journalist Carol Coulter, who grew up in south County Sligo but moved to Dublin in the 1960s, remembers that whereas in Sligo she and her family were "an integral part of the local community," in Dublin she found "a smug and complacent intimate world where networking assured children employment in the arenas of finance, insurance and manufacturing, where the old Protestant middle class still held sway. Its social life was almost hermetically sealed." Far from being exposed to a broader and more tolerant worldview in the city, it was only when moving to south Dublin that she encountered the elitism and Anglophilia sometimes associated with southern Irish Protestants. Later, when Coulter made Catholic friends at university and in her early career, she was shocked by how favorable their view of Protestants was—and how different from her own experience. From the outside, Protestants were seen as "economically comfortable, diligent, hard-working, tolerant, and devoted to slightly eccentric though productive pursuits like market gardening and home-baking"—all of which was completely overturned by Coulter's own neighbors, who had a much loftier view of themselves.[17]

In part, this positive view from the outside may have been because most of the snobbery of Dublin's Protestants was self-inflicted, directed not at

Catholics but at fellow members of the minority. This was not a new development. The writer L. A. G. Strong remembers hearing about how his mother's family was shocked when she was pursued by a suitor "in business" in the 1890s. "From the way her parents talked," he writes, "she might have been proposing to marry a hottentot."[18] This attitude did not change much in the first few decades after independence. Brian Inglis grew up in Malahide, a smaller but almost equally Protestant-filled enclave north of Dublin, and remembers how status trumped even religion. The group he identifies as "Our Set"—another name for the membership roster of the Island Golf Club—included upper-middle-class Catholics such as members of the Jameson family and the relatives of the Dublin surgeon Sir Arthur Chance but excluded fellow Protestants who happened to be "in trade." "[One local Protestant merchant] lived in a pleasant farmhouse near Malahide; his children went to good schools, and gave parties to which we used to go," he remembers, "but they could not become members of the Island; even when one of the daughters became captain of the women's golf team at Trinity College, she was refused membership."[19] Inglis did not even meet his own cousin Dermot Findlater, the owner of the prominent Dublin grocery chain, until after the war because he was "in trade"—although he was allowed to interact with other Findlater relatives who were involved in the more socially acceptable wine business.[20]

But as persistent as this attitude was, it was itself a sign that even before independence, things had already begun to change. Defining oneself by what one does for a living, after all, means that one has to do something for a living. If areas such as Pembroke had really been as aristocratic as their street names suggested, there would have been no need for snobbery in the first place. In some ways, these divisions revealed not so much anxiety as self-confidence. Lionel Fleming notes that the Dublin upper-middle class was the first group of southern Irish Protestants to realize, after independence, that their position in the new state depended on what they did, rather than who they were: "Nearly all of them had ceased to be landowners in any case. They had become a body of professional men (doctors, solicitors, manufacturers and the like) and were fairly quick to see that the new State, whatever its beliefs, was unlikely to be so foolish as to expel or down-grade them."[21] One of the most revealing entries in the *Untold Stories* collection is by Desmond FitzGerald, the 29th Knight of Glin, who is most associated with Glin Castle in Limerick but who also owned a townhouse in Pembroke. In his contribution, FitzGerald observes that despite his service to the state—"as well as having served on numerous committees concerned with heritage issues, I have been a member of the Irish Georgian Society since the 1960s and its President for nine years"—he was never once invited to a state function. "Not one dinner in Dublin Castle in all those years!"[22] The implication is striking: a member of one of the most ancient and distinguished families in Ireland cares a great deal about being recognized by the state—not for his family name but for his considerable contributions to Ireland in the area of historic preservation. On a more positive note, when Patrick Campbell returned to Ireland in 1963 for the funeral of his father, the 2nd Baron Glenavy, what touched his family most of all was the presence of official representatives of the president. Despite the baron's prominent service as secretary to the Department of Industry and Commerce and as a director of the Bank of Ireland, his family was still surprised to see two "high ranking—by the scarlet flashes on their collars—officers of the Irish Army" waiting outside the church in Dun Laoghaire. "I was overwhelmed to find that my father had been recognised by the President and the Prime Minister of the Irish Republic, although of course I should have expected it," his son wrote; "it made him into the public figure that he'd been for many years."[23]

In fact, the same phenomenon explains both the 29th knight's resentment and the 3rd baron's gratitude. The first was out of, the second in, a new social force that had supplanted, if not erased, the memory of those luminaries commemorated on Pembroke's street signs. This new force was the Irish establishment.

By coincidence, two of Smyllie's most accomplished protégés, Brian Inglis and Patrick Campbell, would be in at the birth of the debate over the use of the term *establishment* in postwar Britain. In the mid-1950s, Inglis was on the staff of, and Campbell a contributor to, *The Spectator* when the magazine's political editor, Henry Fairlie, created a minor firestorm by identifying a new ruling class, one whose power was based not primarily on birth or landownership but on social connections. Typical representatives of this class included the warden of All Souls, the editor of the *Times*, the archbishop of Canterbury, the director general of the BBC, the chairman of the Arts Council, and political chatelaines such as Lady Violet Bonham Carter. This new class consisted of the opinion shapers, the power brokers, "the whole matrix of official and social relations within which power is exercised."[24] Fairlie dubbed this new group "The Establishment."

In England, Fairlie's analysis took on a life of its own and was attached to everything from a book of serious essays to a London nightclub. A whole genre of "What's Wrong with Britain" literature was founded on its example, of which Anthony Sampson's *Anatomy of Britain* series is perhaps the most significant product.[25] In the 1960s, opposition to "The Establishment" turned into a rallying cry, to the point that Fairlie spent much of his later career trying to distance himself from the concept.[26]

In post-1922 Ireland, the term entered the political discourse somewhat gradually, reaching critical mass only during the Celtic Tiger and the economic crisis of 2008.[27] In some ways, this seems counterintuitive. The Irish have long been aware of the power of social networks and have been particularly conscious of the way that those networks overlap with political and economic influence; Fairlie's ruminations on "The Establishment" in the 1950s echo Burke's thoughts on "ascendancy" in the 1790s.[28] On the other hand, the sectarian divide may have hindered the term's adoption: because for so long Ireland's ruling class had stood apart from the mass of the population, not just because of its class and its political allegiances but also because of its religion, it may have taken longer for the term to root itself in Irish soil. Nevertheless, as Fergus Campbell's work demonstrates, a recognizable Irish establishment was discernable by the last quarter of the nineteenth century—a "constellation of elite groups" that dominated the political, economic, religious, and administrative worlds of the country, who "were able to influence critically important decision-making in Irish society."[29]

Smyllie, who died in 1954, just missed the furor about the establishment, although he would have loved the idea and almost certainly would have launched his own tongue-in-cheek investigation of its Irish equivalent in his Saturday takeover of "Irishman's Diary." In a way, however, he had already done so more than three decades earlier. One of his first major contributions to the *Irish Times* was a long series of articles titled "Irishmen of To-Day," which appeared in the winter and spring of 1922.

Smyllie, writing as "Nichevo," identified fifteen leaders he believed would play an important role in shaping the new country. Although the list included several nationalists—including Arthur Griffith and Michael Collins—it also identified Protestant and Unionist luminaries. He praised these figures not just because of their principles but because of their willingness to adapt those principles to the realities of Ireland. The earl of Midleton, for instance—educated at Eton and Balliol, active in the War Office during the Boer War, staunchly Unionist where Ireland was concerned—represented on paper anyway, the personification of all the reasons critics of the *Irish Times* were critics of the *Irish Times*. But "Nichevo" lauded him not for his staunch service to the British Empire but for his ability to recognize when that empire was changing and to move with it. As chairman of the Anti-Partition League, for instance, he could hardly support the Government of Ireland Act, but he also recognized that opposing the act would endanger the principle of Irish self-government. So he "refrained from active opposition, and confined his efforts to an attempt to secure important amendments in the House of Lords." Similarly, although he was opposed morally and politically to the IRA, he "saw clearly that the continuation of [the Anglo-Irish War] could lead in the end only to complete anarchy" and urged the government to work with De Valera and Arthur Griffith.[30]

The concept of cooperation was also an important quality of the "Irishman of To-Day," according to "Nichevo." By this he often meant cooperation between seemingly oppositional forces in Irish life: Catholics and Protestants, for instance. In an article highlighting the good relations between the Catholic and the Protestant holders of the title of "Archbishop of Dublin," he praised their cooperation. "All sorts of social as well as religious problems await solution," he wrote, "and if the two Archbishops work together in sympathy, not only Dublin, but Ireland, will reap an abundant harvest of good."[31]

Perhaps the most important quality of all, in making an "Irishman of To-Day," was a kind of clubbability. Midleton, for instance, "helped to hunt down General Smuts in the South African War, [but] hobnobbed with him last year in London, when an Irish settlement was on the carpet."[32] The dual archbishops likewise engaged in a "cordial rivalry in well-doing" that improved the lives of all in Dublin.[33] On paper, H. G. Burgess might appear a forbidding figure, but "as a *raconteur* he excels. He has a fine fund of anecdotes concerning men and matters of the times, and could write a most entertaining book about the humorous side of Irish affairs during the past half century."[34]

In the years following the publication of "Irishmen of To-Day," Smyllie seemed to have spent most of his time following the example of those he profiled. Although he is more commonly associated with the literary and intellectual circle associated with the Palace Bar, he spent as least as much time and energy engaged with the broader Irish establishment. Nearly all of the tributes to Smyllie after his death remarked on the range and significance of his social network. His obituary in the *Irish Times* mentioned how even by the 1920s "he [had] made friends in every political camp. . . . No more 'social' man existed in Dublin; everybody was his friend; information came to him from the most diverse sources."[35] Cathal O'Shannon described him as "a repository of secrets, political and personal, [who] had close friends in all parties, professions and creeds."[36] The *Irish Press* observed that "[t]he number and variety of his friends testified to the urbanity with which he could put forward arguments and listen to their opposites, and also to his ability as raconteur and good companion."[37]

Social life is one of the most difficult historical phenomena to study. Many of its most important interactions go unrecorded; those that are written down are often misleading, occasionally intentionally. Many attempts to chronicle "establishments," Irish or otherwise, fail because the historian simply cannot access the meetings that matter: we know that people must have encountered each other, but we cannot prove it. In Smyllie's case, he thoughtfully provided his own record in the social columns of the *Irish Times*, which faithfully chronicled the comings and goings of its editor, and in "Irishman's Diary." Smyllie's vast social network deserves its own book. It is a truism about Ireland that everyone knows everyone else, but even by Irish standards, Smyllie's connections are surprisingly extensive. It would be interesting to know, for instance, if Controller of Censorship Thomas Coyne's treatment of the *Irish Times* was at all influenced by the fact that Coyne's aunt, Agatha Mary Chilcott, had been one of Smyllie's great friends in Germany before the war.[38]

Judging by his appearances throughout Dublin society, it is hard to comprehend when Smyllie found time to edit a newspaper at all, much less spend hours in the Palace. Some of his activities were entirely appropriate for a prominent opinion maker. He served as president of the Dublin Writers' Club.[39] He hosted talks by Pavel Růžička and Karel Košťál at the Dublin Literary Society.[40] He patronized various university societies, chairing a debate at Trinity on the proposition "This House Is Disgusted with Modern Journalism."[41] He appeared at or hosted benefits for various charities. And he was invited to speak to a bewildering range of different interest groups: Soroptimists, members of the Tomorrow Club, Irish Auctioneers and Estate Agents, Irish Motor Traders, the Junior League of Nations Society, the National Society for the Prevention of Cruelty to Children, and the 32nd Dublin Company of the Boys' Brigade all benefited from Smyllie's insights during the 1930s and 1940s.[42] He also performed duties more specifically related to his own heritage, serving as the head of the Presbyterian

Musical Society, speaking to the Dublin Scottish Benevolent Society of St. Andrew, and being a regular guest of honor at meetings of the St. Andrew's College Old Boy's Union.[43] By the late 1930s, he was such a well-respected figure that the Department of Industry and Commerce recruited him to lead an inquiry into unemployment in the building trade.[44]

But even before attaining such a high public profile, he had become a fixture at the series of "At Homes"—the welcomes to new officials and fare-wells to old ones that marked time in Dublin's diplomatic and social world. Considering his Ruhleben experience, it made sense that he might be in-vited to the German consul-general's "At Home" in August 1927, although the fresh-faced journalist must have felt a bit out of place among a long list of ministers in Free State Government.[45] Similarly, his musical background would have earned him entrée to the "Farewell Recital" given by Jean du Chastain, professor of pianoforte at the Royal Irish Academy of Music, al-though there too a more self-conscious Sligoman would have balked at the prospect of being in the midst of the consul-generals of Poland, Belgium, Italy, the United States, Germany, Sweden, and the Netherlands, not to mention Sarah Purser and the "Misses Jellett."[46] By the early 1930s, Mr. and Mrs. Smyllie were often the only nonofficial figures invited to diplomatic events. Sometimes this necessitated some careful maneuvering. In 1936, Smyllie attended an "At Home" hosted by the wife of the French ambas-sador. Also at the event were Sean T. O'Kelly, de Valera's close advisor and then vice president of the Executive Council; J. P. Walshe, later minister for External Affairs; and James Ryan, minister for Agriculture, all of whom had been the targets of Smyllie's attacks in the editorial pages. How did these bitter political enemies get along? Through their common membership in the establishment, which created a demilitarized zone in which Anglo-Irish and Irish-Irish alike could bond over their common appreciation for good company, a lovely violin recital by Yvonne Astruc, and their gratitude for their hostess, who was wearing a "handsome gown of black ripple crepe."[47]

The paper's mention of Mademoiselle Astruc and "Mrs. R.M. Smyllie" raises another important aspect of the Irish establishment: the prominent place of women in this group. In most of the standard accounts of the Pal-ace Bar literary circle, women play a role that can be generously described only as minimal. Tony Gray was so shocked by the appearance of a female in the Palace in 1943 that, in his memoir published almost fifty years later, he remembered clearly what brand of raincoat she was wearing. But in the ballrooms and Georgian mansions, on the golf and race courses of the Irish establishment, women were not only visible, they were dominant. The pioneer in this regard was the legendary Dublin hostess Sarah Purser, whose soirees at Mespil House (just up the street from Smyllie) included most of the leading figures in the Irish art and literary worlds. But she was one of many: the lists of attendees at events in the social columns of the *Irish Times* often include more women than men.

In the case of Smyllie's wife, for instance, it is the supposedly exclusive establishment, rather than the take-all-comers Palace Bar, that rescues her from historical oblivion. She plays almost no part in the venerable genre of Palace Bar stories: when she appears, she does so only in the persona of an apron-wearing matron, disapproving of Smyllie staggering home in the early hours of the morning. But when seen through the context of the establishment, she becomes a vital force, planning events, organizing fundraisers, and often standing in for Smyllie when the responsibilities of his editorship become too much. In some respects, the social world of the Irish establishment was one of the least sexist places in Ireland in the 1920s and 1930s. In the relatively rare cases when the demands of the *Irish Times* became too great and the Smyllies were unable to attend events together, Mrs. Smyllie would show up in her husband's stead. The crowds gathered at the French, American, and Czechoslovakian legations welcomed her with open arms.[48] It is doubtful she would have received a similar reception at the Palace or the Pearl.

But the social pages of the *Irish Times* capture only part of Smyllie's role in the Irish establishment. "Irishman's Diary" helps to fill in the gaps. The column, which was the work of various hands during the week but returned to Smyllie, or "Nichevo," on Saturdays, had its admirers and detractors—the *Irish Press* praised it as "a list of friendships" while less friendly observers suggested that it should be retitled "'Famous People Who Know Me.'"[49] Later commentators have largely agreed with this sentiment: R. B. McDowell acidly describes the column as "very popular with [Smyllie's] simpler readers" and "impossible to parody."[50] For the historian attempting to trace the Irish establishment of Smyllie's day, however, it is an invaluable source—perhaps never so much as when Smyllie is writing about golf.

One of the most elusive forms of social interaction is what goes on on the golf course. In Smyllie's case, his golf regularly put him in contact with not only friends but also those one might think were his sworn enemies. In some cases this meant his counterparts at other newspapers. Judged strictly by their differing editorial standpoints, it is hard to imagine that the staffs of the *Irish Independent* and the *Irish Times* would have anything to do with one another, but in 1926, perhaps to the surprise of the *Irish Times*'s critics, Smyllie's paper's staff lost a press match against their more middle-class rival, five games to three.[51] The *Irish Times* hosted a regular cup competition in honor of Sir John Arnott, and Smyllie and members of his staff competed in regular "Publicity Club" competitions throughout the period.[52] But golf also allowed Smyllie access to politicians, many of who also would not necessarily be thought of as Smyllie's regular interlocutors. In June 1928, he took part in a stroke competition hosted by the Free State Parliamentary Golf Society, which put him on the course at Kingstown alongside a diverse group that included, among others, Ernest Blythe, Ceann Comhairle, Michael Hayes, Bryan Cooper, members of the Farmers' Party, and Smyllie's future antagonist in the wartime censor's office, Michael Knightly.[53]

But outside of formal competitions, Smyllie's golf gained him access to a wide range of people at the top of Irish—and even international—society. He was a member of the Island Golf Club despite the fact that, in Inglis's words, he regularly appeared on the course "[wearing] his disreputable clothes with an air of someone who has nothing better to wear—not, as other members did, because they kept shabby old clothes in the club house to change into." Characteristically, it was Smyllie's diplomatic friends that probably got him into the club: he typically played in a threesome with the French minister and the Czech consul-general.[54] Even Smyllie had his limits, however. During the war, the Japanese consul was put up for the club by the Department of External Affairs. But, as Smyllie later reported, he "could find nobody willing to play with him in the club" and was forced to maintain his dignity by "entering for nearly all the competitions, employing the local professional to mark his card."[55] Later, Smyllie would become captain of the slightly less grand Delgany Golf Club in Wicklow. Perhaps no posthumous tribute would have meant as much to Smyllie as the notice the club posted in the *Irish Times* shortly after his death announcing that the clubhouse and course would be closed out of respect.[56]

When Smyllie wrote about golf in his "Irishman's Diary" column, he invariably did so in the self-deprecating manner that is characteristic of most golfing literature. Especially once Myles started prodding him from across the page, Smyllie would often end up parodying himself:

> I have pretty well decided to give up the game of golf. . . . I have arrived, after much thought, at the sorrowful conclusion that golf is a snare and a delusion. It is a Will o' the Wisp, an ignis fatuus, a Jack o' Lanthorn, fata morgana, or

whatever you like to call it, so long as you convey the impression that it lures on guileless, merry-hearted lads like myself towards the mirage of a single-figure handicap, and, having caused them to spend oceans of hard-earned money on golf balls, caddies, lessons from distracted pros, new drives, sand-blasters, umbrellas, expensive shoes that always let the water in, and, above all, on multitudinous ones for the road, when one is half-dead with exhaustion, hurls them from the pinnacle of happiness to which they have been elevated by a twenty-yard putt into that slough of despond, whose depths only the man who has failed to break a hundred and twenty can appreciate.[57]

As always, however, reading between the lines demonstrates Smyllie's uncanny ability to run into prominent figures on and around the course. During a golfing trip to Donegal in 1940, for instance, where he observed that "the golf at Bundoran is good—that is to say, it would be good if one could play the absurd game," he also mentioned running into his good friend Karel Košťál; George T. Hamlet, the rugby international and president of the Irish Rugby Football Union; and Joseph Connolly, controller of Censorship. Smyllie's response to this uncomfortable encounter was revealing: "I have a high regard for Mr. Connolly; but I hate the Controller of Censorship. Was it possible that the long arm of the Censor was pursuing me even to Donegal? For a few dreadful moments I contemplated immediate flight, until I realised that Mr. Connolly probably was as glad as I was to get away from his job for a few days, and then I almost warmed—I say 'almost'—to the Censorship."[58] In 1942, he achieved a kind of "Smyllie Style" trifecta, managing to deprecate his own golf game, make a political point about the war, and drop the name of a prominent acquaintance within a few lines: "If there is no rubber for tyres, there will be no rubber for golf balls; and I refuse to believe that a ball stuffed with features will make a suitable substitute—certainly not for my particular style, which once was described rudely by Mr. P.J. Floyd, of the Great Southern Railways, as 'mullicking.'"[59]

Smyllie was aware of the image that he presented as the "At Home"-attending, golfing, Ballsbridge-residing, Wicklow-weekending personification of the Irish establishment. To his credit, however, he never believed his own legend. Famously, even after being appointed editor, he still lined up with the rest of the staff to receive his weekly pay packet from the chief cashier's desk in the *Irish Times* building's lobby.[60] Lionel Fleming remembers meeting Smyllie at Punchestown Races, where the young reporter assumed Smyllie was in his natural element. He was quickly proven wrong:

> [Smyllie] was a magnificent figure, complete with grey top-hat and race-glasses; and I in my baggy flannels felt rather glad that I had no need to go to

him for guidance. But he saw me and shouted "Hi!," waving his silver-knobbed stick. "How are you getting on?" he said. "I've lost four pounds ten so far, and the wife will have the hide off of me." . . . We had some beer. "I'm destroyed with this heat," said Smyllie. I asked rather timidly if it might not be a good idea to take off the overcoat. "Can't be done, old boy; there's only my pullover underneath it."[61]

What Smyllie realized and Fleming did not, at least until that moment, was that the Irish establishment was no aristocracy. Ireland was, after all, a postrevolutionary society and as a result experienced a good deal of social fluidity: one power structure replaced an old one and in the process of that replacement was enriched by many new members who did not share the socioeconomic status of the old. Sean T. O'Kelly, for instance, who railed against the exclusivity of these South Dublin enclaves during the Local Government Act debates in the 1920s, ended up living on Anglesea Road, right across the River Dodder from Smyllie. The strange thing about establishments is that their continued success depends on recruiting new members from different backgrounds: to again paraphrase Edmund Burke, change is the means of their preservation.

Smyllie was acutely aware of this. In one of the most self-revealing passages he ever wrote, he remembered traveling to Cork by train as a young man:

> I was very poor in those [student] days—not, indeed, that I am rich now—and it always was my ambition to travel some day in a first-class carriage. How remote, and even terrifying, those first class carriages used to be! Generally they were occupied by a single traveler, as often as not by an obvious 'County' gentleman, dressed in aggressive tweeds, with, or without, fishing flies in his cap, but invariably making one fellow passenger, at least, feel that his excuse for existence on this planet was pretty tenuous.
>
> I remember the old guard on the Midland Great Western Line, on which I used to travel, invariably addressed any first-class passenger who wore knicker-bockers (in those far-off days, there were no plus-fours) as 'My Lord,' and in nine cases out of ten he was right. The intrusion of any ordinary mortal into a first-class carriage thirty or more years ago was regarded almost as *lése majesté*; and my boyish mind conceived the idea that some day I, too, would travel first-class, and that, *hoi polloi* would make obeisance to me.
>
> Well, part of my ambition was achieved; for I did travel first-class to—and from—Cork; but nobody made the obeisance. . . . There were several of the old 'County' class, male and female, striving bravely to keep up appearances; but one felt that it was they who were making obeisance, or, at least, resigning themselves to the horrid thought that Jack had become as good as his master, and that in an Irish railway train at present class distinctions have become as dead as good coal.[62]

This is hardly the stereotypical voice of the Irish establishment. Or, perhaps, it is the voice of the Irish establishment at its most resilient and its most adaptable.

Notes

1. *Irish Independent*, August 8, 2009.

2. Although some tables in the 1936 census include statistics for Baptists as well, there is little consistency across the census as a whole, with all other Protestant sects categorized as "Other Religions."

3. Irish census 1936, Volume 3, Table 1C, "Number of Persons of Each Religion in Saorstát Éireann at Each Census per 1,000 of Total Persons at that Census"; Table 12, "Number of Persons of Each Religion in Each District Electoral Division in Saorstát Éireann on 26th April, 1936"; and Table 3A, "Number of Persons of Each Religion in Each Province in Saorstát Éireann on 26th April, 1936."

4. And the entire populations of Howth, Clones, Greystones, and Ballybay would still have been less than the Protestant population of Pembroke. Irish census 1936, Volume 3, Table 7, "Number of Persons of Each Religion in Each Town of 1,500 or More Inhabitants (and Smaller Towns Possessing Local Government) in Saorstát Éireann on 26th April 1936, Showing Percentage Changes from 1926 to 1936."

5. Joseph O'Brien, *Dear Dirty Dublin: A City in Distress, 1899–1916* (Berkeley: University of California Press, 1982); Ruth McManus, *Dublin 1910–1940: Shaping the City & Suburbs* (Dublin: Four Courts Press, 2002); and Séamas Ó Maitiú, *Dublin's Suburban Towns: 1834–1930* (Dublin: Four Courts Press, 2003).

6. Dáil Éireann Debates, vol. 33, no. 7, "Local Government (Dublin) Bill, 1929—Second Stage," cols. 973–74.

7. Ciaran Wallace, "Fighting for Unionist Home Rule: Competing Identities in Dublin 1880–1929," *Journal of Urban History* 38, no. 5 (2012): 940–41.

8. James Joyce, *Ulysses* (London: The Bodley Head, 1960), 69.

9. Francis Elrington Ball, *An Historical Sketch of the Pembroke Township* (Dublin: Alex. Thom & Co., Limited, 1907).

10. Adrian Greenwood, *Victoria's Scottish Lion: The Life of Colin Campbell, Lord Clyde* (London: History Press, 2015).

11. Weston St. John Joyce, *The Neighbourhood of Dublin: Its Topography, Antiquities and Historical Associations* (Dublin: M. H. Gill & Son, Ltd., 1921), 23–24.

12. See Kevin Kenny, *Ireland and the British Empire* (Oxford: Oxford University Press, 2006), 72; George Macartney, *An Account of Ireland in 1773 by a Late Chief Secretary of That Kingdom* (London, 1773).

13. "D'Olier Descendant Comes Home," *Irish Times*, August 31, 2002.

14. See Fred Trench, "John Hatch and the Development of Harcourt Street," *Dublin Historical Record* 62, no. 1 (Spring 2009), 70–77; and C. T. McCready, *Dublin Street Names Dated and Explained* (Dublin: Hodges, Figgis and Co., 1892).

15. For the purposes of this exercise, I consulted a 1938 six-inch Ordnance Survey map of Dublin, available at http://sdublincoco.maps.arcgis.com/home/webmap/viewer.html?useExisting=1&layers=5123645c552648fc92b41a39533e202a, accessed November 15, 2016.

16. *Thom's Dublin Street Directory* (Dublin: Alex Thom, 1939), 1473.

17. Colin Murphy and Lynne Adair, *Untold Stories: Protestants in the Republic of Ireland, 1992–2002* (Dublin: Liffey Press, 2002), 65–66.

18. L. A. G. Strong, *Green Memory*. (London: Methuen & Co., Ltd., 1961), 19.

19. Inglis, *West Briton*, 19.

20. Inglis, *Downstart*, 69. See also Alex Findlater, *Findlaters: The Story of a Dublin Merchant Family* (Dublin: A. & A. Farmar, 2001). Thanks to Dr. David Lloyd, whose healthy relationship with his own Findlater relatives allowed him to provide me with this reference without suffering any loss of status himself.

21. Lionel Fleming, *Head or Harp* (London: Barrie & Rockliff, 1965), 93.

22. Murphy and Adair, *Untold Stories*, 84.

23. Patrick Campbell, *My Life and Easy Times* (London: Anthony Blond, Ltd.), 31–32.

24. Henry Fairlie, "Political Commentary," *Spectator*, September 23, 1955, 380.

25. See, among others, Anthony Sampson, *Anatomy of Britain* (London: Hodder and Stoughton, 1962), *The Changing Anatomy of Britain* (London: Hodder and Stoughton, 1982), *The Essential Anatomy of Britain: Democracy in Crisis* (London: Hodder and Stoughton, 1992), and *Who Runs This Place?: The Anatomy of Britain in the 21st Century* (London: John Murray, 2004). More policy-oriented recent studies include Peter Hennessy, *The Great and the Good: An Inquiry into the British Establishment* (London: Policy Studies Institute, 1986); Ian Budge, David McKay, John Bartle and Ken Newton, *The New British Politics* (Abingdon: Routledge, 1999); and Peter Oborne, *The Triumph of the Political Class* (London: Simon and Schuster, 2007). And in recent years the establishment has been reinvigorated again: see Owen Jones, *The Establishment* (London: Allen Lane, 2014).

26. Henry Fairlie, "Evolution of a Term," *The New Yorker*, October 19, 1968.

27. The collected work of David McWilliams and Fintan O'Toole—influential columnists and writers who regularly attack the Irish establishment and are in turn attacked by those who see them as leading apologists for the Irish establishment—testifies to the term's current ubiquity.

28. Edmund Burke, "Letter to Richard Burke, Esq." in *Works of Edmund Burke*, vol. 5 (Boston: Charles C. Little and James Brown, 1839), 307–8.

29. Fergus Campbell, *The Irish Establishment 1879–1914* (Oxford: Oxford University Press, 2009), 6–7.

30. *Irish Times*, February 25, 1922, 9.

31. *Irish Times*, March 18, 1922, 9.

32. *Irish Times*, February 25, 1922, 9.

33. *Irish Times*, March 4, 1922, 9.

34. *Irish Times*, February 4, 1922, 3.

35. *Irish Times*, September 13, 1954, 4.

36. Ibid., 4, 7.

37. *Irish Times*, September 14, 1954, 4.

38. *Irish Times*, April 14, 1945, 3.

39. *Irish Times*, October 29, 1931, 6.

40. *Irish Times*, November 18, 1933, 4.

41. *Irish Times*, February 21, 1934, 4.

42. *Irish Times*, May 22, 1939, 8; *Irish Times*, March 28, 1946, 23; *Irish Times*, December 5, 1946, 3; *Irish Times*, November 23, 1938, 8; *Irish Times*, November 29, 1942, 2; *Irish Times*, April 6, 1945, 3.

43. *Irish Times*, September 16, 1931, 8; *Irish Times*, December 3, 1934, 8; *Irish Times*, December 2, 1938, 5.

44. *Irish Times*, December 21, 1938, 11.

45. *Irish Times*, August 12, 1927, 6.

46. *Irish Times*, December 19, 1939, 11.

47. *Irish Times*, March 16, 1936, 5.

48. *Irish Times*, March 6, 1940, 3; *Irish Times*, February 23, 1937, 9; *Irish Times*, May 1, 1937, 10.

49. *Irish Press* as quoted in *Irish Times*, September 14, 1954, 4; and Gray, *Mr. Smyllie, Sir*, 220.

50. R. B. McDowell, *Crisis and Decline: The Fate of the Southern Unionists* (Dublin: The Lilliput Press, 1997), 176.

51. *Irish Times*, June 17, 1926, 11.

52. *Irish Times*, July 28, 1941, 3.

53. *Irish Times*, June 1, 1928, 14.

54. Inglis, *West Briton*, 38.

55. R. M. Smyllie, "Unneutral Neutral Eire," *Foreign Affairs*, January 1, 1946, 325.

56. *Irish Times*, September 14, 1954, 10.

57. *Times Pictorial*, August 15, 1942, 4.

58. *Irish Times*, March 28, 1940, 4.

59. *Irish Times*, March 14, 1942, 4.

60. Gray, *Mr. Smyllie, Sir*, 68–69.

61. Fleming, *Head or Harp*, 123–24.

62. *Times Pictorial*, December 19, 1942, 4.

CONCLUSION

Smyllie's Ireland

R. M. SMYLLIE FOLLOWED SOUTHERN IRISH PROTESTANT OPINION as much as he led it. This is part of the reason that he serves as such an effective means of understanding the experience of the broader group. But for a moment in the late 1920s, it is quite possible that R. M. Smyllie may have changed Irish history.

The first general election of 1927 had produced an inconclusive result: the government party, Cumann na nGaedhael, had won forty-seven seats while the main party of opposition, Eamon de Valera's Fianna Fáil, had won forty-four. Fianna Fáil, the Labour Party (with twenty-two seats) and the National League Party (with eight seats) shared a critical view of the government and particularly of the government's crackdown on political activity in the wake of the execution of the vice president and minister for External Affairs, Kevin O'Higgins. Because of this, the three parties agreed to support a motion of no confidence in the government. The party whips had done the math, and it seemed a near certainty that the government would be defeated by a vote of 72–71. A coalition government would replace it, with Thomas Johnson, the English-born leader of the Labour Party, becoming taoiseach.[1] It would be a truly revolutionary change—Ireland would be led by Labour for the first time in its history, supported by Fianna Fáil, many of who had fought against the Anglo-Irish Treaty during the Civil War and had only recently deigned to enter the Dáil after a long period of abstention.

On August 16, 1927, the Ceann Comhairle (chairperson or speaker) of the Dáil put the motion to the chamber. Votes were shouted, and Ceann Comhairle Michael Hayes announced that the government had been defeated. A division was called, and TDs began the pro forma process of moving to the yes (Tá) or no (Níl) lobbies. But someone noticed a problem: John Jinks, the National League TD from Sligo, had gone missing. This meant that the erstwhile coalition was short one vote. In this situation Ceann

Comhairle Hayes, a Cumann na nGaedhael TD, was required to cast the deciding vote—which he did, in favor of the government. The revolution was averted. The question—which would torment not just the national but the international press for weeks—was where had John Jinks gone?[2] The *Connacht Tribune*'s treatment was typical: its subheadline read, "The Missing Jinks," and it posited that "to future generations of politicians the verb 'to jinks' may well be as expressive as the verb 'to boycott.'"[3]

The question is one of the great mysteries of Irish political history. According to Jinks's own account after the fact, he had decided at the very last moment that handing the government over to Labour activists and opponents of the Treaty was simply too great a risk. He left the House before the division was called and returned to his hotel.[4]

But gossips circulated a different story. Two southern Protestants, Jasper Wolfe, TD for Cork West, and Bryan Cooper, TD for South Dublin County, had asked Jinks out of the House to discuss his vote.[5] The three TDs had been joined in this discussion by an acquaintance: a young journalist from the *Irish Times*, originally from Sligo himself, whose family had known Jinks for decades. The young journalist had, naturally enough, suggested that the conversation might be more comfortably carried on in the pub, and it was not long before the deciding vote was on a train home to Sligo—full of porter and only vaguely aware of what had happened.

In later years, Smyllie was unusually—even suspiciously—reticent about his role in the "Jinks Affair." In his "Irishman's Diary" column in the early 1940s, he noted that the "Jinks Crisis" ended the career of the Irish Labour Party before it really got started: "it never seemed to recover from that *débâcle*, and hardly can be regarded as a serious political force in Ireland today."[6] In 1944, he reminded his readers of Jinks's abstention, although even then he made no reference to his own part in it, preferring to use it as a hook on which to hang a comical anecdote about Jinks's days as an auctioneer in Sligo.[7] Smyllie's silence on the subject was notable: John Jinks was one of the few names he did not drop.

It is probably impossible to establish exactly what happened that day in 1927. It will likely exist forever in that nexus of historical inaccessibility where Dublin pub lore overlaps with political rumor. But in the not unlikely case that Smyllie realized exactly what he was doing, this kind of intervention would be entirely typical of him. It represented a distinctly local approach to national and international politics; it was exactly the kind of thing that only a well-connected insider could manage; it was an "establishment" solution to a crisis of mass democracy. Above all, it was the action of an Irishman doing what he believed was right for his country.

In some ways, Smyllie's story reveals commonalities among southern Protestants; in others, his life points up areas of difference. Like Smyllie, many postindependence Protestants found strength in older traditions. His lifelong fondness for associationalism, for instance, was shared by the larger group and in fact was one of the keys to their survival in independent Ireland; southern Protestants were joiners. His tendency to continue to think of Ireland as part of a larger British community—one bound by common traditions and practices rather than by ethnic or racial unity—was also fairly common. To Smyllie and many other southern Protestants, Ireland was partly British whether it wanted to be or not. Finally, Smyllie's carefully crafted public persona, which often veered toward self-caricature, was also a part of life for many southern Protestants, who drew heavily on what might be called the "Stage Anglo-Irishman" tradition.

On the other hand, Smyllie's experience revealed divisions and disagreements within southern Protestantism during this period. Some members of the group did in fact hold on to their old ways and refuse to change while others, like Smyllie, adapted and engaged with the new Ireland. Smyllie's unwillingness to keep his opinions to himself was more common within the group than the "grand tragedy" model would imply, but most were more cautious than Smyllie. Also, Smyllie's engagement with the younger generation of southern Protestants—many of who had never known what it meant not to be Irish—meant that he was slightly ahead of the curve. Smyllie's people included not only "Protestants and Protestant-minded Catholics" who shared his views but representatives of the New Ireland, such as Brian O'Nolan. Smyllie's social circle was broader than that of many southern Irish Protestants—or southern Irish Catholics, for that matter. Finally, while many southern Protestants ensconced themselves within Ireland's "establishment," and many others could often be seen behind a pint at the Palace or the Pearl, few were able to move between both worlds. A key part of Smyllie's success was finding a way to combine traditional Protestant sources of strength with an outreach to modern Ireland.

But in doing so, he helped to change what it meant to be Irish. In some ways, Smyllie really was ahead of his time. From the very beginning of his journalistic career, for instance, he insisted on placing Ireland in a wider European context. Many of his critiques of independent Ireland—from Irish-language education to neutrality to social welfare policy—were rooted in his study of and travel in Europe. This set him apart from West Brits and Small Irelanders alike, but in today's Ireland he would fit right in. His politics, too, while idiosyncratic in their own time, anticipated a later consensus. Of all the epithets typically applied to Smyllie, "conservative" is perhaps the least accurate. Except for an occasional Burkean nod to religion and aristocracy, Smyllie was generally progressive, believing that a combination of liberal economic policies and strong welfare and planning efforts were Ireland's best way forward. He criticized the government not because it was doing too much but because it was not doing enough. And, as tolerant as he was in so many ways, he could be dismissive of those who did not share his views—he was bien-pensant decades before it was fashionable. Smyllie's Ireland looks much more like the Ireland of today than it does the country of his father. In this, he reminds us that southern Irish Protestants, too, changed over time; their histories did not end in 1922.

If this has not been a biography of Smyllie, it has been at attempt to show how Smyllie reveals some of the ways in which southern Protestants succeeded in modern Ireland. By holding on to the old ways, by engaging with the new, and by anticipating what Ireland would become, they made their way back into their country. Some might argue they never left.

Notes

1. J. Anthony Gaughan, *Thomas Johnson, 1872–1963: First Leader of the Labour Party in Dáil Éireann* (Mount Merrion: Kingdom Books, 1980).

2. For a summary of English coverage, see *Irish Times*, August 18, 1927, 7.

3. *Connaught Tribune*, August 20, 1927, 8.

4. *Irish Times*, August 18, 1927, 7.

5. Jasper Ungoed-Thomas, *Jasper Wolfe of Skibbereen* (Dublin: Collins Press, 2009); Lennox Robinson, *Bryan Cooper* (London: Constable & Co., 1931).

6. *Irish Times*, July 4, 1942, 4.

7. *Irish Times*, May 13, 1944, 3.

BIBLIOGRAPHY

Primary Sources

Official Documents

Dáil Éireann Debates
Irish Census
Seanad Debates

Archives

NATIONAL LIBRARY OF IRELAND

Ephemera Collection
Irish Large Books
John Patrick Bradshaw Manuscripts
O'Hara Papers

NATIONAL ARCHIVES, DUBLIN

Department of the Taoiseach
Department of Justice
Records of the Office of the Controller of Censorship

UNIVERSITY COLLEGE DUBLIN SPECIAL COLLECTIONS

Frank Aiken Papers
Patrick Kavanagh Papers

NATIONAL PORTRAIT GALLERY, LONDON

Photographs Collection

NATIONAL ARCHIVES, KEW

Cabinet Papers
Dominions Office Papers
Foreign Office Papers

HARVARD LAW SCHOOL LIBRARY, HARVARD UNIVERSITY

Maurice Ettinghausen Collection of Ruhleben Civilian Internment Camp Papers
J. C. Masterman Collection

UNIVERSITY OF SOUTHERN ILLINOIS, CARBONDALE

Brian O'Nolan Papers

UNIVERSITY OF VICTORIA, BRITISH COLUMBIA

John Betjeman Papers

Periodicals

The Bell
Connaught Tribune
Dublin Daily Express
The Economist
Fermanagh Herald
Freemans Journal
Horizon
Irish Independent
Irish Press
Irish Times
Lisburn Herald, and Antrim and Down Advertiser
The New Yorker
Sligo Champion
Sligo Times
Spectator
Strabane Chronicle
Times Pictorial
Tuam Herald
Zvon

Printed

Andrews, C. S. *Man of No Property*. Dublin: Lilliput Press, 2001.
Ball, Francis Elrington. *An Historical Sketch of the Pembroke Township*. Dublin: Alex Thom & Co., Limited, 1907.
Bell, William, and N. D. Emerson, eds. *The Church of Ireland A.D. 432–1932: The Report of the Church of Ireland Conference held in Dublin, 11th–14th October, 1932, to Which Is Appended an Account of the Commemoration by the Church of Ireland of the 1500th Anniversary of the Landing of St. Patrick in Ireland*. Dublin: Church of Ireland Printing and Publishing Co., Ltd., 1932.
Biagini, Eugenio. "The Protestant Minority in Southern Ireland." *Historical Journal* 55, no. 4 (2012): 1172.
Borges, Jose Luis. "The Library of Babel." In *Jorge Luis Borges: Collected Fictions*, translated by Andrew Hurley, 112–18. New York: Penguin Books, 1998.
Bowen, Elizabeth. "The Big House." *The Bell*, October 1940.
———. *Bowen's Court*. New York: Ecco Press, 1979.
Brown, Stephen. *The Press in Ireland: A Survey and a Guide*. New York: Lemma Publishing Corporation, 1971.

Brown, Terence. *The Irish Times: Fifty Years of Influence.* London: Bloomsbury, 2015.

Burke, Edmund. "Letter to Richard Burke, Esq." In *Works of Edmund Burke,* vol. 5, 307–8. Boston: Charles C. Little and James Brown, 1839.

———. "Letter to Richard Burke, Esq., on Protestant Ascendancy in Ireland, 1793." In *The Writings and Speeches of Edmund Burke,* vol. 6, 393. Boston: Little Brown, 1901.

———. *The Writings and Speeches of Edmund Burke.* Vol. 6. Boston: Little Brown, 1901.

Butler, Hubert. "The Bell: An Anglo-Irish View." *Irish University Review* 6, no. 1 (Spring 1976): 66–72.

———. *Independent Spirit: Essays.* New York: Farrar, Strauss and Giroux, 1996.

Cairnes, W. E. "Fox-Hunting in Ireland." *National Review* 40 (1903): 430–42.

Campbell, Patrick. *The Campbell Companion.* London: Pavilion Books Limited, 1994.

———. *My Life and Easy Times.* London: Blond, 1967.

Carlson, Julia. *Censorship and the Irish Writer.* London: Routledge, 1990.

Churchill, Winston. *The Second World War: The Gathering Storm.* Boston: Houghton Mifflin Company, 1948.

Cimino, Hugh. *Behind the Prison Bars in Germany: A Detailed Record of Six Months' Experiences in German Prison and Detention Camps.* London: George Newnes Limited, 1915.

Cohen, Israel. *The Ruhleben Prison Camp: A Record of Nineteen Months' Internment.* London: Methuen & Co., Ltd., 1917.

Cross, Eric. *The Tailor and Ansty.* London: Chapman & Hall, Ltd, 1942.

———. *The Tailor and Ansty.* Cork: Mercier Press, 1999.

Ellison, Wallace. *Escaped! Adventures in German Captivity.* London: W. Blackwood and Sons, 1918.

Fleming, Lionel. *Head or Harp.* London: Barrie and Rockcliff, 1965.

Gerard, James W. *My Four Years in Germany.* New York: George H. Doran Company, 1917.

Glenavy, Beatrice. *Today We Will Only Gossip.* London: Constable, 1964.

Guinness, Desmond. Introduction to *The Irish Georgian Society Records of Eighteenth-Century Domestic Architecture and Decoration in Dublin,* v–ix. Dublin: Irish Georgian Society, 1969.

Hepburn, Allan, ed. *Listening In: Broadcasts, Speeches and Interviews by Elizabeth Bowen.* Edinburgh: Edinburgh University Press, 2010.

Inglis, Brian. *Downstart.* London: Chatto & Windus, 1991.

———. *West Briton.* London: Faber & Faber, 1962.

Joyce, James. *Ulysses.* London: Bodley Head, 1960.

Joyce, Weston St. John. *The Neighbourhood of Dublin: Its Topography, Antiquities and Historical Associations.* Dublin: M. H. Gill & Son, Ltd., 1921.

Ketchum, J. Davidson. *Ruhleben: A Prison Camp Society.* Toronto: University of Toronto Press, 1965.

Lane, Jack, and Clifford, Brendan, eds. *Elizabeth Bowen: "Notes on Eire"; Espionage Reports to Winston Churchill, 1940–2; with a Review of Irish Neutrality in World War 2.* Cork: Aubane Historical Society, 1999.

Macartney, George. *An Account of Ireland in 1773 by a Late Chief Secretary of That Kingdom.* (London: privately printed, 1773.

Masterman, J. C. *On the Chariot Wheel: An Autobiography.* Oxford: Oxford University Press, 1975.

Mayo, the Earl of, and Boulton, W. B. *A History of the Kildare Hunt.* London: St. Catherine Press, 1913.

McCarthy, Daniel J. *The Prisoner of War in Germany: The Care and Treatment of the Prisoner of War with a History of the Development of the Principle of Neutral Inspection and Control.* New York: Moffat, Yard and Company, 1917.

McCready, C. T. *Dublin Street Names Dated and Explained.* Dublin: Hodges, Figgis and Co., 1892.

Mitchell, Angus, ed. *One Bold Deed of Open Treason: The Berlin Diary of Roger Casement, 1914–1916.* Sallins, Co. Kildare: Merrion Press, 2016.

Molony, William O'Sullivan. *Prisoners and Captives.* London: Macmillan and Co., 1933.

Moss, Edward R. *Shores of the Polar Sea: A Narrative of the Arctic Expedition of 1875–6.* London: Marcus Ward & Co., 1878.

Moynihan, Maurice, ed. *Speeches and Statements by Eamon de Valera 1917–73.* Dublin: Gill and Macmillan, 1980.

Powell, Joseph, and Francis Gribble. *The History of Ruhleben: A Record of British Organisation in a Prison Camp in Germany.* London: W. Collins Sons & Company Ltd., 1919.

Smyllie, R. M. ("Nichevo"). *Carpathian Contrasts.* Dublin: Irish Times, 1938.

———. *Carpathian Days—and Nights.* Dublin: Irish Times, 1942.

———. "Unneutral Neutral Eire." *Foreign Affairs* (January 1, 1946): 317–26.

Strong, L. A. G. *Green Memory.* London: Methuen & Co., Ltd., 1961.

Thom's Dublin Street Directory. Dublin: Alex Thom, 1932.

Walshe, Éibhear, ed. *Elizabeth Bowen's Selected Irish Writings.* Cork: Cork University Press, 2011.

Wood-Martin, William Gregory. *History of Sligo, County and Town, from the Revolution of 1688 to the Present Time.* Dublin: Hodges Figgis and Co., 1892.

Secondary Sources

Adams, Michael. *Censorship: The Irish Experience.* Dublin: Scepter Books, 1968.

Akenson, Donald H. "No Petty People: Pakeha History and the Historiography of the Irish Diaspora." In *A Distant Shore: Irish Migration and New Zealand Settlement,* edited by Lyndon Fraser, 13–24. Dunedin, New Zealand: Otago University Press, 2000.

———. *Small Differences: Irish Catholics and Irish Protestants, 1815–1922: An International Perspective.* Montreal: McGill-Queens University Press, 1988.

Baár, Monica. *Historians and Nationalism: East Central Europe in the Nineteenth Century.* Oxford: Oxford University Press, 2010.

Barnard, Toby. *A New Anatomy of Ireland.* New Haven: Yale University Press, 2002.

Barr, Colin. "Giusseppe Mazzini and Irish Nationalism, 1845–70." *Proceedings of the British Academy* 152 (2008): 125–44.

Beckett, J. C. *The Anglo-Irish Tradition.* London: Faber and Faber, 2009.

Bence-Jones, Mark. *Twilight of the Ascendancy.* London: Constable, 1987.

Bielenberg, Andy. "Exodus: The Emigration of Southern Irish Protestants During the Irish War of Independence and the Civil War." *Past and Present* no. 218 (February 2013): 199–233.

———. "Southern Irish Protestant Experiences of the Irish Revolution." In *Atlas of the Irish Revolution,* edited by John Crowley, Donal Ó Drisceoil, and Mike Murphy, 770–80. New York: New York University Press, 2017.

Bowen, Kurt. *Protestants in a Catholic State: Ireland's Privileged Minority*. Montreal: McGill-Queens University Press, 1983.

Brown, Terence. *The Irish Times: Fifty Years of Influence*. London: Bloomsbury, 2015.

Buckland, Patrick. *Irish Unionism: The Anglo-Irish and the New Ireland*. Dublin: Gill and Macmillan, 1978.

Budge, Ian, David McKay, John Bartle, and Ken Newton. *The New British Politics*. Abingdon: Routledge, 1999.

Bury, Robin. *Buried Lives: The Protestants of Southern Ireland*. Dublin: History Press, 2017.

Cabanel, Patrick. "Protestantism in the Czech Historical Narrative and Czech Nationalism in the Nineteenth Century." *National Identities* 11, no. 1 (March 2009): 31–43.

Campbell, Fergus. *The Irish Establishment 1879–1914*. Oxford: Oxford University Press, 2009.

Coakley, John. "Independence Movements and National Minorities: Some Parallels in the European Experience." *European Journal of Political Research* 8 (1980): 215–47.

——. "A Political Profile of Protestant Minorities in Europe." *National Identities* 11 (2009): 9–30.

——. "Religion, Ethnic Identity and the Protestant Minority in the Republic." In *Ireland and the Politics of Change*, edited by William Crotty and David E. Schmitt, 86–106. Harlow, UK: Addison Wesley Longman Limited, 1998.

Cole, Robert. *Propaganda, Censorship and Neutrality in the Second World War*. Edinburgh: Edinburgh University Press, 2006.

Comerford, R. V. "Patriotism as Pastime: The Appeal of Fenianism in the mid-1860s." *Irish Historical Studies* 22, no. 87 (March 1981): 239–50.

Corcoran, Neil. *Elizabeth Bowen: The Enforced Return*. Oxford: Oxford University Press, 2008.

Cowell, John. *No Profit but the Name: The Longfords and the Gate Theatre*. Dublin: The O'Brien Press, 1988.

Crawford, Heather W. *Outside the Glow: Protestants and Irishness in Independent Ireland*. Dublin: University College Dublin Press, 2010.

Cronin, Anthony. *No Laughing Matter: The Life and Times of Flann O'Brien*. New York: Fromm International Publishing Corporation, 1989.

Curran, Steven. "'Could Paddy Leave off from Copying Just for Five Minutes': Brian O'Nolan and Eire's Beveridge Plan." *Irish University Review* 31, no. 2 (2001): 353–75.

d'Alton, Ian. "A Protestant Paper for a Protestant People: The Irish Times and the Southern Irish Minority." *Irish Communications Review* 12, no. 1 (January 2010): 65–73.

——. "Religion as Identity: The Church of Ireland's 1932 Patrician Celebrations." In *Representing Irish Religious Histories: Historiography, Ideology and Practice*, edited by Jacqueline Hill and Mary Ann Lyons, 197–210. Cham, Switzerland: Palgrave Macmillan, 2017.

——. "Southern Irish Unionism: A Study of Cork Unionists, 1884–1914." *Transactions of the Royal Historical Society* 23 (1973): 71–88.

——. "'A Vestigial Population'?: Perspectives on Southern Irish Protestants in the Twentieth Century." *Éire-Ireland* 44, nos. 3–4 (fall/winter 2009): 9–42.

Day, Jon. "Cuttings from Cruiskeen Lawn: Bibliographical Issues in the Republication of Myles na gCopaleen's Journalism." In *"Is It about a Bicycle?": Flann O'Brien in the Twenty-First Century*, edited by Jennika Baines, 32–48. Dublin: Four Courts Press, 2011.

Deignan, Patrick. "The Protestant Community in Sligo, 1914–1949." PhD thesis, National University of Ireland Maynooth, 2008.

de Vere White, Terence. *The Anglo-Irish*. London: Victor Gollancz Ltd., 1972.

Devine, Karen. "A Comparative Critique of the Practice of Irish Neutrality in the 'Unneutral' Discourse." *Irish Studies in International Affairs* 19 (2008): 73–97.

Dickson, David. "County Histories, National Narratives and Missing Pieces: A Report from Ireland," accessed June 1, 2017. https://webcache.googleusercontent.com/search? q=cache:ULQVEpl5_XsJ:https://www.victoriacountyhistory.ac.uk/sites/default/files /page-attachments/dickson_-_local_histories.doc+&cd=1&hl=en&ct=clnk&gl=us.

Diment, Galya. *A Russian Jew of Bloomsbury: The Life and Times of Samuel Koteliansky*. Montreal: McGill-Queens University Press, 2011.

Doerries, Reinhard R. *Prelude to the Easter Rising: Sir Roger Casement in Imperial Germany*. London: Frank Cass Publishers, 2000.

Doherty, Richard. *Irish Men and Women in the Second World War*. Dublin: Four Courts Press, 1999.

Dolan, Anne. "Divisions and Divisions and Divisions: Who to Commemorate?" In *Towards Commemoration: Ireland in War and Remembrance 1912–1923*, edited by John Horne and Edward Madigan, 145–53. Dublin: Royal Irish Academy, 2013.

Dooley, Terence. *The Decline of the Big House in Ireland: A Study of Irish Landed Families 1860–1960*. Dublin: Wolfhound Press, 2001.

Eatough, Matt. "Bowen's Court and the Anglo-Irish World System." *Modern Language Quarterly* 73, no. 1 (2012): 69–94.

Fahey, Tony, Bernadette C. Hayes, and Richard Sinnott. *Conflict and Consensus: A Study of Values and Attitudes in the Republic of Ireland and Northern Ireland*. Dublin: Institute of Public Administration, 2005.

Fanning, Ronan. *Éamon de Valera: A Will to Power*. London: Faber & Faber, 2015.

Fanning, Tim. *The Fethard-on-Sea Boycott*. Dublin: Collins Press, 2010.

Findlater, Alex. *Findlaters: The Story of a Dublin Merchant Family*. Dublin: A. & A. Farmar, 2001.

Fisk, Robert. *In Time of War: Ireland, Ulster and the Price of Neutrality 1939–45*. London: André Deutsch Limited, 1983.

Fitzpatrick, David. *Descendancy: Irish Protestant Histories since 1795*. Cambridge: Cambridge University Press, 2014.

———. *Politics and Irish Life 1913–1921: Provincial Experience of War and Revolution*. Dublin: Gill and Macmillan, 1977.

Forth, Gordon. "'No Petty People': The Anglo-Irish Identity in Colonial Australia." In *The Irish World Wide*, vol. 2, edited by Patrick O'Sullivan, 128–42. Leicester: Leicester University Press, 1992.

Foster, R. F. *Luck and the Irish: A Brief History of Change, 1970–2000*. London: Allen Lane, 2007.

———. *Paddy and Mr. Punch*. London: Penguin, 1993.

———. *W. B. Yeats: A Life II: The Arch-Poet*. Oxford: Oxford University Press, 2003.

Garvin, John. "Sweetscented Manuscripts." In *Myles: Portraits of Brian O'Nolan*, edited by Timothy O'Keefe, 54–61. London: Martin Brian and O'Keefe Ltd., 1973.

Gaughan, J. Anthony. *Thomas Johnson, 1872–1963: First Leader of the Labour Party in Dáil Éireann*. Mount Merrion: Kingdom Books, 1980.

Girvin, Brian. *The Emergency: Neutral Ireland 1939–45*. London: Macmillan UK, 2007.

Glascott, J. R. M. Symes. *Sir John Keane and Cappoquin House in Time of War and Revolution*. Dublin: Four Courts Press, 2016.

Glendinning, Victoria. *Love's Civil War: Elizabeth Bowen and Charles Ritchie, Letters and Diaries 1941–1973*. London: Simon & Schuster UK, 2010.

Gray, Tony. *Mr. Smyllie, Sir*. Dublin: Gill and MacMillan, 1991.

Greenwood, Adrian. *Victoria's Scottish Lion: The Life of Colin Campbell, Lord Clyde*. London: History Press, 2015.

Hanna, Erika. *Modern Dublin: Urban Change and the Irish Past, 1957–73*. Oxford: Oxford University Press, 2013.

Hart, Peter. "The Protestant Experience of Revolution in Southern Ireland." In *Unionism in Modern Ireland: New Perspectives on Politics and Culture*, edited by Richard English and Graham Walker, 81–98. London: Macmillan Press Ltd, 1996.

Hennessy, Peter. *The Great and the Good: An Inquiry into the British Establishment*. London: Policy Studies Institute, 1986.

Hoenselaars, Ton. "In Exile with Shakespeare: British Civilian Internee Theatre at Ruhleben Camp, 1914–1918." *Shakespeare in Southern Africa* 23 (2011): 1–10.

Holmes, Andrew R., and Eugenio F. Biagini. "Protestants." In *The Cambridge Social History of Modern Ireland*, edited by Eugenio F. Biagini and Mary E. Daly, 88–111. Cambridge: Cambridge University Press.

Holquist, Peter. "'Conduct Merciless Mass Terror': Decossackization on the Don, 1919." *Cahiers de Monde Russe* 38, nos. 1–2 (1997): 127–62.

Hopkinson, Michael. "President Woodrow Wilson and the Irish Question." *Studia Hibernica*, no. 27 (1993): 89–111.

Horgan, John. "Saving Us from Ourselves: Contraception, Censorship and the 'Evil Literature' Controversy of 1926." *Irish Communication Review* 5, no. 1 (January 1995): 61–67.

Hunt, Tristram. *Ten Cities That Made an Empire*. London: Allen Lane, 2013.

Hylton, Raymond. *Ireland's Huguenots and Their Refuge, 1662–1745: An Unlikely Haven*. Brighton: Sussex Academic Press, 2005.

Inglis, Tom. "Local Belonging, Identities and Sense of Place in Contemporary Ireland." IBIS Discussion Paper #4, Institute for British-Irish Studies, University College Dublin. Accessed May 15, 2017. http://www.ucd.ie/ibis/publications/discussionpapers/localbelo ngingidentitiesandsenseofplaceincontemporaryireland/p%26d_disscussion_paper_4 .pdf.

James, Dermot. *From the Margin to the Centre: A History of the Irish Times*. Dublin: Woodfield Press, 2008.

Jones, Heather. "A Missing Paradigm? Military Captivity and the Prisoner of War, 1914–1918." *Immigrants and Minorities* 26:1–2, 19–48.

Jones, Owen. *The Establishment*. London: Allen Lane, 2014.

Jordan, Heather Bryant. *How Will the Heart Endure? Elizabeth Bowen and the Landscape of War*. Ann Arbor: University of Michigan Press, 1992.

Keating, Anthony. "Censorship: The Cornerstone of Catholic Ireland." *Journal of Church and State* 57, no. 2: 298.

Kelly, Anne. "The Lane Bequest: A British-Irish Cultural Conflict Revisited." *Journal of the History of Collections* 16, no. 1 (May 2004): 89–110.

Kelly, Matthew. "Languages of Radicalism, Race, and Religion in Irish Nationalism: The French Affinity, 1848-1871." *Journal of British Studies* 49, no. 4 (2010): 801-25.

———. "The Politics of Protestant Street Preaching in 1890s Ireland." *Historical Journal* 48, no. 1 (2005): 101-25.

Kenny, Herbert A. *Literary Dublin: A History*. Dublin: Gill and Macmillan, 1974.

Kenny, Kevin. *Ireland and the British Empire*. Oxford: Oxford University Press, 2006.

Keogh, Dermot. *Ireland and Europe, 1919-1948*. Dublin: Gill and MacMillan, 1988.

———. *Ireland and the Vatican: The Politics and Diplomacy of Church-State Relations, 1922-1960*. Cork University Press, 1995.

Kiberd, Declan. *Inventing Ireland*. Cambridge: Harvard University Press, 1995.

Legg, Marie-Louise. *Newspapers and Nationalism: The Irish Provincial Press, 1850-1892*. Dublin: Four Courts Press, 1999.

Ludewig, Alexandra. "Visualising a Community in Incarceration: Images from Civilian Internees on Rottnest Island and in Ruhleben during the First World War." *War & Society* 35, no. 1 (February 2016): 54-74.

Ludington, Charles C. "Between Myth and Margin: The Huguenots in Irish History." *Historical Research* 73, no. 180 (2000): 1-19.

MacMaster, Norma. *Over My Shoulder: A Memoir*. Dublin: Columba Press, 2008.

Maguire, Martin. "'Our People': The Church of Ireland in Dublin Since Disestablishment." In *The Laity and the Church of Ireland, 1000-2000*, edited by Raymond Gillespie and W. G. Neely, 277-303. Dublin: Four Courts Press, 2002.

———. "'Remembering Who We Are': Identity and Class in Protestant Dublin and Belfast, 1868-1905." In *Essays in Irish Labour History: A Festschrift for Elizabeth and John W Boyle*, edited by Francis Devine, Fintan Lane and Niamh Puirséil, 49-64. Dublin: Irish Academic Press, Dublin, 2008.

Martin, David. "Notes for a General Theory of Secularisation." *European Journal of Sociology/ Archives Européennes de Sociologie* 10, no. 2 (1969): 192-201.

Martin, James. *The Irish Times Past and Present: A Record of the Journal Since 1859*. Belfast: Belfast Historical and Educational Society, 2008.

Martin, John. *The Irish Times Past and Present: A Record of the Journal Since 1859*. Belfast: Belfast Historical and Educational Society, 2008.

Mattinson, Miles Walker. *The Law Relating to Corrupt Practices at Elections*. London: Waterlow and Sons Limited, 1883.

Mayhew, Robert. *Enlightenment Geography: The Political Languages of British Geography, 1650-1850*. New York: St. Martin's Press, 2000.

Mays, J. C. C. "Brian O'Nolan: Literalist of the Imagination." In *Myles: Portraits of Brian O'Nolan*, edited by Timothy O'Keefe, 79-92. London: Martin Brian and O'Keefe Ltd., 1973.

McAuley, James, and Jonathan Tonge. "Britishness and Irishness in Northern Ireland since the Good Friday Agreement." *Parliamentary Affairs* 63, no. 2 (2010): 266-85.

McConville, Michael. *Ascendancy to Oblivion: The Story of the Anglo-Irish*. London: Quartet Books, 1986.

McDowell, R. B. *Crisis and Decline: The Fate of the Southern Unionists*. Dublin: Lilliput Press, 1997.

———. *The Irish Convention 1917-18*. London: Routledge and Keegan Paul, 1970.

McKee, Eamonn. "Church-State Relations and the Development of Irish Health Policy: The Mother and Child Scheme, 1944-1953." *Irish Historical Studies* 25, issue 98 (November 1986): 159-94.

McManus, Ruth. *Dublin 1910–1940: Shaping the City & Suburbs*. Dublin: Four Courts Press, 2002.

McWilliams, David. *The Pope's Children: Ireland's New Elite*. Dublin: Gill and Macmillan, 2005.

Meehan, Niall. "Shorthand for Protestants: Sectarian Advertising in the *Irish Times*." *History Ireland* 17, no. 5 (September/October 2009): 46–49.

Mennell, Stephen. Introduction to *Untold Stories: Protestants in the Republic of Ireland 1922–2002*, edited by Colin Murphy and Lynn Adair, 8–11. Dublin: Liffey Press, 2002.

Mennell, Stephen, Mitchell Elliott, Paul Stokes, Aoife Rickard, and Ellen O'Malley-Dunlop. "Protestants in a Catholic State—A Silent Minority in Ireland." In *Religion and Politics: East-West Contrasts from Contemporary Europe*, edited by Tom Inglis, Zdzisław Mach, and Rafał Manzanek, 68–92. Dublin: University College Dublin Press, 2000.

Mollan, R. Charles. *Some People and Places in Irish Science and Technology*. Dublin: Royal Irish Academy, 1985.

Mullen, Michael. *Mayo: The Waters and the Wild*. Donaghadee: Cottage Publications, 2004.

Murphy, Colin, and Lynne Adair. *Untold Stories: Protestants in the Republic of Ireland, 1992–2002*. Dublin: The Liffey Press, 2002.

Murphy, John A. "Irish Neutrality in Historical Perspective." In *Ireland and the Second World War: Politics, Society and Remembrance*, edited by Brian Girvin and Geoffrey Roberts, 9–23. Dublin: Four Courts Press, 2000.

Oborne, Peter. *The Triumph of the Political Class*. London: Simon and Schuster, 2007.

O'Brien, Joseph. *Dear Dirty Dublin: A City in Distress, 1899–1916*. Berkeley: University of California Press, 1982.

O'Brien, Mark. *The Fourth Estate: Journalism in Twentieth-Century Ireland*. Manchester: Manchester University Press, 2017.

———. *The Irish Times: A History*. Dublin: Four Courts Press, 2008.

O'Connor, Catherine. "Southern Protestantism: The Inter-relationship of Religious, Social and Gender Identity in the Diocese of Ferns 1945–65." PhD thesis, University of Limerick, 2007.

Ó Corráin, Daithí. *Rendering to God and Caesar: The Irish Churches and the Two States in Ireland, 1949–73*. Manchester: Manchester University Press, 2006.

Ó Drisceoil, Donal. *Censorship in Ireland, 1939–1945: Neutrality, Politics and Society*. Cork: Cork University Press, 1996.

O'Halloran, Claire. *Partition and the Limits of Irish Nationalism: An Ideology under Stress*. Atlantic Highlands, NJ: Humanities International Press, 1987.

Ó Maitiú, Séamas. *Dublin's Suburban Towns: 1834–1930*. Dublin: Four Courts Press, 2003.

Oram, Hugh. *Paper Tigers: Stories of Irish Newspapers by the People Who Make Them*. Belfast: Appletree Press, 1993.

Ó Riagáin, Pádraig. "Relationships between Attitudes to Irish, Social Class, Religion and National Identity in the Republic of Ireland and Northern Ireland." *International Journal of Bilingual Education and Bilingualism* 10, no. 4 (2007): 369–93.

Ranger, Pierre. "The World in Paris and Ireland Too: The French Diplomacy of Sinn Féin." *Études Irlandaises* 36, no. 2 (2011): 39–57.

Richardson, Caleb. "Patrick Campbell's Easy Times: Humour and Southern Irish Protestants." In *Irish And Protestant*, edited by Ian d'Alton and Ida Milne, 268–82. Cork: Cork University Press, 2018.

———. "Transforming Anglo-Ireland: R. M. Smyllie and the *Irish Times*." *New Hibernia Review* 11, no. 4 (geimhreadh/winter 2007): 17–36.

Robinson, Lennox. *Bryan Cooper*. London: Constable & Co., 1931.

Ruane, Joseph, and David Butler. "Southern Irish Protestants: An Example of De-ethnicization?" *Nations and Nationalism* 13, no. 4 (2007): 619–35.

Salmon, Trevor C. *Unneutral Ireland*. Oxford: Oxford University Press, 1989.

Samek, Daniel. *Czech-Irish Cultural Relations 1900–1950*. Prague: Centre for Irish Studies, Charles University, 2009.

Sampson, Anthony. *Anatomy of Britain*. London: Hodder and Stoughton, 1962.

———. *The Changing Anatomy of Britain*. London: Hodder and Stoughton, 1982.

———. *The Essential Anatomy of Britain: Democracy in Crisis*. London: Hodder and Stoughton, 1992.

———. *Who Runs This Place?: The Anatomy of Britain in the 21st Century*. London: John Murray, 2004.

Sinclair, Andrew. *The Last of the Best: The Aristocracy of Europe in the Twentieth Century*. London: Macmillan Company, 1969.

Stibbe, Matthew. *British Civilian Internees in Germany: The Ruhleben Camp, 1914–1918*. Manchester: Manchester University Press, 2008.

Teekell, Anna. "Elizabeth Bowen and Language at War." *New Hibernia Review/Iris Éireannach Nua* 15, no. 3 (fómhar/autumn 2011): 61–79

Thompson, E. P. *The Making of the English Working Class*. New York: Vintage Books, 1966.

Tobin, Robert. *The Minority Voice: Hubert Butler and Southern Irish Protestantism, 1900–1991*. Oxford: Oxford University Press, 2012.

Trench, Fred. "John Hatch and the Development of Harcourt Street." *Dublin Historical Record* 62, no. 1 (spring 2009): 70–77.

Ungoed-Thomas, Jasper. *Jasper Wolfe of Skibbereen*. Dublin: Collins Press, 2009.

Wallace, Ciaran. "Fighting for Unionist Home Rule: Competing Identities in Dublin 1880–1929." *Journal of Urban History* 38, no. 5 (2012): 940–41.

Wheatley, Michael. *Nationalism and the Irish Party*. Oxford: Oxford University Press, 2006.

Whelan, Ruth. "The Huguenots and the Imaginative Geography of Ireland: A Planned Immigration Scheme in the 1680s." *Irish Historical Studies* 35, no. 140 (2007): 477–95.

White, Jack. *Minority Report: The Protestant Community in the Irish Republic*. Dublin: Gill and Macmillan, 1975.

White, Terence de Vere. *The Anglo-Irish*. London: Victor Gollancz, 1972.

Wilson, T. K. *Frontiers of Violence: Conflict and Identity in Ulster and Upper Silesia, 1918–1922*. Oxford: Oxford University Press, 2010.

Wilson, Tim. "Ghost Provinces, Mislaid Minorities: the Experience of Southern Ireland and Prussian Poland Compared, 1918–1923." *Irish Studies in International Affairs* 13, no. 1 (2002): 61–86.

INDEX

CALEB WOOD RICHARDSON is Assistant Professor of History at the University of New Mexico, Albuquerque. This is his first book.